SpringerBriefs in Computer Science

SpringerBriefs present concise summaries of cutting-edge research and practical applications across a wide spectrum of fields. Featuring compact volumes of 50 to 125 pages, the series covers a range of content from professional to academic.

Typical topics might include:

- A timely report of state-of-the art analytical techniques
- A bridge between new research results, as published in journal articles, and a contextual literature review
- A snapshot of a hot or emerging topic
- An in-depth case study or clinical example
- A presentation of core concepts that students must understand in order to make independent contributions

Briefs allow authors to present their ideas and readers to absorb them with minimal time investment. Briefs will be published as part of Springer's eBook collection, with millions of users worldwide. In addition, Briefs will be available for individual print and electronic purchase. Briefs are characterized by fast, global electronic dissemination, standard publishing contracts, easy-to-use manuscript preparation and formatting guidelines, and expedited production schedules. We aim for publication 8–12 weeks after acceptance. Both solicited and unsolicited manuscripts are considered for publication in this series.

**Indexing: This series is indexed in Scopus, Ei-Compendex, and zbMATH **

Linfeng Zhang

Knowledge Distillation in Computer Vision

 Springer

Linfeng Zhang
School of Artificial Intelligence
Shanghai Jiao Tong University
Shanghai, China

ISSN 2191-5768　　　　　　　ISSN 2191-5776　(electronic)
SpringerBriefs in Computer Science
ISBN 978-981-95-0366-7　　　ISBN 978-981-95-0367-4　(eBook)
https://doi.org/10.1007/978-981-95-0367-4

© The Editor(s) (if applicable) and The Author(s), under exclusive license to Springer Nature Singapore Pte Ltd. 2025

This work is subject to copyright. All rights are solely and exclusively licensed by the Publisher, whether the whole or part of the material is concerned, specifically the rights of translation, reprinting, reuse of illustrations, recitation, broadcasting, reproduction on microfilms or in any other physical way, and transmission or information storage and retrieval, electronic adaptation, computer software, or by similar or dissimilar methodology now known or hereafter developed.
The use of general descriptive names, registered names, trademarks, service marks, etc. in this publication does not imply, even in the absence of a specific statement, that such names are exempt from the relevant protective laws and regulations and therefore free for general use.
The publisher, the authors and the editors are safe to assume that the advice and information in this book are believed to be true and accurate at the date of publication. Neither the publisher nor the authors or the editors give a warranty, expressed or implied, with respect to the material contained herein or for any errors or omissions that may have been made. The publisher remains neutral with regard to jurisdictional claims in published maps and institutional affiliations.

This Springer imprint is published by the registered company Springer Nature Singapore Pte Ltd.
The registered company address is: 152 Beach Road, #21-01/04 Gateway East, Singapore 189721, Singapore

If disposing of this product, please recycle the paper.

Foreword

Knowledge distillation embodies a computational extension of the teacher-student dynamic inherent in human education systems. In human society, students can achieve accelerated learning by assimilating knowledge from more experienced teachers—a process that artificial intelligence researchers have ingeniously transposed to neural networks. This paradigm positions compact "student models" to learn from sophisticated "teacher models," leveraging the teacher's refined representations to achieve superior learning efficiency compared to training solely on raw data. This conceptual bridge between human cognitive strategies and machine learning mechanisms represents a fascinating convergence of biological and artificial intelligence.

Yet like many developments in deep learning, knowledge distillation research has predominantly evolved through empirical experimentation rather than systematic theoretical analysis. While achieving remarkable practical successes, the field currently lacks rigorous theoretical foundations or systematic frameworks to guide architectural design and knowledge transfer protocols. This empirical nature has constrained the development of universal principles applicable across diverse domains and model architectures.

This book addresses this critical gap by establishing a structured methodology for knowledge distillation. We first deconstruct the process into two fundamental challenges: (1) the quantification and characterization of transferable knowledge, and (2) the optimization of knowledge transmission efficiency between heterogeneous architectures. For each challenge, we present theoretically grounded solutions supported by rigorous mathematical analysis. Subsequent chapters explore domain-specific adaptations across high-level and low-level computer vision, supplemented by empirical design principles for practitioners developing task-optimized distillation frameworks.

At its core, this work engages with profound questions underlying artificial intelligence: What constitutes "knowledge" in machine learning models? How is it generated, organized, and transferred between intelligent systems? While focusing specifically on visual knowledge distillation, our systematic analysis of feature representation dynamics and information bottleneck theories provides foundational insights relevant to broader AI research. The methodologies presented here may serve as stepping stones toward answering these grand challenges in machine intelligence - challenges that will likely occupy researchers for decades to come.

Through this dual lens of theoretical rigor and practical implementation, we aim to elevate knowledge distillation from an empirical art to a structured science of machine knowledge transfer. The resulting framework not only advances current compression techniques but also deepens our understanding of how artificial neural networks acquire, process, and communicate semantic information—a crucial step toward developing truly explainable and efficient AI systems.

During the completion of this monograph, numerous scholars have provided contributions that merit special recognition. I extend my heartfelt gratitude and profound respect for their intellectual generosity. Hope that the "knowledge" contained within these pages can be "distilled" to you.

Shanghai, China Linfeng Zhang
April 2025

Contents

Background of Knowledge Distillation 1
1 Challenges on the Deployment of AI Models 1
2 Classic Knowledge Distillation 3
3 Structured Knowledge Distillation 4
4 Contributions and Organization 4
References 6

Student and Teacher Models in KD 9
1 Problem Definition 9
   1.1 Previous Methods 10
   1.2 Remaining Problems 11
2 Self-Distillation: Teacher-Free KD 12
   2.1 Knowledge from Deep Layers to Shallow Layers 13
   2.2 Dynamic Inference 16
   2.3 Rationality of Self-Distillation 18
3 Evaluation and Discussion 19
   3.1 Evaluation on Distilled Neural Networks 19
   3.2 Evaluation on Dynamic Inference 21
   3.3 Analysis of Self-Distillation 24
4 Brief Summary 27
References 28

Distilled Knowledge in KD 31
1 Problem Definition 31
   1.1 Previous Methods 31
   1.2 Remaining Problems 32
2 Task-Oriented Feature Distillation 33
   2.1 Extracting and Distilling Task-Oriented Knowledge 34
   2.2 Evaluation and Discussion 37

3	Task-Irrelevant KD	40
	3.1 Extracting and Distilling Task-Irrelevant Knowledge	42
	3.2 Evaluation and Discussion	44
4	Brief Summary	46
References		49

Application of KD in High-Level Vision Tasks 53
1 KD for 2D Object Detection and Instance Segmentation 53
   1.1 Attention-Guided Distillation and Non-local Distillation 54
   1.2 Evaluation and Discussion 58
2 KD for Point Cloud-based 3D Object Detection 68
   2.1 Local Distillation and Reweighted Learning Strategy 69
   2.2 Evaluation and Discussion 72
3 KD for Multi-View Images based 3D Object Detection 78
   3.1 Distilling Crucial Knowledge in Multi-view Images 80
   3.2 Evaluation and Discussion 83
4 Brief Summary 83
References 86

Application of KD in Low-Level Vision Tasks 91
1 Wavelet KD for Image-to-Image Translation 92
   1.1 Distilling High-Frequency Information in Images 93
   1.2 Evaluation and Discussion 94
2 Region-aware KD for Image-to-Image Translation 99
   2.1 Distilling Knowledge in Crucial Regions 101
   2.2 Evaluation and Discussion 103
3 KD for Diffusion-based Image Generation 107
   3.1 From One Teacher to Multiple Students 109
   3.2 Evaluation and Discussion 111
4 Brief Summary 114
References 114

Application of KD Beyond Model Compression 117
1 Robust Computer Vision with Self-Distillation 117
   1.1 Training Auxiliary Classifiers with Self-Distillation 119
   1.2 Evaluation and Discussion 123
2 Efficient Model Updating via KD 129
   2.1 Reducing the Number of Updated Parameters 131
   2.2 Evaluation and Discussion 132
3 Brief Summary 134
References 134

Conclusion and Challenges 137
1 Conclusion 137
2 Challenges 138
   2.1 Automatic Design for KD 138
   2.2 Training-Efficient KD 139
References 140

Background of Knowledge Distillation

Abstract The rapid evolution of deep neural networks in computer vision has driven unprecedented performance gains, yet their growing complexity poses critical deployment barriers in latency-sensitive scenarios like autonomous systems and edge devices. Knowledge distillation (KD) emerges as a pivotal paradigm to bridge this gap by transferring knowledge from cumbersome teacher models to compact student models. This chapter introduces the background of KD, providing a comprehensive overview of its motivation, evolution, methodologies, and applications in computer vision. It sets the foundation for understanding the systematic approaches and innovations discussed throughout this book.

1 Challenges on the Deployment of AI Models

The last ten years have witnessed a significant evolution in computer vision techniques, characterized by a notable shift toward the widespread adoption of neural networks. This shift has been supported by significant advancements in deep learning algorithms, marked by the emergence of convolutional neural networks (CNNs) [1, 2], recurrent neural networks (RNNs) [3, 4], Vision Transformers (ViT) [5], and their variants. Drawing inspiration from the complex mechanisms of the human visual system, these models have demonstrated remarkable performance in a myriad of visual recognition tasks such as image recognition [1, 2, 6, 7], object detection [8, 9], image segmentation [10–12], image generation [13, 14], face recognition [15], visual reasoning [16], 3D vision [17, 18], video recognition [19, 20] and so on. The integration of neural networks within computer vision pipelines has been further catalyzed by the unprecedented growth in computational resources, enabling the training of increasingly complex models on vast repositories of visual data. Notable datasets such as ImageNet [21], COCO [22], Open Images [23], Kinetics [19] and ModelNet [24], LAION [25] have emerged as pivotal catalysts, providing researchers with richly annotated visual data for training and evaluation. Based on the advanced neural networks and datasets, magnificent breakthroughs have been achieved in computer vision, which facilitate applications such as intelligent cities, intelligent monitoring, autonomous driving, AIGC, and so on.

As neural network architectures have evolved and grown in complexity over the past decade, one notable trend has been the exponential increase in the number of parameters within these models. This surge in the number of parameters, often facilitated by deeper, wider, and more complex neural network architectures, has been driven by the pursuit of improved performance on various computer vision tasks. For instance, Swin-L, one of the advanced vision transformers [26], contains 197M parameters and 103.9G FLOPs for a single inference. However, although larger neural networks have demonstrated impressive capabilities in tasks such as image classification and semantic segmentation, they are not without their drawbacks. One significant disadvantage of excessively large models is the computation and storage burden during the inference phase.

Firstly, the enormous parameters in neural networks incur a substantial inference cost, posing significant challenges for widespread adoption and scalability. The improvements of parameters exponentially increase the computational resources required for model inference, resulting in higher hardware infrastructure costs and operational expenses. This high inference cost not only limits the accessibility of AI technologies to resource-constrained environments but also hampers their feasibility for large-scale deployment in commercial products or services.

Secondly, the enormous parameters in neural networks render them unsuitable for deployment on edge devices, which have very limited computational and storage abilities. Edge devices such as smartphones, IoT devices, and embedded systems typically operate under stringent constraints in terms of processing power, memory capacity, and energy consumption. The enormous parameters of large AI models exacerbate these limitations, rendering their deployment on edge devices.

Thirdly, the enormous parameters in neural networks pose significant challenges for their deployment in applications with real-time requirements, such as self-driving vehicles. The computational burden imposed by large models with numerous parameters inhibits timely decision-making, a critical aspect of safety-critical systems like autonomous vehicles. Real-time responsiveness is essential for detecting and responding to dynamic environmental cues, such as pedestrians, obstacles, and traffic signals, to ensure safe navigation. However, the extensive computational resources required to process the enormous parameters hinder the ability of AI models to meet stringent latency constraints inherent in safety-critical applications. Consequently, deploying overly complex models in contexts where split-second decisions can impact human lives introduces unacceptable risks and compromises safety assurances.

The above observations demonstrate that there is a significant gap between the neural networks in academic research and the neural networks for industrial applications. To address this problem, abundant methods for model compression and acceleration have been proposed to bridge this gap. For instance, neural network pruning and neural network architecture searching have been proposed to obtain an efficient and lightweight architecture of neural networks [27, 28]. Neural network quantization has been introduced to represent the value of parameters and features with fewer bits [27]. Despite these advancements, model compression usually results in diminished accuracy and precision. To address this challenge, Hinton et al. proposed knowledge distillation (KD) in 2014 as a training strategy that ensures compressed models retain comparable accuracy to their pre-compression versions [29]. Currently, KD has become an indispensable component in the pipeline of model compression in various domains.

2 Classic Knowledge Distillation

Before the booming research of neural networks in the 2010s, the idea of "teaching machines with machines" has been proposed by Vapnik et al. in their research for support vector machine [30], known as "learning with privilege information". Besides, in 2008, Buciluă et al. introduced the idea of transferring the knowledge from the ensemble of multiple neural networks into a single neural network for compression and acceleration [31]. However, limited by the development of the machine learning field at that time, these efforts were not successfully extended to deep neural networks and some more complex tasks.

In 2014, Hinton et al. first proposed KD to compress a single deep neural network by transferring the knowledge learned by a single large neural network to a single lightweight neural network. Concretely, Hinton's KD first trains a cumbersome and over-parameterized model as the teacher model with the standard training process. After that, a lightweight student model is trained to give similar prediction results (i.e. the category probability distribution for a classification task) with the teacher model. In this process, the predictions from the teacher model serve as a guide to enhance the training of the student model, thereby allowing the student to assimilate the "dark knowledge" from the teacher. Ideally, following the KD process, the student model is capable of producing predictions identical to those of the teacher model, achieving equivalent accuracy. Consequently, during the inference phase, the student model can be utilized to replace the teacher model to achieve compression and acceleration. Hinton et al. effectively demonstrated the efficacy of KD across both linguistic and visual tasks at the time of its proposal.

Mathematically, by denoting the training set of an image classification task as $\mathcal{X} = \{x_i\}_{i=1}^{N}$ and the corresponding one-hot label set as $\mathcal{Y} = \{y_i\}_{i=1}^{N}$, the student and the teacher networks can be written as f_s and f_t, respectively. Then, in the first stage, KD trains the teacher network with the standard cross-entropy loss, which can be formulated as follows.

$$f_t^* = \arg\min_{f_t} \frac{1}{N} \sum_{i=1}^{N} L_{\text{CE}}(f_t(x_i), y_i), \tag{1}$$

where L_{CE} indicates the cross-entropy loss. Then, with the pre-trained teacher network f_t^*, the training loss of the student network is a weighted combination between the standard cross-entropy loss and the KD loss, which can be formulated as

$$\min_{f_s} \frac{1}{N} \sum_{i=1}^{N} \left(L_{\text{CE}}\left(f_s\left(x_i\right), y_i\right) + \alpha \cdot L_{\text{KL}}\left(\frac{f_s}{\tau}, \frac{f_t^*}{\tau}\right) \right), \qquad (2)$$

where τ is a temperature hyper-parameter to soften the distribution of predicted categorical probability distribution. α is a hyper-parameter to balance the influence between the two loss items. L_{KL} denotes Kullback–Leibler divergence.

3 Structured Knowledge Distillation

With the development of KD, recent works have gradually formed the concept of structured knowledge distillation. Currently, there is no clear definition of structured KD. In this book, we argue that structured KD is distinguished from previous KD methods from the following characteristics:

- Firstly, structured KD adopts a more systematic KD strategy, distilling different types of teacher knowledge rather than a single type of knowledge, to achieve more comprehensive performance improvements. For example, in an early work of structured KD for semantic segmentation by Liu et al. [32], feature-based, relation-based, and probability-based KD are simultaneously utilized.
- Secondly, structured KD usually employs a more systematic design methodology with a relatively mature research philosophy. Early endeavors in KD research are usually designed by intuitive thoughts rather than structured research frameworks. In contrast, in this book, we introduce a framework that decomposes KD into two fundamental problems and then designs specific KD methods for different tasks based on these two fundamental problems.
- Thirdly, structured KD is usually utilized to tackle more challenging tasks. The early KD methods are usually introduced for simple vision and language tasks such as classification. In contrast, structured KD is utilized to solve the more challenging problems in complex application scenarios.

4 Contributions and Organization

In this book, we study the structured KD methods for the compression and acceleration of deep neural networks on computer vision tasks. As shown in Fig. 1, the contributions of this book can be summarized as follows.

- We introduce the two fundamental problems in KD, including "how to build the student model and the teacher model", and "what kind of knowledge should

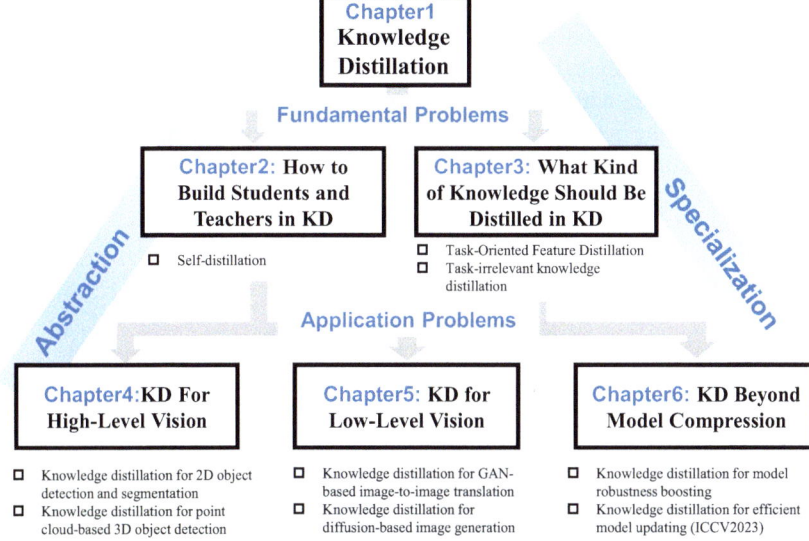

Fig. 1 The contribution and organization of this book

be distilled". To address the first problem, we introduce self-distillation, which first shows that the teacher model is not indispensable in KD. To address the second problem, we introduce the task-oriented KD and task-irrelevant KD, which demonstrate the influence of distilling different kinds of knowledge. These methods have achieved state-of-the-art performance and profoundly helped researchers in the field to obtain a better understanding of KD.
- We introduce the KD method for challenging tasks in real-world applications. Different from traditional works which mainly focus on image classification, we applied KD to all kinds of real-world tasks, including 2D object detection and instance segmentation, point cloud-based 3D object detection, and conditional and unconditional image generation with GANs and diffusion models. Besides, based on these findings, we formed a systematic methodology for the design of KD tailored to different tasks.
- We have studied the application of KD for purposes besides model compression. Concretely, we show that KD can also be utilized to improve model robustness for image corruptions and be employed for efficient software updating. These findings may break the barrier of KD and provide insights for future research.

The organization of this book is as follows: In chapter "Background of Knowledge Distillation", we introduce the background of KD, including the motivation, formulation, and related works. In chapters "Student and Teacher Models in KD" and "Distilled Knowledge in KD", we present the insights into addressing two fundamental problems in KD. Chapters "Application of KD in High-Level Vision Tasks" and "Application of KD in Low-Level Vision Tasks" shed light on the practical applications of KD in confronting complex tasks within real-world scenarios. Chapter "Application of KD Beyond Model Compression" introduces applications of KD beyond model compression. In chapter "Conclusion and Challenges" we conclude with a comprehensive summary of the presented work, while also introducing the possible challenges and opportunities for future research in KD and AI model compression.

References

1. Krizhevsky, A., Sutskever, I., Hinton, G.E.: Imagenet classification with deep convolutional neural networks. In: Advances in Neural Information Processing Systems (NeurIPS), pp. 1097–1105 (2012)
2. He, K., Zhang, X., Ren, S., Sun, J.: Deep residual learning for image recognition. In: IEEE/CVF Conference on Computer Vision and Pattern Recognition(CVPR), pp. 770–778 (2016)
3. Schuster, M., Paliwal, K.K.: Bidirectional recurrent neural networks. IEEE Trans. Signal Process. **45**(11), 2673–2681 (1997)
4. Hochreiter, S., Schmidhuber, J.: Long short-term memory. Neural Comput. **9**(8), 1735–1780 (1997)
5. Dosovitskiy, A., Beyer, L., Kolesnikov, A., Weissenborn, D., Zhai, X., Unterthiner, T., Dehghani, M., Minderer, M., Georg, H., Gelly, S., et al.: An image is worth 16×16 words: Transformers for image recognition at scale. In: The International Conference on Learning Representations (ICLR) (2020)
6. Simonyan, K., Zisserman, A.: Very deep convolutional networks for large-scale image recognition. In: The International Conference on Learning Representations (ICLR) (2015)
7. Xie, S., Girshick, R., Piotr Dollár, Tu, Z., He, K.: Aggregated residual transformations for deep neural networks. In: The IEEE/CVF Conference on Computer Vision and Pattern Recognition (CVPR), pp. 5987–5995 (2017)
8. Ren, S., He, K., Girshick, R., Sun, J.: Faster r-cnn: Towards real-time object detection with region proposal networks. In: Advances in Neural Information Processing Systems (NIPS), pp. 91–99 (2015)
9. Lin, T. -Y., Goyal, P., Girshick, R., He, K., Dollár, P.: Focal loss for dense object detection. IEEE Trans Pattern Anal Mach Intell **42**(2), 318–327 (2020). https://doi.org/10.1109/TPAMI.2018.2858826
10. Long, J., Shelhamer, E., Darrell, T.: Fully convolutional networks for semantic segmentation. In: The IEEE/CVF Conference on Computer Vision and Pattern Recognition (CVPR), pp. 3431–3440 (2015)
11. He, K., Gkioxari, G., Dollar, P., Girshick, R.: Mask r-cnn. In: International Conference on Computer Vision (ICCV). IEEE (Oct 2017)
12. Ronneberger, O., Fischer, P., Brox, T.: U-net: Convolutional networks for biomedical image segmentation. In: International Conference on Medical Image Computing and Computer Assisted Intervention (MICCAI), pp. 234–241. Springer (2015)
13. Goodfellow, I., Pouget-Abadie, J., Mirza, M., Xu, B., Warde-Farley, D., Ozair, S., Courville, A., Bengio, Y.: Generative adversarial nets. In: Advances in Neural Information Processing Systems (NIPS), vol. 27 (2014)
14. Ho, J., Jain, A., Abbeel, P.: Denoising diffusion probabilistic models. Adv. Neural Inf. Proces. Syst. **33**, 6840–6851 (2020)
15. Schroff, F., Kalenichenko, D., Philbin, J.: Facenet: A unified embedding for face recognition and clustering. In: Proceedings of the IEEE Conference on Computer Vision and Pattern Recognition, pp. 815–823 (2015)

References

16. Perez, E., Strub, F., De Vries, H., Dumoulin, V., Courville, A.: Film: Visual reasoning with a general conditioning layer. In: Proceedings of the AAAI Conference on Artificial Intelligence, vol. 32 (2018)
17. Qi, C.R., Su, H., Mo, K., Guibas, L.J.: Pointnet: Deep learning on point sets for 3d classification and segmentation. In: IEEE/CVF Conference on Computer Vision and Pattern Recognition (CVPR), pp. 652–660 (2017)
18. Qi, C.R., Yi, L., Su, H., Guibas, L.J.: Pointnet++: Deep hierarchical feature learning on point sets in a metric space. In: Advances in Neural Information Processing Systems (NIPS), vol. 30 (2017)
19. Carreira, J., Zisserman, A.: Quo vadis, action recognition? A new model and the kinetics dataset. In: Proceedings of the IEEE Conference on Computer Vision and Pattern Recognition, pp. 6299–6308 (2017)
20. Feichtenhofer, C., Fan, H., Malik, J., He, K.: Slowfast networks for video recognition. In: Proceedings of the IEEE/CVF International Conference on Computer Vision, pp. 6202–6211 (2019)
21. Deng, J., Dong, W., Socher, R., Li, L.-J., Li, K., Fei-Fei, L.: Imagenet: A large-scale hierarchical image database. In: IEEE/CVF Conference on Computer Vision and Pattern Recognition (CVPR), pp. 248–255 (2009)
22. Lin, T.-Y., Maire, M., Belongie, S., Hays, J., Perona, P., Ramanan, D., Dollár, P., Zitnick, C.L.: Microsoft coco: Common objects in context. In: The European Conference on Computer Vision (ECCV), pp. 740–755. Springer (2014)
23. Kuznetsova, A., Rom, H., Alldrin, N., Uijlings, J., Krasin, I., Pont-Tuset, J., Kamali, S., Popov, S., Malloci, M., Kolesnikov, A., et al.: The open images dataset v4: Unified image classification, object detection, and visual relationship detection at scale. Int. J. Comput. Vis. **128**(7), 1956–1981 (2020)
24. Wu, Z., Song, S., Khosla, A., Yu, F., Zhang, L., Tang, X., Xiao, J.: 3d shapenets: A deep representation for volumetric shapes. In: Proceedings of the IEEE Conference on Computer Vision and Pattern Recognition, pp. 1912–1920 (2015)
25. Schuhmann, C., Beaumont, R., Vencu, R., Gordon, C., Wightman, R., Cherti, M., Coombes, T., Katta, A., Mullis, C., Wortsman, M., et al.: Laion-5b: An open large-scale dataset for training next generation image-text models. Adv. Neural Inf. Proces. Syst. **35**, 25278–25294 (2022)
26. Liu, Z., Lin, Y., Cao, Y., Hu, H., Wei, Y., Zhang, Z., Lin, S., Guo, B.: Swin transformer: Hierarchical vision transformer using shifted windows. In: IEEE/CVF International Conference on Computer Vision (ICCV), pp. 9992–10002 Montreal, QC, Canada (2021). https://doi.org/10.1109/ICCV48922.2021.00986
27. Han, S., Mao, H., Dally, W.J.: Deep compression: Compressing deep neural networks with pruning, trained quantization and huffman coding. In: The International Conference on Learning Representations (ICLR) (2016)
28. He, Y., Lin, J., Liu, Z., Wang, H., Li, L.-J., Han, S.: Amc: Automl for model compression and acceleration on mobile devices. In: The European Conference on Computer Vision (ECCV), pp. 784–800 (2018)
29. Hinton, G., Vinyals, O., Dean, J.: Distilling the knowledge in a neural network. In: Advances in Neural Information Processing Systems (NeurIPS) (2014)
30. Vapnik, V., Vashist, A.: A new learning paradigm: Learning using privileged information. Neural Netw. **22**(5-6), 544–557 (2009)
31. Buciluǎ, C., Caruana, R., Niculescu-Mizil, A.: Model compression. In: ACM SIGKDD International Conference on Knowledge Discovery and Data Mining (KDD), pp. 535–541. ACM (2006)
32. Liu, Y., Chen, K., Liu, C., Qin, Z., Luo, Z., Wang, J.: Structured knowledge distillation for semantic segmentation. In: IEEE/CVF Conference on Computer Vision and Pattern Recognition (CVPR), pp. 2604–2613 (2019)

Student and Teacher Models in KD

Abstract This chapter addresses the foundational challenge of constructing student-teacher architectures in KD. Traditional KD frameworks rely on pre-trained teacher models to guide smaller student networks, but face two critical limitations: (1) the two-stage training process incurs excessive computational overhead, particularly prohibitive for modern large-scale models, and (2) performance instability arises from suboptimal teacher selection, where high-accuracy teachers may paradoxically degrade student performance. To solve these issues, we propose self-distillation as an innovative paradigm that eliminates external teacher dependency. This approach introduces shallow classifiers at intermediate layers to form a multi-exit architecture, enabling intra-model knowledge transfer through hierarchical layer-wise supervision. These findings position self-distillation as a unified solution addressing computational efficiency, deployment flexibility, and performance stability in KD frameworks.

1 Problem Definition

The objective of KD is to transfer knowledge from a teacher model to a student model. Therefore, the prerequisite for implementing KD lies in the initial construction of both a teacher model and a student model within a computational system. Intuitively, to ensure the effectiveness of KD in improving the performance of the student model, the teacher model must exhibit higher accuracy than the student model. Thus, in the classic KD framework proposed by Hinton [1], a pre-trained model with a larger number of parameters is employed as the teacher, while a model with fewer parameters is utilized as the student. However, subsequent research has revealed that this approach may not always be the optimal student-teacher configuration. As a result, numerous alternative approaches for constructing student-teacher pairs have been proposed by researchers, aiming to improve the performance of KD and extend its applicability to different objectives.

1.1 Previous Methods

1.1.1 Learning from Multiple Teachers

Traditional KD distills the knowledge from a single teacher model. However, it is obvious that the knowledge from multiple teacher models may provide more knowledge for the students. Hence, abundant methods have been proposed to train a single student to learn from multiple teachers. For instance, Park et al. propose to employ non-linear transformation to the features from multiple teacher models for KD [2]. Shen et al. introduce adaptive knowledge amalgamation to perform KD from multiple heterogeneous teacher models [3]. Similarly, Luo et al. propose to train a lightweight student model which can learn the integrated knowledge from heterogeneous-structure teachers without accessing annotations [4]. You et al. propose to distill the dissimilarity relationships at intermediate layers from multiple teachers [5]. Xiang et al. propose to aggregate the knowledge from multiple teachers for different categories for long-tailed classification [6]. Besides, Sau et al. propose to simulate the effect of KD from the ensemble of teachers by injecting random noise into the prediction of teachers [7]. In summary, these works show that the teacher model can be an ensemble between multiple models.

1.1.2 Online KD

In traditional KD, the teacher model is trained before the training of the student. After that, abundant methods have been proposed to train the students and the teachers at the same time. For instance, deep mutual learning [8] has been proposed to train multiple students to learn from each other simultaneously. Guo et al. propose a similar idea but use different data augmentation for different students [9]. Chen et al. introduce online KD with diverse peers, which trains multiple student classifiers and takes the ensemble of these student classifiers as the teacher [10]. Zhu et al. train a multi-branch neural network while simultaneously establishing the ensemble from different branches controlled by a gate [11]. Zheng et al. introduce online KD for efficient pose estimation by training a single multi-branch network and then taking the aggregated heatmap from different branches as the teacher heatmap [12]. In summary, these works demonstrate that the student model and the teacher model can be trained at the same time.

1.1.3 Teacher-free KD

The teacher model in KD is utilized to provide the learning target for the student model. Recently, abundant works reveal that the teacher model in KD is not indispensable. For instance, the Born-again neural network first shows that the sequential self-teaching of students allows them to gradually achieve higher accuracy [13]. Then, based on the born-again network, Yang et al. further introduce a loss function that facilitates the student to distribute confidence to a few secondary classes [14]. After that, Clark et al. extend born-again networks to multi-task neural networks for language understanding, where single-task models are distilled sequentially to a multi-task model [15]. Besides, fruitful research works focus on replacing the prediction results of the teacher by applying different data augmentations. For instance, Xu et al. propose to transfer knowledge between different augmentations of the same images, which does not rely on any accompanying teacher models [16]. Then, Lee et al. further validate this idea on the few-shot and imbalanced classification scenarios [17]. In summary, these works show that the teacher model in KD is not always necessary. In other words, the learning targets for the student models in KD do not have to be provided by another teacher model.

1.1.4 Teacher-Assistant KD

The original KD transfers the knowledge from the teacher to the student in one step. However, both theoretical and experimental results show that sometimes the overlarge accuracy gap between students and teachers may harm the performance of students. To address this problem, teacher-assistant KD is proposed to first distill the knowledge from the teacher to a teacher-assistant, and then distill the knowledge from the teacher-assistant to the student model [18]. Based on the same observation, Jin et al. propose RKD, where the student models in different epochs are taught by teacher models in different epochs [19]. Then, Son et al. propose the densely guided KD which uses multiple teacher assistants in a densely-connected manner [20]. After that, Zhu et al. propose to examine the capacity mismatch between teacher models and student models with the metric of gradient similarity, which allows the teacher to transfer its knowledge to the student model when the student can benefit from learning such knowledge [21]. In summary, these works show that KD can be performed gradually.

1.2 Remaining Problems

Although previous methods have introduced all kinds of methods for building students and teachers. However, there remain two problems that have not been solved.

Training Overhead Since KD is a two-stage training method, it has much more training overhead than the traditional one-stage training method. Concretely, besides the training cost of the student. KD additionally trains the teacher model in the first training stage and infers the teacher model in the second training stage. Since the teacher model usually has many more parameters than the student model, the additional training cost of KD is not affordable. This problem becomes more fatal for the advanced large models, whose training overhead is more expensive.

Instability from the Teacher Model The other problem of original KD is that the choice of teacher models has a significant and unstable influence on the performance of the student. Recently, researchers have found that the choice of teacher models has a great impact on the accuracy of student models. Sometimes, the teacher model with high accuracy may not improve, but rather reduce the efficiency of KD [18, 22, 23]. As a result, substantial experiments are required to search for the optimal teacher model for distillation, which can be very time-consuming.

2 Self-Distillation: Teacher-Free KD

As a two-stage training method, traditional KD suffers from excessively large training overhead and unstable performance. To address these problems, a novel KD method named self-distillation is proposed in this section. Self-distillation first attaches several attention-based shallow classifiers after the intermediate layers of neural networks at different depths. Then, in the training period, the deeper classifiers are regarded as the teacher models and they are utilized to guide the training of student models by a KL divergence loss on the outputs and a L2 loss on the feature maps. In the inference period, all of the additional shallow classifiers can be dropped so they don't bring additional parameters and computation. It is worth noting that different shallow classifiers correspond to the student models of different sizes. As a result, student models of different sizes can be obtained by training once.

Self-distillation reduces the training overhead compared with conventional KD. Since both teacher models and student models in self-distillation are the classifiers in the same neural network, substantial experiments for searching the teacher model in conventional KD can be avoided. Moreover, conventional KD is a two-stage training method where we have to train a teacher first and then use the teacher to train the student. In contrast, self-distillation is a one-stage training method where the teacher model and student models can be trained together. The one-stage property of self-distillation further reduces training overhead.

Self-distillation achieves higher accuracy, acceleration, and compression compared with conventional KD. Different from the conventional KD which focuses on knowledge transfer among different models, self-distillation tries to transfer the knowledge within one model. Experiments show that self-distillation outperforms other KD methods by a large margin. Moreover, we also find that the self-distillation and conventional knowledge distillation methods can be utilized together to achieve better results. Self-distillation allows neural networks to perform dynamic inference based on the input image, which leads to a higher acceleration ratio. In the multi-classifier neural networks trained by self-distillation, the deep classifiers can provide more accurate classification results while the shallow classifiers can give quick classification results with slightly lower accuracy. Based on these observations, we further present a dynamic inference mechanism that allows the shallow classifiers to give prediction to the easy images and the deep classifiers to predict images that are more difficult to be classified. For example, more than 95% of the images in CIFAR100 can be classified by the shallowest classifier of ResNet18 with 3% higher accuracy and 3 times acceleration than the baseline model.

2.1 Knowledge from Deep Layers to Shallow Layers

Figure 1 shows the details of self-distillation on ResNet18. Compared with the original model, self-distillation does not change the architecture of backbone layers yet add several early exit branches after the intermediate layers of neural networks.

Each early exit branch is composed of an attention module and a shallow classifier. In the training period, all the classifiers are trained by self-distillation, which regards the deeper classifiers as teacher models and the shallower classifiers as student models. In the inference period, all the additional attention modules and shallow classifiers are dropped so there are no additional parameters or computation penalty for the deployed model. The left part of this section gives a detailed introduction to this content.

Let $c : \mathbb{R}^N \mapsto \mathbb{R}^M$ be a given backbone classifier such as ResNets, VGG, or MobileNets, we introduce several shallow classifiers by using the intermediate information in the backbone classifier F. More specifically, assume $F = g \circ f$ where g is the final classier and f is the feature extractor operator, and $f = f_K \circ f_{K-1} \circ \cdots \circ f_1$ where K denotes the number of stages in f. At each feature extraction stage i, we attach a classifier g_i for early prediction. Thus, we have K classifiers in total which have the form:

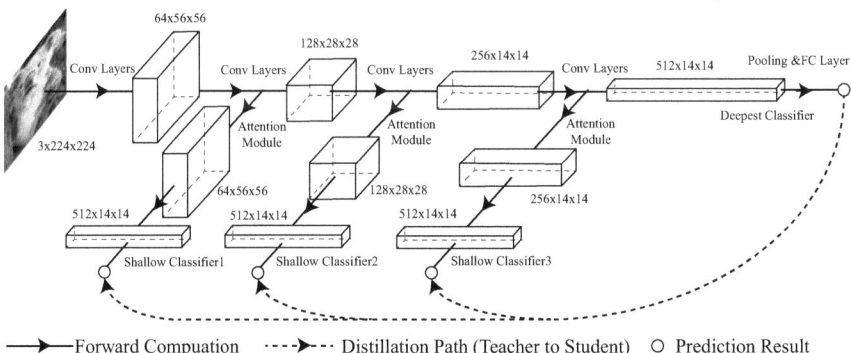

Fig. 1 The architecture of ResNet18 trained by self-distillation. (i) The whole neural network can be divided into three sections: backbone, attention modules, and shallow classifiers. (ii) The backbone section is just identical to the original model. (iii) Additional attention modules are attached after the intermediate features of the backbone. (iv) Features refined by attention modules will be fed into the shallow classifiers, which consist of a bottleneck layer and a fully connected layer. (v) All the attention modules and shallow classifiers are dropped in the inference period, indicating that there are no additional parameters and computation penalty in self-distillation

$$c_1(x) = g_1 \circ f_1(x),$$
$$c_2(x) = g_2 \circ f_2 \circ f_1(x),$$
$$\dots, \tag{1}$$
$$c_K(x) = g_K \circ f_K \circ f_{K-1} \circ \cdots \circ f_1(x).$$

By defining $h_i = f_i \circ f_{i-1} \circ \cdots \circ f_1$, we have $c_i = g_i \circ h_i$ for all $i = 1, \dots, K$ and $c_K = c$ if g_K is chosen as $g_K = g$. Here, we call $g_1, \dots, g_{K-1}$ as shallow classifiers, and g_K as the final classifier. Each shallow classifier contains a feature alignment layer and a softmax layer. The feature alignment layer is to guarantee that the feature dimension in the shallow layer is equal to the feature dimension of the last layer, and the softmax layer is to smooth the label distribution with temperature T. In other words, for each $i = 1, 2, \dots, K-1$, g_i is represented as $g_i = q_T \circ F_i$ where F_i is the feature alignment layer and q_T is defined as

$$q_T(x) = \frac{\exp(x/T)}{\sum \exp(x/T)}. \tag{2}$$

Given n training samples $X = \{(x_j, y_j)\}_{j=1}^n$ where $x_j \in \mathbb{R}^N$ is the input image and $y_j \in \mathbb{R}^M$ is the corresponding label. Define $c_i^j = c_i(x_j)$ to be the predicted label of sample x_j by the i-th classifier and $F_i^j = F_i \circ h_i(x_j)$ be the feature vector of the j-th sample given by i-th classifier, we construct the distillation loss of j-th sample:

$$L_{\text{dis}}^j = \frac{1}{K} \sum_{i=1}^K \left((1 - \alpha_i) L_{\text{CE}}(c_i^j, y_j) + \alpha_i L_{\text{KL}}(c_i^j, c_{\text{re},i}^j) \right), \tag{3}$$

where L_{CE} is the cross entropy loss, L_{KL} is the Kullback-Leibler (KL) divergence, $\alpha_i \in [0, 1], \forall i = 1, \dots, K$ are the imitation parameters and $c_{\text{re},i}^j$ is the reference label of the j-th sample for i-th classifer. Besides, motivated by the hint loss in FitNet [24], we add a penalty for the shallow features:

$$L_{\text{pen}}^j = \frac{1}{K} \sum_{i=1}^K \lambda_i L_2(F_i^j, F_{\text{re},i}^j), \tag{4}$$

where L_2 is the squared ℓ_2-norm loss, $\lambda_i > 0, i = 1, \dots, K$ are trade-off parameters and $F_{\text{re},i}^j$ is the reference feature of j-th sample for i-th classifier. It is noted that the final classifier g_K is only trained by the L_{CE} loss, i.e. $\alpha_K = \lambda_K = 0$. In summary, the total loss of the self-distillation is

$$L = \frac{1}{n} \sum_{j=1}^n L_{\text{dist}}^j + \lambda L_{\text{pen}}^j. \tag{5}$$

Since there are several classifiers in the self-distillation framework, there are multiple choices of the reference labels c_{re} and the reference features F_{re}.

1. **Deepest Teacher Distillation.** The deepest classifier is used as the reference labels and the reference features for all shallow classifiers, i.e. $c_{\text{re},i} = c_K$ and $F_{\text{re},i} = F_K \circ h_K$ for all $i = 1, 2, \ldots, K-1$.
2. **Ensemble Teacher Distillation.** An ensemble of labels and features produced by all classifiers are used as the reference labels and the reference features, i.e. $c_{\text{re},i} = \mathcal{S}(\{c_i\})$ and $F_{\text{re},i} = \mathcal{S}(\{F_i \circ h_i\})$ for all $i = 1, 2, \ldots, K-1$, where $\mathcal{S}$ denotes some ensemble operation.
3. **Transitive Teacher Distillation.** This distillation chooses the reference label and the reference feature transitively, i.e. $c_{\text{re},i} = c_{i+1}$ and $F_{\text{re},i} = F_{i+1} \circ h_{i+1}$ for all $i = 1, 2, \ldots, K-1$. This distillation approach is similar to the distillation by teacher assistant [18].
4. **Dense Teacher Distillation.** The dense distillation connects all the label and feature information among all classifiers, i.e. $c_{\text{re},i} = \{c_k | k \neq i\}$ and $F_{\text{re},i} = \{F_k \circ h_k | k \neq i\}$ for all $i = 1, 2, \ldots, K-1$. Thus, the KL loss in (3) is

$$L_{\text{KL}}(c_i^j, c_{\text{re},i}^j) = \sum_{k=i+1}^{K} L_{\text{KL}}(c_i^j, c_k^j). \tag{6}$$

In this section, we choose the deepest teacher distillation throughout all experiments and the comparison study of four distillation methods is presented in Table 6 (Fig. 2).

Remark Compared with the conventional distillation methods where the teacher and student are two or several individual neural networks, self-distillation method simultaneously trains all classifiers $c_i, i = 1, 2, \ldots, K$, and enables us to perform KD within one neural network.

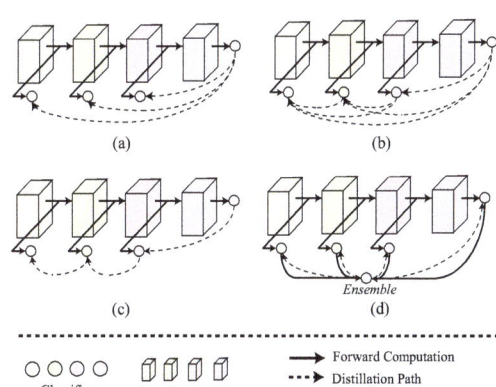

Fig. 2 Four kinds of distillation paths in self-distillation. Each distillation path indicates a scheme for how to choose the teacher and student classifiers. A →B indicates that the classifier A is the teacher of the classifier B. (**a**) Best teacher distillation. (**b**) Dense connected distillation. (**c**) Transitive distillation. (**d**) Ensemble teacher distillation

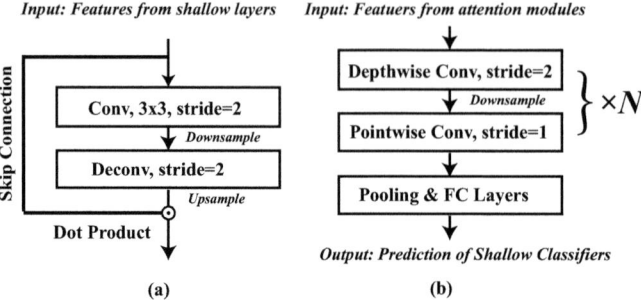

Fig. 3 The architecture of attention modules and shallow classifiers. (i) The attention module consists of a convolution layer for downsampling and a deconvolution layer for upsampling. The attention mask learned by these two layers is utilized to enhance the original features by a dot product operation. (ii) The shallow classifier is composed of several pairs of depthwise and pointwise layers which are designed to downsample the feature with few parameters and computation. N in the figure is decided by the depth of the shallow classifiers. (**a**) Attention module. (**b**) Shallow classifier

Shallow Classifiers As mentioned earlier, each shallow classifier g_i is the composition of the softmax layer q_T and the feature alignment layer F_i. Since the shallow classifiers only use the intermediate information of the backbone network at different depths, the feature alignment layer F_i firstly extracts the useful intermediate features by the attention module, followed by an alignment network. The alignment network is to adjust the feature size such that the squared ℓ_2-norm loss between the shallow features and the reference feature can be used for improving the accuracy of shallow classifiers. The proposed attention module is shown in Fig. 3a which is composed of a depthwise-pointwise layer and bilinear interpolation. The features from the shallow convolution layers are fed into the attention module to obtain the attention mask. Then, a dot product is performed between the attention mask and the input features.

The architecture of align nets is shown in Fig. 3b. The depthwise and pointwise convolution layers proposed in MobileNet are utilized to replace the vanilla convolution layers to reduce the training overhead. Each depthwise-pointwise convolutional layer performs two times downsampling on feature maps. The number of depthwise-pointwise convolutional layers for the shallow classifiers is set as N_i. Take $K = 4$ as an example, $N_i = 4 - i, i = 1, 2, 3$ for the three shallow classifiers.

2.2 Dynamic Inference

It is generally acknowledged that the prediction of neural networks with higher confidence (softmax value) is more likely to be right. In this section, we exploit this observation to determine whether a classifier gives a right or wrong prediction. As

Algorithm 1 Scalable inference

Input: Images x, Thresholds $\{\sigma_i\}^N$, Classifiers $\{c_i\}^N$
Output: Prediction Result $\hat{y}$
1: **for** i from 1 to N **do**
2:      $\hat{y}_i = c_i(x)$
3:      **if** $\max(\hat{y}) > \sigma_i$ **then**
4:          **return** $\hat{y}_i$
5:      **end if**
6: **end for**
7: **return** ensemble$(y_1, \ldots, y_N)$

---

described in Algorithm 1, we set different thresholds for shallow classifiers. If the maximal output of softmax in the shallow classifier is larger than the corresponding threshold, its results will be adopted as the final prediction so much computation can be reduced. Otherwise, the neural networks will employ a deeper classifier to predict. If there is no shallow classifier that can provide confident prediction, the ensemble of all the classifiers is regarded as the final result. Since all the classifiers in self-distillation share the same backbone layers, there is not much extra computation introduced in the dynamic inference. Moreover, experiments show that most images can be classified by the shallowest classifier correctly, which reduces the computation cost significantly.

Moreover, threshold-based dynamic inference provides more flexibility in real-world application. It permits models to dynamically adjust their trade-offs between response time and accuracy on the fly by adjusting the thresholds of shallow classifiers. Since the value of thresholds determines which classifier is utilized as the final prediction, it has a direct influence on the accuracy and acceleration results of dynamic inference. A lower threshold for shallow classifiers results in the fact that most samples will be predicted by shallow classifiers, indicating more rapid response yet lower accuracy. Similarly, a higher threshold leads to a phenomenon that most samples will be determined by deeper classifiers, indicating precise prediction yet longer response time. In self-distillation, we have applied a genetic algorithm to find the best thresholds as shown in Algorithm 2. The values of thresholds in different shallow classifiers are encoded into binary codes as the genes. The accuracy and acceleration results are utilized to measure the fitness of the threshold.

$$\text{fitness} = \text{acceleration ratio} + \beta \cdot (\text{accuracy-baseline}) \quad (7)$$

where β is a hyper-parameter to balance the impact of these two elements. Adjustment of β leads to trade-offs between accuracy and acceleration.

Algorithm 2 Threshold searching

Input: Images x, Classifiers $\{c_i\}^N$, Max Generations g
Output: Optimal Thresholds $\Sigma = \{\sigma_i\}^N$
1: Randomly Initialize G as the set of genes
2: **for** i from 1 to g **do**
3:   Get fitness of G according to Eq. 7.
4:   Sample genes with high fitness from G as $\hat{G}$
5:   $G :=$ crossover and mutate $\hat{G}$
6: **end for**
7: $\Sigma :=$ decode G from binary codes to numbers
8: **return** Σ

2.3 Rationality of Self-Distillation

In this subsection, we interpret our model from the perspective of the generalized distillation [25], which unifies KD and privileged information. In generalized distillation, each training sample x_j associates with additional information x_j^* provided by "intelligent teachers". In the context of the traditional distillation framework, the additional information is given by a teacher network.

Given a function $g \in \mathcal{G}$, define $|\mathcal{G}|_C$ to be an appropriate function capacity measure, e.g. VC-dimension and $R(g)$ to be the generalization error. Let $f\mathcal{F}$ be the target function, the generalized distillation framework [25] assumes the student network $f_s \in \mathcal{F}_s$ learn the oracle classifier at a slow rate and the teacher network $f_t \in \mathcal{F}_t$ learn it at a fast rate, i.e.

$$R(f_s) - R(f) \leq O(|\mathcal{F}_s|_C/\sqrt{N}) + \epsilon_s, \tag{8}$$

$$R(f_t) - R(f) \leq O(|\mathcal{F}_s|_C/N) + \epsilon_t, \tag{9}$$

where ϵ_s and ϵ_t denote the approximation error of the function class $\mathcal{F}_s$ and $\mathcal{F}_t$ to f, respectively. It assumes that the student learns from the teacher at a medium rate, i.e.

$$R(f_s) - R(f_t) \leq O(|\mathcal{F}_s|_C/N^\alpha) + \epsilon_l, \tag{10}$$

where $\alpha \in (1/2, 1]$ and ϵ_l is the approximation error of the function class $\mathcal{F}_s$ to f_t. Combining (9) with (10), we arrive at an estimation error of the student network:

$$R(f_s) - R(f) \leq O\left(\frac{|\mathcal{F}_s|_C + |\mathcal{F}_t|_C}{N^\alpha}\right) + \epsilon_l + \epsilon_t. \tag{11}$$

Therefore, we have to analyze the if the inequality

$$O\left(\frac{|\mathcal{F}_s|_C + |\mathcal{F}_t|_C}{N^\alpha}\right) + \epsilon_l + \epsilon_t \leq O\left(\frac{|\mathcal{F}_s|_C}{\sqrt{N}}\right) + \epsilon_s \tag{12}$$

holds. Consider $K = 2$ in self-distillation framework, i.e. there is one shallow classifier c_1 and a final classifier c_2. When the capacity of classifier c_2 is much larger than c_1, we can treat $c_1 = f_s$ and $c_2 = f_t$, which implies the (12). This is also the main assumption in classical KD [1]. When the capacity of the shallow classifier c_1 is large enough to approximate the target function, we can treat $f_s = c_2$ and $f_t = c_1$. In this case, $\epsilon_l = 0$ and $\epsilon_t \approx \epsilon_s$ but $|\mathcal{F}_s|_C \gg |\mathcal{F}_t|_C$, which also implies (12). Thus, the features provided by the shallow classifier are the so-called privileged information. In this sense, instead of the teacher-student structure, self-distillation network is more likely to be the "student-student" which may accelerate the knowledge communication.

3 Evaluation and Discussion

3.1 Evaluation on Distilled Neural Networks

3.1.1 Experiment Settings

self-distillation is evaluated in two benchmark datasets: CIFAR100 [26] and ImageNet (ILSVRC2012) [27] and six kinds of neural networks: ResNet [28], WideResNet [29], ResNeXt [30], SENet [31], MobileNetV2 [32] and ShuffleNet [33].

3.1.2 Experimental Results

Table 1 shows the experiment results of self-distillation in CIFAR100. It is observed that (i) On average, self-distillation leads to a 3.49% accuracy boost. (ii) In 5 of

Table 1 Experiment results of accuracy (%) on CIFAR100 with AotuAugment

Models	Baseline	Classifier1	Classifier2	Classifier3	Classifier4	Ensemble
ResNet18	79.01	76.31	79.32	81.24	81.76	82.64
ResNet50	80.88	82.60	83.55	84.42	83.66	85.42
ResNet101	82.37	81.64	82.73	84.12	84.03	85.48
ResNet152	82.92	81.25	82.94	84.37	84.52	85.41
WRN50-2	81.26	82.85	84.02	84.91	84.33	85.78
WRN101-2	82.37	82.56	83.79	84.87	84.33	86.03
SeNet18	79.53	75.60	79.81	81.77	81.84	83.10
SeNet50	81.01	81.80	82.93	83.91	83.51	85.21
SeNet101	82.75	82.20	82.69	83.17	82.97	84.82
ResNeXt50-4	82.65	82.03	83.50	83.78	83.42	85.12
ResNeXt101-8	82.96	82.84	83.70	84.70	84.31	85.81
MobileNetV2	65.49	62.93	66.03	67.95	67.17	68.87
ShuffleNetV2	71.61	73.20	73.87	75.66	/	76.45

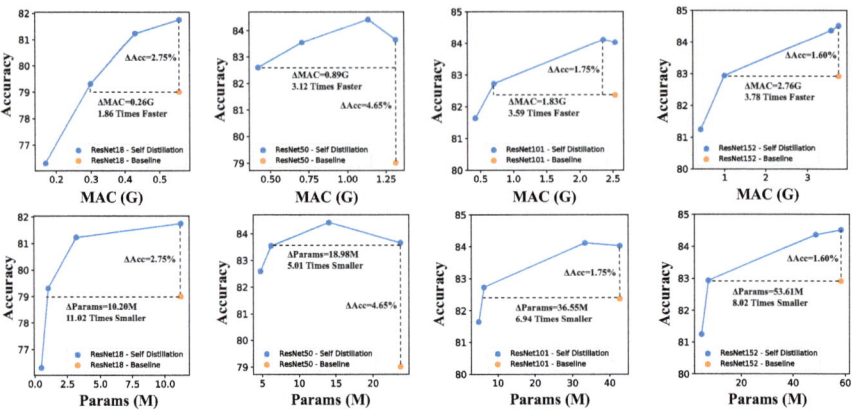

Fig. 4 Experiment results of self-distillation on CIFAR100. MAC indicates the multiply-accumulation operation of neural networks

Table 2 Experiment results of accuracy (%) on ImageNet with AotuAugment

Models	Baseline	Classifier1	Classifier2	Classifier3	Classifier4	Ensemble
ResNet18	69.21	55.03	60.94	64.70	70.51	70.63
ResNet50	76.30	71.72	74.58	77.45	77.89	78.28
ResNet101	77.03	71.75	74.39	79.47	79.70	78.87
ResNet152	77.62	71.50	75.36	80.22	80.32	80.56
ResNeXt50-4	77.29	71.95	75.76	79.02	79.96	80.32
WideResNet50	77.46	72.37	75.99	79.22	79.87	80.17

13 neural networks, the shallowest classifier, which has much fewer parameters and computations, achieves higher accuracy than their baseline models. (iii) In all the neural networks, the second shallowest classifier achieves higher accuracy than their baseline models. (iv) There are 3.38% and 4.84% accuracy improvements on MobileNetV2 and ShuffleNetV2, indicating that self-distillation also works on lightweight neural networks.

Figure 4 shows the comparison of computation, parameters, and accuracy of four ResNet models on CIFAR100. The blue dots indicate the three shallow classifiers and the deepest classifier in neural networks and the orange dot indicates the baseline model. It is observed that significant accuracy improvements and acceleration can be achieved simultaneously by replacing the baseline model with shallow classifiers.

Table 2 shows the experiment results on ImageNet with Auto Augment and Fig. 5 shows the parameters, computation, and accuracy of ResNet models. It is observed that (i) On average, a 2.84% accuracy boost can be observed in neural networks trained by self-distillation on ImageNet, ranging from 2.47% on ResNet18 as the minimum to 4.24% on ResNet50 as the maximum. (ii) More benefits can be found in neural networks with more layers. (iii) Significant acceleration and compression

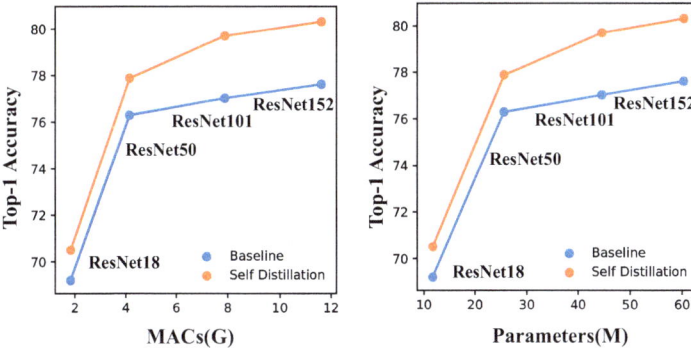

Fig. 5 Experiment results of self-distillation on ImageNet. MAC indicates the multiply-accumulation operation of neural networks

Table 3 Comparison with other KD methods on CIFAR100. The numbers are reported by the accuracy of the deepest classifier

KD method	Accuracy
Student (ResNet18) w/o KD	79.01
Teacher (ResNet50) w/o KD	80.88
KD [1]	80.49
KD + Self-Distillation	82.23
FitNet [24]	80.67
FitNet + Self-Distillation	82.17
AT [34]	80.43
AT + Self-Distillation	82.34
DML [8]	80.52
DML + Self-Distillation	82.09
Self-Distillation	81.76

can be achieved by replacing the deep ResNet with shallow ResNet trained by self-distillation.

The comparison between self-distillation and the other three kinds of KD methods on CIFAR100 is shown in Table 3. It is observed that (i) Self-distillation achieves the highest accuracy compared with the other KD methods. 0.98% accuracy boost can be found in the comparison between self-distillation and the second-best KD method (DML). (ii) Self-distillation and other KD methods can be utilized together to attain more improvements in accuracy. 1.74, 1.50, and 1.57% accuracy boosts can be achieved by combining KD, AT, and DML with self-distillation.

3.2 Evaluation on Dynamic Inference

Experiment results of the proposed threshold-controlled dynamic inference method are shown in Tables 4 and 5. It is observed that the proposed dynamic inference leads

Table 4 Experiment results of dynamic inference on CIFAR100 with different thresholds. Accuracy and acceleration in this table indicate the accuracy increment and the acceleration ratio compared with baseline models, respectively

ResNet18		ResNet50		ResNet101		ResNet152	
Accuracy	Acceleration	Accuracy	Acceleration	Accuracy	Acceleration	Accuracy	Acceleration
+3.10	1.4X	+4.04	1.8X	+2.48	+4.0X	+1.69	4.8X
+3.06	1.6X	+4.01	2.0X	+2.47	+4.2X	+1.78	5.4X
+3.06	1.8X	+4.10	2.2X	+2.37	+4.4X	+1.71	5.8X
+2.98	2.0X	+4.10	2.4X	+2.31	+4.6X	+1.82	6.2X
+2.87	2.2X	+3.92	2.6X	+2.05	+4.8X	+1.50	6.6X
+2.82	2.4X	+3.45	2.8X	+2.07	+5.0X	+1.16	7.4X
+2.17	2.6X	+2.68	3.0X	+1.93	+5.2X	+0.37	7.8X

3 Evaluation and Discussion

Table 5 Experiment results of dynamic inference on ImageNet with different thresholds. Accuracy and acceleration in this table indicate the accuracy increment and the acceleration ratio compared with baseline models, respectively

ResNet18		ResNet50		ResNet101		ResNet152	
Accuracy	Acceleration	Accuracy	Acceleration	Accuracy	Acceleration	Accuracy	Acceleration
+1.40	1.10X	+0.13	1.74X	+2.32	1.92X	+2.63	2.17X
+1.26	1.15X	+0.87	1.66X	+2.17	2.01X	+2.26	2.59X
+0.88	1.20X	+1.28	1.60X	+1.71	2.15X	+2.03	2.71X
+0.04	1.25X	+1.36	1.56X	+1.42	2.21X	+1.74	2.82X
/	/	+1.54	1.42X	+0.98	2.30X	+0.24	3.17X

Fig. 6 The relation between the threshold and the number of images classified by this classifier. Note that there are 10K images in the testing set

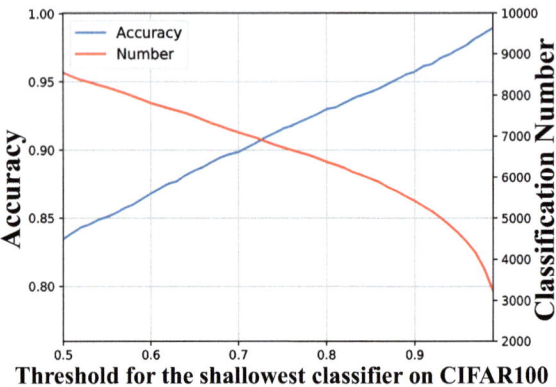

Threshold for the shallowest classifier on CIFAR100

to benefits for both model accuracy and acceleration. With different thresholds, the trade-offs between them can be adjusted flexibly.

Figure 6 gives a comparison between the proposed method and three related dynamic inference methods including ACT, SCAT [35], and BlockDrop [36]. Experiments are conducted on ImageNet with ResNet101. It is observed that the dynamic inference in self-distillation has outperformed other related methods by a large margin. The thresholds of shallow classifiers have a great impact on the classification results. With a lower threshold, most images can be predicted by shallow classifiers, indicating more rapid responses yet lower accuracy. With a higher threshold, most images can be determined by deeper classifiers, indicating precise prediction yet longer response time. The relation among thresholds, classification accuracy, and the number of images classified are shown in Fig. 6. The X axis is the threshold of the shallowest classifier on ResNet18. The left Y-axis indicates its classification accuracy while the right Y-axis indicates how many images are classified by the shallowest classifier. It is observed that (i) The higher the threshold is, the more classification accuracy is achieved, and the less images can be classified. (ii) Even with a very high threshold (0.99), there are more than 30% of images can be classified. (iii) Even with a very low threshold (0.5), the shallowest classifier can achieve higher classification accuracy than the baseline model (79.01%).

3.3 Analysis of Self-Distillation

3.3.1 Influence from Different Distillation Paths

The experiment results of these four kinds of distillation schemes are shown in Table 6. It is observed that (i) All of the four distillation paths have achieved significant accuracy boosts over the baselines, especially on the shallow classifiers. (ii) There is no obvious difference among the four kinds of distillation schemes,

3 Evaluation and Discussion

Table 6 Experiments of different distillation paths in self-distillation

Distillation path	Classifier1	Classifier2	Classifier3	Classifier4	Ensemble
No distillation	75.85	78.73	81.27	81.26	82.65
Best teacher distillation	76.22	79.81	81.93	81.29	82.32
Densely connected distillation	77.52	79.98	81.32	81.37	82.42
Transitive distillation	76.31	79.32	81.24	81.76	82.64
Ensemble teacher distillation	76.50	78.90	82.01	81.86	83.33

Table 7 Ablation study on the loss function with ResNet18 on CIFAR100

Loss	Baseline			Self-distillation	
L_{KL}	×	✓	×	✓
L_2	×	×	✓	✓
Accuracy	79.01	81.58	80.37	81.76

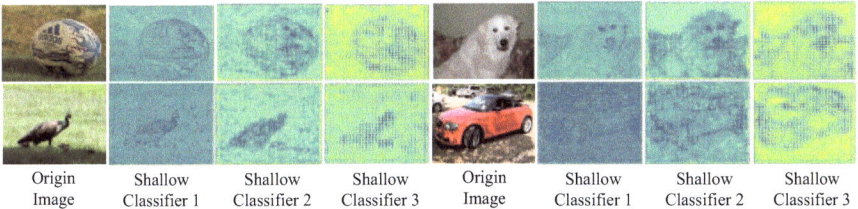

Origin Image | Shallow Classifier 1 | Shallow Classifier 2 | Shallow Classifier 3 | Origin Image | Shallow Classifier 1 | Shallow Classifier 2 | Shallow Classifier 3

Fig. 7 Visualization of attention maps in shallow classifiers on ImageNet

indicating that self-distillation is not sensitive to the choice of teacher and student models.

3.3.2 Ablation Study

Compared with the standard training, two distillation loss L_{KL} and L_2 are introduced in self-distillation. As shown in Table 7, an ablation study is conducted to demonstrate their effectiveness. It is observed that (i) Self-distillation with only one of the two losses still outperforms the baseline model by a large margin. (ii) Self-distillation achieves best accuracy when the two loss functions are utilized together.

3.3.3 Visualization of Attention Map

In self-distillation, attention modules are introduced to obtain classifier-specific features, leading to a significant performance gain on shallow classifiers. We further visualize the spatial attention maps as depicted in Fig. 7. The heat maps indicate learned attention maps where the value of each pixel is computed as the average value of pixels in the same position of all channels.

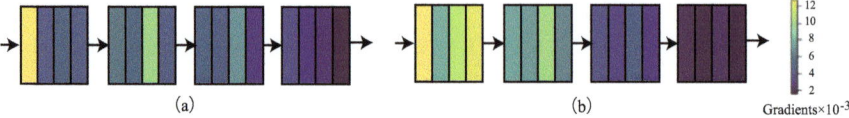

Fig. 8 The visualization of the average absolute value of gradients in the training period of ResNet18 on CIFAR100. The blocks in the figure indicate the convolutional layers. (**a**) Without self distillation. (**b**) With self distillation

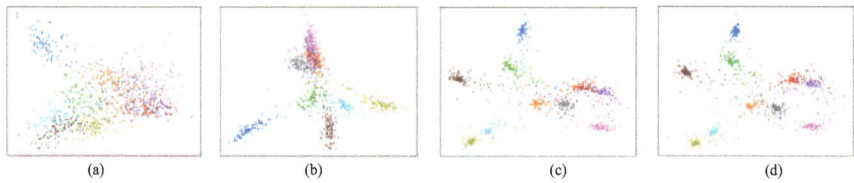

Fig. 9 Principal component analysis (PCA) of the feature distribution in four classifiers. (**a**) Classifier1. (**b**) Classifier2. (**c**) Classifier3. (**d**) Classifier4

As depicted in Fig. 7, all the classifiers pay their attention to the same spatial position while ignoring the backgrounds, which indicates that all of the attention modules have learned to find the most informative pixels. The attention maps in shallow classifier 1 seem to concentrate on the details of the shark's and cat's features such as their outlines. In contrast, the attention maps in shallow classifier 3 focus more on the texture features, which indicates that deep classifiers with larger receptive fields are more likely to predict based on global and low-frequency information while shallow classifiers are inclined to be dominated by local and high-frequency information (Figs. 8 and 9).

3.3.4 Model Interpretation by Integrated Gradients

As shown in Fig. 10, the output of shallow classifiers is interpreted by integrated gradients [37]. The bright pixels in the figure indicate that the pixels have a large impact on the prediction result of the image. It is observed that the shallow classifiers and the deepest classifier have similar interpretation results—the pixels containing objects have a high value while the pixels of the background have a low value.

3.3.5 Visualization of Feature Map

More discriminating features are extracted with deeper classifiers in self-distillation. Since there are multiple classifiers in self-distillation, the features of each classifier can be computed and analyzed to demonstrate their discriminating principles. As depicted in Fig. 9, experiments on WideResNet trained on CIFAR100 are conducted to compare features of different classifiers. Figure 9 visualizes the distances of

4 Brief Summary

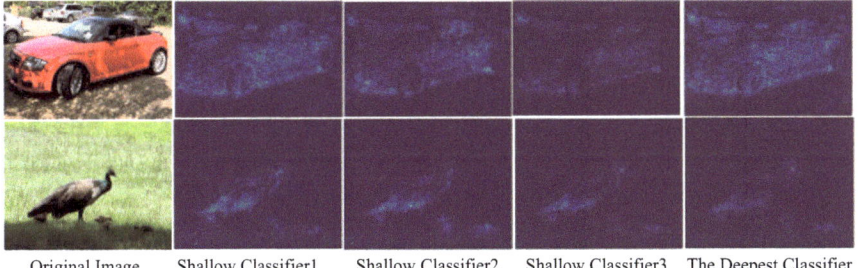

Original Image   Shallow Classifier1   Shallow Classifier2   Shallow Classifier3   The Deepest Classifier

Fig. 10 The interpretation map of classifiers by the integrated gradients [37]. The brightness of each pixel indicates its influence on the prediction results of the classifier

features in different classifiers. To begin with, it is obvious that the deeper the classifier is, the more concentrated clusters are observed. In addition, the changes of the distances in shallow classifiers, as shown in Fig. 9a, b, are more severe than those in deep classifiers, as demonstrated in Fig. 9c, d.

3.3.6 Vanishing Gradients

Self-distillation can prevent models from vanishing gradients. It is generally acknowledged that deep neural networks are difficult to train due to the problem of vanishing gradients. In self-distillation, the supervision of the neural networks is injected into different depths. DSN [38] has proven that multi-exit neural networks can alleviate the problem of vanishing gradients mathematically. We conduct the following experiments to support this view. Two 18-layer ResNets are trained, one of them is equipped with self-distillation and the other is not. We compute the mean magnitude of gradients in each convolutional layer as shown in Fig. 8. It is observed that the magnitude of gradients of the model with self-distillation (Fig. 8a) is larger than the one without self-distillation (Fig. 8b), especially in the first and second ResBlocks.

4 Brief Summary

This chapter studies the first fundamental problem in KD—"how to build the student models and teacher models". It introduces self-distillation, which performs KD from the deeper layers to the shallow layers, leading to benefits in model accuracy, model acceleration, and model compression simultaneously. Based on the multi-exit neural network in self-distillation, the threshold-controlled dynamic inference can be utilized to achieve higher acceleration. There are two main insights provided in self-distillation. Firstly, the knowledge transfer within one neural network is very promising. Different from conventional KD, which transfers knowledge among different models, self-distillation has proved that the knowledge transfer inside one model can be utilized to improve the performance of neural networks. Secondly, the success of dynamic inference in this section shows that the bottleneck of dynamic inference is how to train a high-performance early exit in the neural network, instead of how to control different exit paths. In summary, self-distillation provides an alternative to build students and teachers in KD.

References

1. Hinton, G., Vinyals, O., Dean, J.: Distilling the knowledge in a neural network. In: Advances in Neural Information Processing Systems (NeurIPS) (2014)
2. Park, S., Kwak, N.: Feed: Feature-level ensemble for knowledge distillation. arXiv preprint arXiv:1909.10754 (2019)
3. Shen, C., Xue, M., Wang, X., Song, J., Sun, L., Song, M.: Customizing student networks from heterogeneous teachers via adaptive knowledge amalgamation. In: Proceedings of the IEEE/CVF International Conference on Computer Vision, pp. 3504–3513 (2019)
4. Luo, S., Wang, X., Fang, G., Hu, Y., Tao, D., Song, M.: Knowledge amalgamation from heterogeneous networks by common feature learning. arXiv preprint arXiv:1906.10546 (2019)
5. You, S., Xu, C., Xu, C., Tao, D.: Learning from multiple teacher networks. In: Proceedings of the 23rd ACM SIGKDD International Conference on Knowledge Discovery and Data Mining, pp. 1285–1294 (2017)
6. Xiang, L., Ding, G., Han, J.: Learning from multiple experts: Self-paced knowledge distillation for long-tailed classification. In: Computer Vision–ECCV 2020: 16th European Conference, Glasgow, UK, August 23–28, 2020, Proceedings, Part V 16, pp. 247–263. Springer (2020)
7. Sau, B.B., Balasubramanian, V.N.: Deep model compression: Distilling knowledge from noisy teachers. arXiv preprint arXiv:1610.09650 (2016)
8. Zhang, Y., Xiang, T., Hospedales, T.M., Lu, H.: Deep mutual learning. In: IEEE/CVF Conference on Computer Vision and Pattern Recognition (CVPR), pp. 4320–4328 (2018)
9. Guo, Q., Wang, X., Wu, Y., Yu, Z., Liang, D., Hu, X., Luo, P.: Online knowledge distillation via collaborative learning. In: Proceedings of the IEEE/CVF Conference on Computer Vision and Pattern Recognition, pp. 11020–11029 (2020)
10. Chen, D., Mei, J.-P., Wang, C., Feng, Y., Chen, C.: Online knowledge distillation with diverse peers. In: Proceedings of the AAAI conference on artificial intelligence, vol. 34, pp. 3430–3437 (2020)
11. Zhu, X., Gong, S., et al.: Knowledge distillation by on-the-fly native ensemble. Advances in neural information processing systems, 31 (2018)
12. Li, Z., Ye, J., Song, M., Huang, Y., Pan, Z.: Online knowledge distillation for efficient pose estimation. In: Proceedings of the IEEE/CVF international conference on computer vision, pp. 11740–11750 (2021)
13. Furlanello, T., Lipton, Z.C., Tschannen, M., Itti, L., Anandkumar, A.: Born again neural networks. In: Proceedings of the International Conference on Machine Learning (ICML) (2018)
14. Yang, C., Xie, L., Qiao, S., Yuille, A.L.: Training deep neural networks in generations: A more tolerant teacher educates better students. In: Proceedings of the AAAI Conference on Artificial Intelligence, vol. 33, pp. 5628–5635 (2019)
15. Clark, K., Luong, M.-T., Khandelwal, U., Manning, C.D., Le, Q.V.: Bam! Born-again multi-task networks for natural language understanding. arXiv preprint arXiv:1907.04829 (2019)

References

16. Xu, T.-B., Liu, C.-L.: Data-distortion guided self-distillation for deep neural networks. In: Proceedings of the AAAI Conference on Artificial Intelligence, vol. 33, pp. 5565–5572 (2019)
17. Lee, H., Hwang, S.J., Shin, J.: Rethinking data augmentation: Self-supervision and self-distillation. arXiv preprint arXiv:1910.05872 (2019)
18. Mirzadeh, S.-I., Farajtabar, M., Li, A., Ghasemzadeh, H.: Improved knowledge distillation via teacher assistant: Bridging the gap between student and teacher. arXiv preprint arXiv:1902.03393 (2019)
19. Jin, X., Peng, B., Wu, Y., Liu, Y., Liu, J., Liang, D., Yan, J., Hu, X.: Knowledge distillation via route constrained optimization. In: International Conference on Computer Vision (ICCV), October (2019)
20. Son, W., Na, J., Choi, J., Hwang, W.: Densely guided knowledge distillation using multiple teacher assistants. In: Proceedings of the IEEE/CVF International Conference on Computer Vision, pp. 9395–9404 (2021)
21. Zhu, Y., Wang, Y.: Student customized knowledge distillation: Bridging the gap between student and teacher. In: Proceedings of the IEEE/CVF International Conference on Computer Vision, pp. 5057–5066 (2021)
22. Cho, J.H., Hariharan, B.: On the efficacy of knowledge distillation. In: International Conference on Computer Vision (ICCV), October (2019)
23. Kang, M., Mun, J., Han, B.: Towards oracle knowledge distillation with neural architecture search. In: AAAI Conference on Artificial Intelligence (AAAI) (2020)
24. Romero, A., Ballas, N., Kahou, S.E., Chassang, A., Gatta, C., Bengio, Y.: Fitnets: Hints for thin deep nets. In: International Conference on Learning Representations (ICLR) (2015)
25. Lopez-Paz, D., Bottou, L., Schölkopf, B., Vapnik, V.: Unifying distillation and privileged information. In: International Conference on Learning Representations (ICLR) (2016)
26. Krizhevsky, A., Hinton, G.: Learning multiple layers of features from tiny images. Technical report, Citeseer (2009)
27. Deng, J., Dong, W., Socher, R., Li, L.-J., Li, K., Fei-Fei, L.: Imagenet: A large-scale hierarchical image database. In: IEEE/CVF Conference on Computer Vision and Pattern Recognition (CVPR), pp. 248–255 (2009)
28. He, K., Zhang, X., Ren, S., Sun, J.: Deep residual learning for image recognition. In: IEEE/CVF Conference on Computer Vision and Pattern Recognition (CVPR), pp. 770–778 (2016)
29. Zagoruyko, S., Komodakis, N.: Wide residual networks. In: British Machine Vision Conference (BMVC) (2016)
30. Xie, S., Girshick, R., Dollár, P., Tu, Z., He, K.: Aggregated residual transformations for deep neural networks. In: IEEE/CVF Conference on Computer Vision and Pattern Recognition (CVPR), pp. 5987–5995 (2017)
31. Hu, J., Shen, L., Sun, G.: Squeeze-and-excitation networks. In: IEEE/CVF Conference on Computer Vision and Pattern Recognition (CVPR), pp. 7132–7141 (2018)
32. Sandler, M., Howard, A., Zhu, M., Zhmoginov, A., Chen, L.-C.: Mobilenetv2: Inverted residuals and linear bottlenecks. In: IEEE/CVF Conference on Computer Vision and Pattern Recognition (CVPR), pp. 4510–4520 (2018)
33. Ma, N., Zhang, X., Zheng, H.-T., Sun, J.: Shufflenet v2: Practical guidelines for efficient cnn architecture design. In: European Conference on Computer Vision (ECCV), pp. 116–131 (2018)
34. Zagoruyko, S., Komodakis, N.: Paying more attention to attention: Improving the performance of convolutional neural networks via attention transfer. In: International Conference on Learning Representations (ICLR) (2017)
35. Figurnov, M., Collins, M.D., Zhu, Y., Zhang, L., Huang, J., Vetrov, D., Salakhutdinov, R.: Spatially adaptive computation time for residual networks. In: IEEE/CVF Conference on Computer Vision and Pattern Recognition (CVPR), pp. 1039–1048 (2017)
36. Wu, Z., Nagarajan, T., Kumar, A., Rennie, S., Davis, L.S., Grauman, K., Feris, R.: Blockdrop: Dynamic inference paths in residual networks. In: IEEE/CVF Conference on Computer Vision and Pattern Recognition (CVPR), pp. 8817–8826 (2018)

37. Sundararajan, M., Taly, A., Yan, Q.: Axiomatic attribution for deep networks. In: Proceedings of the 34th International Conference on Machine Learning, vol. 70, pp. 3319–3328. JMLR. org (2017)
38. Lee, C.-Y., Xie, S., Gallagher, P., Zhang, Z., Tu, Z.: Deeply-supervised nets. In: International Conference on Artificial Intelligence and Statistics (AISTATS), pp. 562–570 (2015)

Distilled Knowledge in KD

Abstract This chapter systematically discusses the second fundamental problem in KD—what knowledge to be distilled. While traditional KD focuses on logits (soft predictions), subsequent research reveals richer information in feature maps and relational patterns. However, the optimal knowledge type remains unclear, as neural networks lack explicit metrics to evaluate knowledge utility. This chapter studies the influence from the distilled knowledge in KD, from the perspectives of both task-oriented KD and task-irrelevant KD. Our findings demonstrate that task-oriented KD is able to transfer the most crucial knowledge for the given task, while task-irrelevant KD is more beneficial in all kinds of downstream tasks, such as classification, detection, and segmentation on images and videos.

1 Problem Definition

The second fundamental problem of KD is what kind of teacher knowledge should be distilled. In original KD, the student model learns the knowledge from the prediction results of the teacher. After that, extensive works show that the features of the teacher model carry more beneficial knowledge for the student. As a result, abundant methods have been proposed to distill the knowledge in the features and the variants of features. However, since the knowledge of a neural network is difficult to measure, there is still no clear answer on what kind of knowledge should be distilled.

1.1 Previous Methods

1.1.1 Logit-based KD

In KD, logits refer to the prediction results of a neural network after the softmax layer, which usually indicates the categorical probability distribution for image classification. Logits are considered to carry richer information than the one-hot labels and hence the student models are usually trained to the logits from the teachers [1–3]. Besides, Zhao et al. have improved logit-based KD by decoupling it into the target class KD and non-target class KD [4]. Recently, Hao et al. find that the performance gap between logit-based KD and the other well-designed KD can be decreased by simply leveraging stronger data augmentation [5].

1.1.2 Feature-based KD

Since the features of teacher models have more information than logits, feature distillation enables student models to learn richer information and always leads to more accuracy improvements. FitNet has been proposed to train the student models with the feature map of teacher models instead of the logit [6]. Zagoruyko et al. apply feature distillation on the attention map of neural networks at different layers [7]. Heo et al. give a comprehensive overhaul of feature distillation which shows that distilling the positive value of features is more beneficial [8]. Ahn et al. propose to distill the variational information from the teacher features [9]. Xu et al. introduce the kernel-based progressive distillation for AdderNet by mapping the features into high-dimension space and then distilling them [10]. Kim et al. propose to distill the correlation between features at different layers [11]. Jin et al. introduce the global kernel alignment to measure the distance between features of different sizes [12].

1.1.3 Relation-based KD

Besides distilling the knowledge for the single input, relation-based KD methods have been proposed to distill the relation for different inputs [13, 14]. Since the relation information carries the high-order semantic information, it can be utilized as the complement for predication-based and feature-based KD methods. For instance, Park et al. propose relational KD by measuring the relation between the features of two images with their angle distance [15]. Besides the relation between different inputs, abundant works show that it is possible to distill the relation between the information on different pixels [16] and patches [17] and so on. For example, Dai et al. propose to apply KD to object detection by distilling teacher knowledge at different objects in the same image [18].

1.2 Remaining Problems

Fruitful works have studied logit-based, feature-based, and relation-based KD. Nonetheless, the determination of which type of knowledge yields the most significant benefits remains ambiguous. To obtain the highest compression and acceleration performance, it is necessary to study how to extract the most beneficial knowledge from the teacher model.

2 Task-Oriented Feature Distillation

In 2024, Hinton et al. first propose the concept of distillation, where a lightweight student model is trained to mimic the softmax outputs (i.e. logit) of an overparameterized teacher model [21]. Later, abundant feature distillation methods are proposed to encourage the student models to mimic the features of teacher models [2, 6–8, 22]. Since the features of teacher models have more information than logit, feature distillation enables student models to learn richer information and always leads to more accuracy improvements. As shown in Fig. 1, instead of directly learning all the features of the teacher models, most of the feature distillation methods first apply a transformation function to the features to convert them into an easy-to-distill form and then distill them to students. In this progress, some unimportant information are filtered, as shown in Table 1. However, what still remains unknown is which form of information is the best to distill and which kind of transformation function can extract this form of information.

In this section, *we assume that the task-oriented information is the information which is the most essential to distillation.* Based on this assumption, we propose a novel knowledge distillation method named task-oriented feature distillation (short as TOFD). Different from previous feature distillation methods whose transfor-

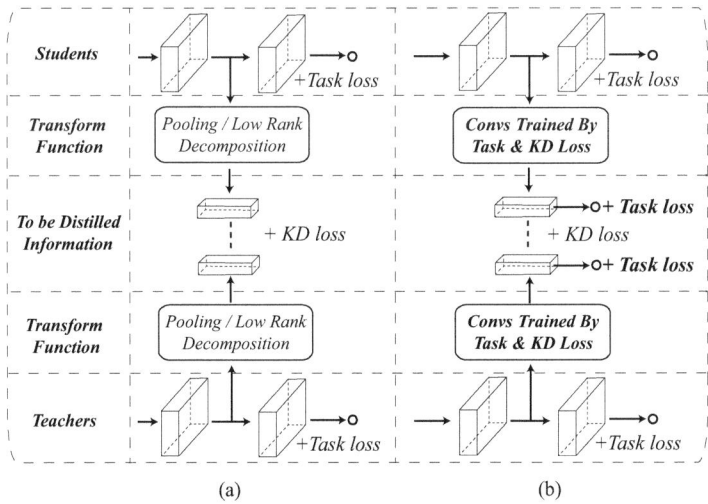

Fig. 1 Comparison between previous feature distillation and task-oriented feature distillation. (**a**) Previous feature distillation. (**b**) Task-oriented feature distillation

Table 1 A survey of previous feature distillation methods and task-oriented feature distillation

Method	Transformation	Lost information
AT [7]	Channelwise pooling	Channel dims
FSP [11]	FSP matrix	Spatial dims
Jacobian [19]	Gradients	Channel dims
SVD [20]	SVD decomposition	Spatial dims
Heo et al. [8]	Margin ReLU	Negative feature
Task-oriented	Convolutional layers	Non-task-oriented
Feature distillation	Trained by task loss	Features

mation functions are manually designed, the transformation function in TOFD is convolutional layers which are trained in a data-driven manner by both distillation loss and the task loss. In the training period of TOFD, several auxiliary classifiers are attached at different depths to the backbone layers. Each auxiliary classifier consists of several convolutional layers, a pooling layer and a fully connected layer. They are trained to perform the same task as the whole neural network does. As a result, the auxiliary classifiers help to capture the task-oriented information from the whole features in the backbone layers, leading to high-efficiency knowledge distillation.

In most situations of knowledge distillation, the features of students and teachers have different widths, heights and channels. Usually, a convolutional layer or a fully connected layer is applied to match their sizes. However, this leads to one problem that some useful information of teachers may be lost in the progress of feature resizing. To address this problem, an orthogonal loss has been introduced in TOFD to regularize the weights of the feature resizing layer. With the property of orthogonality, more supervision from teachers can be exploited in students training.

2.1 Extracting and Distilling Task-Oriented Knowledge

The details of the proposed task-oriented feature distillation are shown in Fig. 2. It is observed that several auxiliary classifiers are attached at different depths of the convolutional neural networks. Each auxiliary classifier is composed of several convolutional layers, a pooling layer and a fully connected layer. They are trained to perform the same task as the whole neural network does. As a result, the convolutional layers in the auxiliary classifiers can capture the task-oriented information from the whole features. Then, these task-oriented information is distilled to the student models by L_2 loss. Moreover, to facilitate the training of auxiliary classifiers, a logit distillation loss is also applied to each pair of auxiliary classifiers between teacher models and student models. Note that these auxiliary classifiers are only utilized in the training period for knowledge distillation. They are not involved in the inference period, so there is no additional computation and parameters.

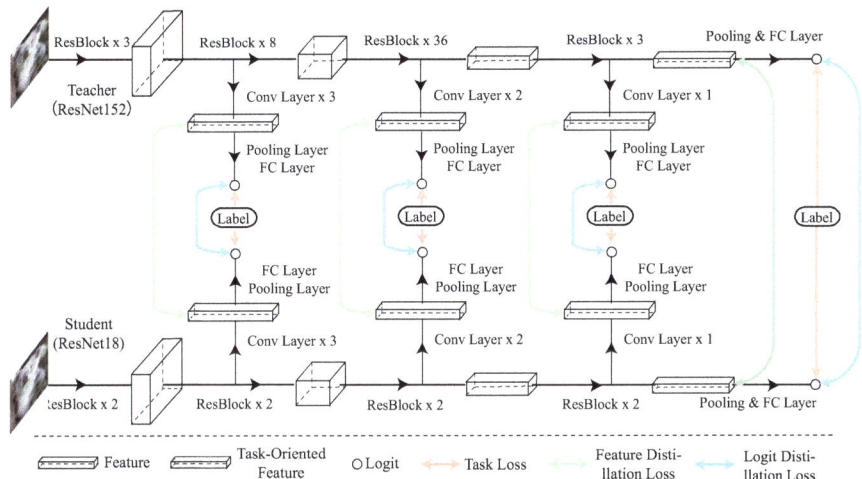

Fig. 2 The overview of TOFD. Best viewed in color. (i) Several auxiliary classifiers are attached at different depths of the neural network. Each auxiliary classifier is composed of several conventional layers, a pooling layer and a fully connected layer. (ii) Each auxiliary classifier is trained by task loss so that it can capture the task-oriented information from the features. (iii) Feature distillation loss is applied between the task-oriented information of students and teachers. (iv) Logit distillation loss is also introduced to facilitate the training of auxiliary classifiers. (v) Auxiliary classifiers are dropped in the inference period to avoid additional computation and parameters

Another crucial problem is how to decide the number and the exact position of the auxiliary classifier. Recent progress in object detection and segmentation [23, 24] demonstrates that features with different resolutions have different information—low resolution features contain more information of the large objects while high resolution features contain more information of the small objects. Inspired by the above conclusion, we choose to perform TOFD before each downsampling layer in neural networks. As a result, different auxiliary classifiers can distill features of teacher models with different resolution. Note that the number of auxiliary classifiers is decided by the number of downsampling layers in the neural networks.

2.1.1 Formulation

Let $\mathcal{X} = \{x_i\}_{i=1}^m$ be a set of training images, $\mathcal{Y} = \{y_i\}_{i=1}^m$ be the corresponding labels. Denote $F_i(\cdot)$ to be the feature map of the i_{th} convolution block and $c_i(\cdot)$ to be the fully connected classifier in the i_{th} convolution block. The superscript t and s denote the teacher model and student model respectively. In a neural network with N convolutional blocks, the logit distillation [21] loss can be formulated as

$$\frac{1}{m}\sum_{i=1}^{m} \cdot L_{KL}(c_N^s(F_N^s(x_i)), c_N^t(F_N^t(x_i))), \qquad (1)$$

where L_{KL} is the KL divergence loss. The loss function of feature distillation can be formulated as

$$\frac{1}{m}\sum_{i=1}^{m}\sum_{j=1}^{N} L_2(T_j(F_j^s(x_i)), T_j(F_j^t(x_i))), \qquad (2)$$

where L_2 is the L_2-norm loss and T indicates the transformation function on the features. In most previous feature distillation methods, T is a non-parametric transformation such as pooling and low rank decomposition. In contrast, T in the proposed TOFD is several convolutional layers whose parameters are trained by both the task loss and the distillation loss. The proposed task-oriented feature distillation loss can be formulated as

$$\frac{1}{m}\sum_{i=1}^{m}\left\{\sum_{j=1}^{N}\alpha \cdot \underbrace{L_2(T_j(F_j^s(x_i)), T_j(F_j^t(x_i)))}_{\mathcal{L}_{\text{feature}}} + \underbrace{L_{CE}(c_j(T_j(F_N^s(x_i))), y_i))}_{\mathcal{L}_{\text{task}}}\right\}, \qquad (3)$$

where α is a hyper-parameter to balance the two kinds of loss. Besides, we could further introduce the logit distillation loss to facilitate the training of the conventional transformation T and the fully connected layer c, which can be formulated as

$$\frac{1}{m}\sum_{i=1}^{m}\sum_{j=1}^{N}\underbrace{L_{KL}(c_j^s(T_j^s(F_N^s(x_i))), c_j^t(T_j^t(F_N^t(x_i))))}_{\mathcal{L}_{\text{logit}}}. \qquad (4)$$

2.1.2 Orthogonal Loss

In most distillation situations, the features of teachers and students have different sizes so their distance can not be directly minimized. To solve this problem, a convolutional or fully connected layer is always introduced to adjust their sizes. However, the information of teachers' features may be lost in this progress, which reduces the effectiveness of feature distillation. In this section, we apply an orthogonal loss to the weights of the feature resizing layer to alleviate this problem. Denotes the distilled features of teacher models as the vector **x** and the weights of feature resizing layer as **W**, the resized feature can be written as **Wx**. To keep the feature information during the feature resizing process and inspired by Bansal et al. [25], we introduce an orthogonal loss that simultaneously penalizes the orthogonality of the row space and column space spanned by **W** in the feature resizing layer, which is defined as

$$\beta \cdot \underbrace{(\|\mathbf{W}^T\mathbf{W} - \mathbf{I}\| + \|\mathbf{W}\mathbf{W}^T - \mathbf{I}\|)}_{\mathcal{L}_{\text{orthogonal}}}, \tag{5}$$

where β is a hyper-parameter to balance its magnitude and other loss. If a convolutional layer instead of a fully connected layer is utilized as the feature resizing layer, its weights can be first reshaped from $S \times H \times C \times M$ to $SHC \times M$ where S, H, C, M are width, height, input channel number and output channel number, respectively. To summarize, the overall loss function can be formulated as

$$\mathcal{L}_{\text{overall}} = \mathcal{L}_{\text{feature}} + \mathcal{L}_{\text{logit}} + \mathcal{L}_{\text{task}} + \mathcal{L}_{\text{orthogonal}}. \tag{6}$$

The overall loss function includes the feature distillation loss, logit distillation loss, task loss, orthogonal loss and two hyper-parameters.

2.2 Evaluation and Discussion

2.2.1 Experiment Setting

The experiments of image classification are conducted with nine kinds of convolutional neural networks, including ResNet [26], PreActResNet [27], SENet [28], ResNeXt [29], MobileNetV1 [30], MobileNetV2 [31], ShuffleNetV1 [32], ShuffleNetV2 [33], WideResNet [34] and three datasets, including CIFAR100 and CIFAR10 [35], ImageNet [36]. The experiments of point cloud classification are conducted with ResGCN [37] of different depths on two datasets including ModelNet10 and ModelNet40 [38]. Four kinds of knowledge distillation methods have been utilized for comparison, including KD [21], FitNet [6], DML [39] and self-distillation [40]. All these experiments are reproduced by ourselves.

2.2.2 Experimental Results

Tables 2 and 3 show the accuracy of student networks on CIFAR100 and CIFAR10. It is observed that: **(a)** The proposed TOFD leads to significant accuracy boost compared with the baseline models. In CIFAR100, 5.46% accuracy boost can be found on the eleven models on average, ranging from 6.75% at SENet50 as the maximum to 3.78% at ShuffleNetV1 as the minimum. In CIFAR10, 2.49% accuracy boost can be found on the eleven models on average, ranging from 3.77% at MobileNetV1 as the maximum to 1.40% at ShuffleNetV1 as the minimum. **(b)** In all the models, the proposed TOFD outperforms the second best distillation method by a large margin. On average, 3.13% and 1.28% accuracy boost compared with the second best distillation method can be observed on CIFAR100 and CIFAR10,

Table 2 Experiment results ((accuracy %)) on CIFAR100

Model	Baseline	KD [21]	FitNet [6]	DML [39]	SD [40]	TOFD
ResNet18	77.09	78.34	78.57	78.72	78.64	**82.92**
ResNet50	77.42	78.58	78.62	79.18	80.56	**84.74**
PreactResNet18	76.05	77.41	78.79	77.03	78.12	**82.06**
PreactResNet50	77.74	78.26	79.12	78.48	80.12	**83.33**
SEResNet18	77.27	78.43	78.49	78.58	79.01	**83.06**
SEResNet50	77.69	78.89	78.82	79.72	80.56	**84.44**
ResNeXt50-4	79.49	80.46	79.54	80.39	82.45	**84.67**
MobileNetV1	67.82	67.55	71.78	67.73	71.39	**72.82**
MobileNetV2	69.04	70.16	70.21	68.79	71.45	**73.57**
ShuffleNetV1	72.26	73.54	72.78	72.72	74.30	**76.04**
ShuffleNetV2	72.38	72.86	74.36	72.66	73.32	**76.68**

Numbers in bold indicate the highest accuracy

Table 3 Experiment results on CIFAR10 (top-1 accuracy/%). Numbers in bold are the highest

Model	Baseline	KD [21]	FitNet [6]	DML [39]	SD [40]	TOFD
ResNet18	94.25	94.67	95.57	95.19	95.87	**96.92**
ResNet50	94.69	94.56	95.83	95.73	96.01	**96.84**
PreactResNet18	94.20	93.74	95.22	94.80	95.08	**96.49**
PreactResNet50	94.39	93.53	94.98	95.87	95.82	**96.93**
SEResNet18	94.78	94.53	95.64	95.37	95.51	**96.80**
SEResNet50	94.83	94.80	95.31	94.83	95.45	**97.02**
ResNeXt50-4	94.49	95.41	95.78	95.41	96.01	**97.09**
MobileNetV1	90.16	91.70	90.53	91.65	91.98	**93.93**
MobileNetV2	90.43	92.86	90.49	90.49	91.02	**93.34**
ShuffleNetV1	91.33	92.57	92.23	91.40	92.47	**92.73**
ShuffleNetV2	90.88	92.42	91.83	91.87	92.51	**93.74**

respectively. (**c**) The proposed TOFD not only works on the over-parameters models such as ResNet and SENet, but also shows significant effectiveness in the lightweight models such as MobileNet and ShuffleNet. On average, 4.40% and 2.74% accuracy boost of the lightweight models can be observed on CIFAR100 and CIFAR10 datasets.

Table 4 shows the experiment results of TOFD on ImageNet. ResNet152 model is utilized as the teacher model across all these experiments. It is observed that (**a**) On average, TOFD leads to 1.18% accuracy improvements across the 6 neural networks. (**b**) The distilled ResNet50 and ResNet101 have higher accuracy than the baselines of ResNet101 and ResNet152 respectively. By replacing the distilled ResNet50 and ResNet101 with ResNet101 and ResNet152 respectively, TOFD achieves 1.57 times compression and 1.81 acceleration with no accuracy loss.

Tables 5 and 6 show the experiment results of TOFD on ModelNet10 and ModelNet40. It is observed that (**a**) In 3D classification tasks, knowledge distillation methods are not as effective as they do in image classification tasks. In the five

Table 4 Experiment results on ImageNet (top-1 accuracy/%)

Model	Baseline	TOFD	MAC(G)	Param(M)
ResNet18	69.76	70.92	1.82	11.69
ResNet50	76.13	77.52	4.11	25.56
ResNet101	77.37	78.64	7.83	44.55
ResNet152	78.31	79.21	11.56	60.19
ResNeXt50-32-4	77.62	78.93	4.26	25.03
WideResNet50-2	78.47	79.52	11.43	68.88

Table 5 Experiments results of the 3D classification task on ModelNet10 (top-1 accuracy/%)

Model	Baseline	KD [21]	FitNet [6]	DML [39]	SD [40]	TOFD
ResGCN8	92.73	93.50	94.05	93.61	93.17	**94.38**
ResGCN12	93.50	93.28	93.17	94.05	92.40	**94.16**
ResGCN16	92.40	92.84	93.39	93.17	92.62	**93.83**

Numbers in bold indicate the highest accuracy

Table 6 Experiments results of the 3D classification task on ModelNet40 (top-1 accuracy/%)

Model	Baseline	KD [21]	FitNet [6]	DML [39]	SD [40]	TOFD
ResGCN8	90.76	91.29	90.76	91.69	90.60	**91.77**
ResGCN12	90.32	91.21	90.80	91.41	90.80	**91.65**
ResGCN16	91.33	91.45	**91.45**	91.33	91.25	**91.45**

Numbers in bold indicate the highest accuracy

distillation methods, only DML and TOFD can achieve consistent accuracy boost than the baseline. (**b**) TOFD outperforms other knowledge distillation methods on all models and datasets. Compared with the baselines, 1.25% and 0.82% accuracy boost can be found in ModelNet10 and ModelNet40 with TOFD on average.

2.2.3 Visualization on Task-Oriented Information

The auxiliary classifiers in TOFD are introduced to capture the task-oriented information from the features of both students and teachers. As shown in Fig. 3, we have visualized the features in the backbone layers and the task-oriented features captured by the auxiliary classifiers with the Gram-Cam method [41]. It is observed that: (**a**) Except the features of the last layer (sub-figure d), the features in the backbone layers have no direct relation with the classification task. The attention of convolutional layers are paid to the whole figure uniformly, indicating there is much non-task-oriented information in the features of backbone layers. (**b**) In the heatmaps of the auxiliary classifier, the pixels of the dog have much more attention value than the background, indicating that auxiliary classifiers really capture the task-oriented information from the original features.

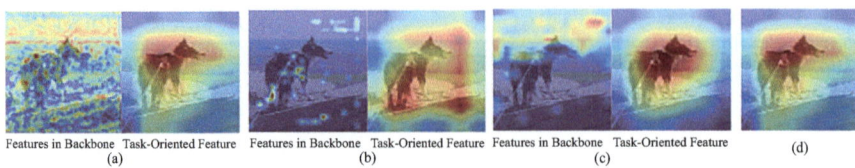

Features in Backbone Task-Oriented Feature   Features in Backbone Task-Oriented Feature   Features in Backbone Task-Oriented Feature   (d)
(a)   (b)   (c)

Fig. 3 Comparison on the Grad-CAM [41] visualization results between the features of the backbone layers and the task-oriented features captured by auxiliary classifiers. (**a**) ResNet Stage 1. (**b**) ResNet Stage 2. (**c**) ResNet Stage 3. (**d**) The final conv

Table 7 Ablation study with ResNet18 on CIFAR100 (top-1 accuracy/%)

$\mathcal{L}_{\text{logit}}$	×	✓	×	✓	×	✓	✓
$\mathcal{L}_{\text{feature}}$	×	×	✓	✓	×	✓	✓
$\mathcal{L}_{\text{task}}$	×	×	×	×	✓	✓	✓
$\mathcal{L}_{\text{orthogonal}}$	×	×	×	×	×	×	✓
Accuracy	77.09	78.34	78.57	78.81	79.99	82.31	82.92

2.2.4 Ablation Study

As shown in Table 7, an ablation study on CIFAR100 with ResNet18 is conducted to show the individual effectiveness of different components in TOFD. It is observed that (**a**) Compared with the combination between feature distillation and logit distillation, 3.50% (82.31–78.81%) accuracy boost can be obtained with the auxiliary classifiers, indicating that the task-oriented information is beneficial to knowledge distillation. (**b**) With only the auxiliary classifier, 2.90% (77.09–79.99%) accuracy boost can be observed compared with the baseline, indicating that the multi-exit training itself can facilitate model training. (**c**) The orthogonal loss on feature resizing layer leads to 0.61% (82.92–82.31%) accuracy boost.

3 Task-Irrelevant KD

The increasing depth of neural networks introduces challenges in their training process. Traditional supervised training method only applies the supervision to the last layer and then propagates the error from the last layer to the shallow layers (Fig. 4a), which leads to hardship in optimizing the intermediate layers, such as gradient vanishing [42]. Recently, deep supervision has been proposed to address this issue by optimizing the intermediate layers directly [43]. As shown in Fig. 4b, deep supervision adds several auxiliary classifiers to the intermediate layers at different depths. During the training phase, these classifiers are optimized with the original final classifier together by the same training loss (e.g. cross entropy for classification tasks). Both experimental and theoretical analyses have demonstrated its effectiveness in facilitating model convergence [44]. However,

3 Task-Irrelevant KD

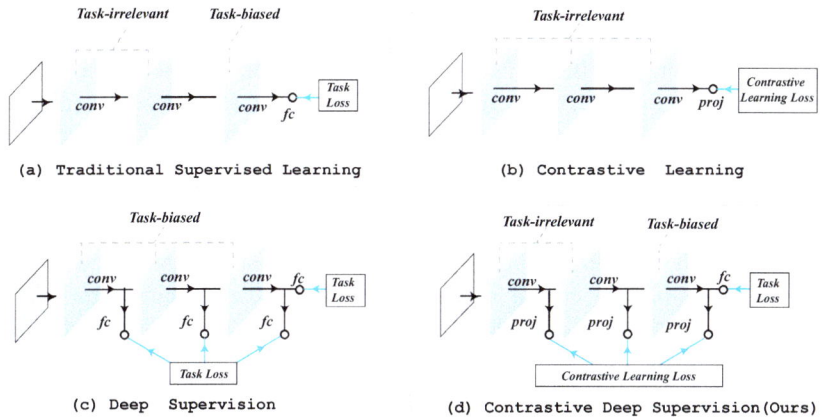

Fig. 4 The overview of the four methods. " $\rightarrow$ " and " $\dashrightarrow$ " indicate the path of forward computation and the backward computation for gradients. "proj" and "fc" indicate the projection heads and the fully connected classifiers, respectively. The *gray dashed line* indicates whether the feature is task-irrelevant or task-biased. (**a**) Traditional supervised learning only applies supervision to the last layer and propagates it to the previous layers, leading to gradient vanishing. (**b**) Contrastive learning. (**c**) Deep supervision trains both the last layer and the intermediate layers directly, which addresses gradient vanishing but makes all the layers biased to the task. (**d**) Our method introduces contrastive learning to supervise the intermediate layer and thus avoids these problems

success comes with remaining obstacles. In general, different layers in convolutional neural networks tend to learn features at different levels. Usually, the shallow layers learn low-level features such as colors and edges, while the last several layers learn more high-level task-related semantic features such as categorical knowledge for classification tasks [45]. However, deep supervision forces the shallow layers to learn the task-related knowledge, which disobeys the original feature extraction process in neural networks. As pointed out in MSDNet [46], this conflict sometimes leads to accuracy degradation in the final classifier. This observation indicates that the supervised task loss is probably not the best supervision for optimizing the intermediate layers.

In this section, we argue that *contrastive learning can provide better supervision for intermediate layers than the supervised task loss*. Contrastive learning is one of the most popular and effective techniques in representation learning [47–49]. Usually, it regards two augmentations from the same image as a positive pair and different images as negative pairs. In the training period, the neural network is trained to minimize the distance of a positive pair while maximizing the distance of a negative pair. As a result, the network can learn the invariance of various data augmentations, such as color jittering and random gray scaling. Considering that these data augmentation invariances are usually low-level, task-irrelevant, and transferable to various vision tasks [50, 51], we argue that they are more beneficial knowledge to be learned by intermediate layers. Motivated by these observations, we propose a novel training framework named *Contrastive Deep Supervision*. It optimizes the intermediate layers with contrastive learning instead of traditional supervised learning. As shown in Fig. 4d, several projection heads are attached in the intermediate layers of the neural network and trained to perform contrastive learning. Besides, since contrastive learning can be performed on unlabeled data, the proposed contrastive deep supervision can also be easily extended in the semi-supervised learning paradigm.

Moreover, contrastive deep supervision can be further utilized to boost the performance of another deep learning technique—KD. Recently, abundant research has found that distilling the "crucial knowledge" inside the backbone features, such as attention and relation [7, 13, 15] leads to better performance than directly distilling all the backbone features. In this section, we show that the data augmentation invariances learned by the intermediate layers in contrastive deep supervision are more beneficial for knowledge for distillation. By combining contrastive deep supervision with the naïve feature distillation, we introduce task-irrelevant KD, which enables the distilled ResNet18 to achieve 73.23% accuracy on ImageNet, outperforming the baseline and the second-best KD method by 4.02% and 2.16%, respectively.

3.1 Extracting and Distilling Task-Irrelevant Knowledge

3.1.1 Deep Supervision

In this subsection, we revisit the formulation of deep supervision methods. Let c be a given backbone classifier. Deep supervision introduces several shallow classifiers by using the intermediate features in c. More specifically, assume $c = g \circ f$ where g is the final classifier, f is the feature extractor operator, and $f = f_K \circ f_{K-1} \circ \cdots \cdot f_1$. K denotes the number of convolutional stages in f. At each feature extraction stage i, deep supervision adds an auxiliary classifier g_i for providing intermediate supervision. Thus, there are K classifiers in total which have the following form:

$$c_1(x) = g_1 \circ f_1(x)$$
$$c_2(x) = g_2 \circ f_2 \circ f_1(x)$$
$$\cdots$$
$$c_K(x) = g_K \circ f_K \circ f_{K-1} \circ \cdots \circ f_1(x). \tag{7}$$

Given a set of training samples $\mathcal{X} = \{x_i\}_{i=1}^n$ and its corresponding labels $\mathcal{Y} = \{y_i\}_{i=1}^n$, the training loss of deep supervision $\mathcal{L}_{\text{DS}}$ can be formulated as

$$\mathcal{L}_{\text{DS}} = \underbrace{\mathcal{L}_{\text{CE}}(c_K(\mathcal{X}), \mathcal{Y})}_{\text{from standard training}} + \alpha \cdot \sum_{i=1}^{K-1} \underbrace{\mathcal{L}_{\text{CE}}(c_i(\mathcal{X}), \mathcal{Y})}_{\text{from deep supervision}}, \tag{8}$$

where $\mathcal{L}_{CE}$ indicates the cross entropy loss. The first and the second items in the loss function indicate the standard training loss and the additional loss from deep supervision for the intermediate layers, respectively. α is a hyper-parameter to balance the two loss items. Recently, some methods have been proposed to apply layer-wise consistency on deep supervision, which additionally minimizes the KL divergence between the prediction of auxiliary classifiers and the final classifier [52, 53]. These methods can also be considered as the KD which regards the final classifier as the teacher and the auxiliary classifiers as the students. Their training loss can be formulated as

$$\mathcal{L}_{DS} + \beta \cdot \sum_{i=1}^{K-1} \mathcal{L}_{KL}(c_i(\mathcal{X}), c_K(\mathcal{X})), \qquad (9)$$

where β is a hyper-parameter to balance the two loss functions.

3.1.2 Contrastive Deep Supervision

In this subsection, we first introduce the formulation of contrastive learning. For a minibatch of N images $\{x_1, x_2, \ldots, x_N\}$, we apply stochastic data augmentation to each image twice, resulting in a batch of $2N$ images. For convenience, we denote x_i and x_{N+i} images as the two augmentations from the same image, which is regarded as a positive pair. Denote $z = c(x)$ as the normalized projection head outputs, contrastive learning loss (*a.k.a.* NT-Xtent [47]) can be formulated as

$$\mathcal{L}_{Contra} = -\sum_{i=1}^{N} \log \frac{\exp(z_i \cdot z_{i+N})/\tau}{\sum_{k=1}^{2N} \mathbb{1}_{[k \neq i]} \exp(z_i \cdot z_k)/\tau}, \qquad (10)$$

where $\mathbb{1} \in \{0, 1\}$ is an indicator function evaluating to 1 if $k \neq i$ and τ is a temperature hyper-parameter. Intuitively, $\mathcal{L}_{Contra}$ encourages the encoder network to learn similar representations for different augmentations from the same image while increasing the difference between representations of the augmentations from different images.

The main difference between deep supervision and our method is that deep supervision trains the auxiliary classifiers by the cross entropy loss while our method trains them with the contrastive loss $\mathcal{L}_{Contra}$. By denoting the contrastive loss at c_i as $\mathcal{L}_{Contra}(\mathcal{X}; c_i)$, then the training loss of our contrastive deep supervision $\mathcal{L}_{CDS}$ can be formulated as

$$\mathcal{L}_{CDS} = \underbrace{\mathcal{L}_{CE}(c_K(\mathcal{X}), \mathcal{Y})}_{\text{from standard training}} + \lambda_1 \sum_{i=1}^{K-1} \underbrace{\mathcal{L}_{Contra}(\mathcal{X}; c_i)}_{\text{from our method}}, \qquad (11)$$

where the first and the second items indicate the standard training loss and the additional loss in our method for the intermediate layers, respectively. λ_1 is a hyper-parameter to balance the two loss items.

3.1.3 Distilling Task-Irrelevant Knowledge

The intermediate layers in contrastive deep supervision are supervised with contrastive learning and thus they can learn the invariance of different data augmentation. As shown in previous research, this data augmentation invariance is beneficial to various downstream tasks [54]. In this section, we further propose to improve KD with contrastive deep supervision by transferring the data augmentation invariance learned by the teachers to the students. Denote the student model and the teacher model in knowledge distillation as f^S and f^T respectively. The naïve feature-based KD directly minimizes the distance between the backbone features of the student and the teacher, which can be formulated as

$$\sum_{i=1}^{K} \|f_i^T(X) - f_i^S(X)\|_2. \tag{12}$$

In contrast, KD with contrastive deep supervision minimizes the distance between the embedding vectors (the output of the projection heads) of the student and the teacher, which can be formulated as

$$\mathcal{L}_{\text{CDS for KD}} = \sum_{i=1}^{K-1} \|c_i^T(X) - c_i^S(X)\|_2. \tag{13}$$

Now we can formulate the overall training loss of the student as

$$\mathcal{L}_{\text{DCDS}} = \mathcal{L}_{\text{CDS}} + \lambda_2 \cdot \mathcal{L}_{\text{CDS for KD}} + \lambda_3 \cdot \mathcal{L}_{\text{KL}}\left(c_K^T(X), c_K^S(X)\right), \tag{14}$$

where λ_2 and λ_3 are the hyper-parameters to balance different loss items. Following previous works in deep supervision, we do not set an individual hyper-parameter for each projection head for convenience in hyper-parameter tuning.

3.2 Evaluation and Discussion

3.2.1 Experiment Setting

Three previous deep supervision methods are utilized for comparison, including DSN [43], DKS [52], and DHM [53]. In KD experiments, we have evaluated our

3.2.2 Experiment Results

Object Detection Table 8 shows the performance of our method on object detection. In these experiments, We firstly pretrain the ResNets on ImageNet with standard training (Baseline), three deep supervision methods and our method, and then finetune them as the backbone for object detection models, including RetinaNet and Faster RCNN. It is observed that with backbones pre-trained with our method, there are 0.9 and 0.8 AP improvements on Faster RCNN and RetinaNet, respectively, which outperforms the second-best method by 0.6 AP, indicating that the representation learned with our method is more beneficial to downstream tasks.

Fine-grained Image Classification Experiments on fine-grained image classification are shown in Tables 9 and 10. It is observed that: (**a**) Contrastive deep supervision leads to consistent and significant accuracy improvements on the five datasets. On average, it leads to 3.80%, 2.43%, 1.73%, 4.77%, and 2.25% accuracy

Table 8 Experiments on different object detection models on COCO2017

Model	Method	AP	AP_S	AP_M	AP_L
Faster RCNN	Baseline	37.4	21.2	41.0	48.1
	DSN	$37.3_{-0.1}$	$21.0_{-0.2}$	$40.8_{-0.2}$	$48.3_{-0.2}$
	DKS	$37.5_{+0.1}$	$21.2_{+0.0}$	$41.5_{+0.5}$	$47.6_{-0.5}$
	DHM	$37.6_{+0.2}$	$21.3_{+0.1}$	$41.3_{+0.3}$	$48.2_{+0.1}$
	Ours	$\mathbf{38.3_{+0.9}}$	$\mathbf{21.6_{+0.4}}$	$\mathbf{42.0_{+1.0}}$	$\mathbf{50.1_{+2.0}}$
RetinaNet	Baseline	36.5	20.4	40.3	48.1
	DSN	$36.3_{-0.2}$	$20.1_{-0.3}$	$40.0_{-0.3}$	$48.1_{0.0}$
	DKS	$36.7_{+0.2}$	$20.1_{-0.3}$	$40.9_{+0.6}$	$48.2_{+0.1}$
	DHM	$36.7_{+0.2}$	$20.0_{-0.4}$	$40.7_{-0.4}$	$48.5_{+0.4}$
	Ours	$\mathbf{37.3_{+0.8}}$	$\mathbf{21.2_{+0.8}}$	$\mathbf{41.0_{+0.7}}$	$\mathbf{47.9_{-0.2}}$

Numbers in bold indicate the highest accuracy

Table 9 Comparison (top-1 acc./%) with deep supervision methods with ResNet50 for fine-grained classification. Models are trained from scratch

Method	CUB	Cars	Flowers	Dogs	Aircrafts
Baseline	60.65	79.86	87.52	64.00	74.07
DSN	$62.37_{+1.72}$	$81.04_{+1.18}$	$88.54_{+1.02}$	$66.32_{+2.32}$	$74.49_{+0.42}$
DKS	$63.59_{+2.94}$	$81.52_{+1.66}$	$88.94_{+0.40}$	$68.31_{+4.31}$	$75.07_{+1.00}$
DHM	$64.01_{+3.36}$	$81.49_{+1.63}$	$89.03_{+1.51}$	$68.38_{+4.38}$	$75.00_{+0.93}$
Ours	$\mathbf{64.65_{+4.00}}$	$\mathbf{82.07_{+2.21}}$	$\mathbf{89.26_{+1.74}}$	$\mathbf{69.02_{+5.02}}$	$\mathbf{75.43_{+1.36}}$

Numbers in bold indicate the highest accuracy

Table 10 Comparison (top-1 acc. %) with deep supervision methods with ResNet50 for fine-grained classification. Models are finetuned from ImageNet pre-trained weights

Method	CUB	Cars	Flowers	Dogs	Aircrafts
Baseline	78.50	90.25	97.68	76.47	87.43
DSN	$80.14_{+1.64}$	$91.32_{+1.07}$	$98.64_{+0.96}$	$77.21_{+0.74}$	$89.31_{+1.88}$
DKS	$81.34_{+2.84}$	$92.54_{+2.29}$	$99.01_{+1.33}$	$78.32_{+1.85}$	$89.20_{+1.77}$
DHM	$81.27_{+2.77}$	$92.31_{+2.06}$	$98.84_{+1.16}$	$78.20_{+1.73}$	$89.57_{+2.14}$
Ours	**$82.10_{+3.60}$**	**$92.90_{+2.65}$**	**$99.39_{+1.71}$**	**$80.99_{+4.52}$**	**$90.52_{+3.09}$**

Numbers in bold indicate the highest accuracy

improvements on the five datasets, respectively. (**b**) Besides, the benefits of our method in *"finetuning from ImageNet"* and *"training from scratch"* are very similar (except on Aircraft), which indicates that the effectiveness of our method is consistent in different training settings.

Task-Irrelevant KD KD experiments on ImageNet and CIFAR are shown in Tables 11 and 12, respectively. It is observed that: (**a**) Our method achieves 5.07% and 2.20% top-1 accuracy improvements on CIFAR100 and CIFAR10 on average, outperforming the second-best KD method by 1.40% and 0.87% on the two datasets, respectively. (**b**) The similar results can also be observed in ImageNet experiments. Our method leads to 4.02%/2.55%, 3.48%/2.14%, and 3.38%/2.22% top-1/top-5 accuracy improvements on ResNet18, ResNet34, and ResNet50, respectively. On average, it outperforms the baseline and the second-best method by 3.62% and 1.76% top-1 accuracy, respectively (Table 13).

4 Brief Summary

In this chapter, we study the second fundamental problem in KD—"what kind of knowledge should be distilled". Most of the previous works simply conduct experiments to evaluate the performance of distilling different teacher knowledge. In contrast, we have introduced representation learning methods to extract the beneficial knowledge from the teacher, and then distill it to the student. Concretely, we propose *task-oriented feature distillation* and *task-irrelevant KD*, two KD methods that focus on distilling the task-relevant and task-irrelevant knowledge obtained by supervised and unsupervised learning, achieving satisfactory performance for the given task and the downstream tasks, respectively.

4 Brief Summary

Table 11 Comparison experiments (top-1 and top-5 accuracy/%) with the other eight KD methods on ImageNet with ResNet. Numbers in bold indicate the highest

Metric	Model	Base	KD	AT	RKD	SP	CRD	CC	OKD	SSKD	Ours
Top-1	ResNet18	69.21	70.52	70.74	70.63	70.61	71.07	69.96	70.55	71.62	**73.23**
	ResNet34	73.17	74.44	74.69	74.61	74.60	74.99	–	–	–	**76.65**
	ResNet50	75.30	76.62	76.79	76.92	76.88	77.21	–	–	–	**78.68**
Top-5	ResNet18	89.01	89.88	90.00	89.71	89.80	91.06	89.17	89.59	90.67	**91.56**
	ResNet34	91.24	92.07	92.18	92.14	92.10	92.58	–	–	–	**93.38**
	ResNet50	92.20	93.36	93.51	93.60	93.58	93.88	–	–	–	**94.42**

Table 12 Comparison with the other KD methods on CIFAR100

Model	Base	KD	FitNet	AT	RKD	SP	CRD	Ours
ResNet18	77.45	78.68	78.15	78.09	78.21	78.19	81.41	**83.31**
ResNet50	77.81	79.19	78.42	78.34	78.94	78.81	82.45	**83.53**
ResNet101	78.65	80.40	80.78	80.97	81.24	80.94	82.57	**84.80**
ResNeXt50	79.85	81.41	82.67	82.59	83.71	82.67	83.41	**84.41**
ResNeXt101	80.67	82.03	82.51	82.43	83.01	82.64	84.50	**85.37**
WRNet50	79.46	81.02	81.29	81.16	82.06	82.07	82.94	**84.27**
WRNet101	79.98	81.82	82.07	82.16	82.54	82.49	83.07	**85.04**
SENet18	77.46	78.92	79.09	79.15	79.41	79.31	81.22	**82.68**
SENet50	78.02	79.78	80.13	80.45	80.69	80.71	81.79	**83.36**
SENet101	78.92	80.31	80.54	80.53	80.74	80.52	82.75	**84.15**
MobileNetV1	68.32	70.04	70.25	70.17	70.89	70.19	72.68	**73.79**
MobileNetV2	69.34	70.58	70.64	70.51	70.83	70.68	71.82	**72.61**
ShuffleNetV1	72.46	74.08	74.19	74.11	74.56	74.68	75.11	**75.77**
ShuffleNetV2	72.81	74.39	74.47	74.51	74.82	74.67	75.62	**76.11**
PreActNet18	76.84	78.25	78.34	78.67	79.01	79.12	81.62	**82.83**
PreActNet50	77.31	79.04	79.27	79.54	79.82	79.76	81.27	**83.42**

Numbers in bold indicate the highest accuracy

Table 13 Comparison with the other KD methods on CIFAR10

Model	Base	KD	FitNet	AT	RKD	SP	CRD	Ours
ResNet18	94.96	95.24	95.31	95.26	95.31	95.27	95.81	**96.84**
ResNet50	95.07	95.31	95.45	95.47	95.33	95.29	96.21	**97.08**
ResNet101	95.13	95.39	95.71	95.49	95.43	95.18	96.37	**97.40**
ResNeXt50	95.09	95.27	95.36	95.68	95.59	95.37	96.49	**97.15**
ResNeXt101	95.34	95.68	95.92	95.78	95.81	95.38	96.51	**97.40**
WRNet50	95.01	95.34	95.38	95.34	95.61	95.73	96.17	**97.37**
WRNet101	95.27	95.51	95.48	95.71	95.99	95.82	96.34	**97.39**
SENet18	94.86	95.21	95.30	95.47	95.34	95.41	96.00	**96.96**
SENet50	95.11	95.39	95.44	95.64	95.57	95.47	96.21	**97.19**
SENet101	95.30	95.64	95.81	95.78	95.81	95.77	96.19	**97.36**
MobileNetV1	90.24	91.27	92.59	92.87	93.01	92.90	93.27	**93.94**
MobileNetV2	90.76	91.09	91.57	91.75	91.82	91.83	92.17	**92.87**
ShuffleNetV1	91.57	91.99	92.30	92.19	92.47	92.38	93.08	**94.04**
ShuffleNetV2	91.19	91.87	92.23	92.41	92.30	92.54	92.90	**93.16**
PreActNet18	94.78	95.08	95.28	95.39	95.51	95.69	96.07	**96.70**
PreActNet50	94.89	95.21	95.57	95.49	95.37	95.48	96.11	**96.93**

Numbers in bold indicate the highest accuracy

References

1. Mirzadeh, S-I., Farajtabar, M., Li, A., Ghasemzadeh, H.: Improved knowledge distillation via teacher assistant: bridging the gap between student and teacher. arXiv preprint arXiv:1902.03393 (2019)
2. Chen, G., Choi, W., Yu, X., Han, T., Chandraker, M.: Learning efficient object detection models with knowledge distillation. In: Advances in Neural Information Processing Systems (NeurIPS), pp. 742–751 (2017)
3. Zhu, X., Gong, S.: Knowledge distillation by on-the-fly native ensemble. Adv. Neural Inf. Process. Syst. **31**, 1–11 (2018)
4. Zhao, B., Cui, Q., Song, R., Qiu, Y., Liang, J.: Decoupled knowledge distillation. In: Proceedings of the IEEE/CVF Conference on Computer Vision and Pattern Recognition, pp. 11953–11962 (2022)
5. Hao, Z., Guo, J., Han, K., Hu, H., Xu, C., Wang, Y.: Revisit the power of vanilla knowledge distillation: from small scale to large scale. Adv. Neural Inf. Process. Syst. **36**, 1–14 (2024)
6. Romero, A., Ballas, N., Kahou, S.E., Chassang, A., Gatta, C., Bengio, Y.: Fitnets: hints for thin deep nets. In: International Conference on Learning Representations (ICLR) (2015)
7. Zagoruyko, S., Komodakis, N.: Paying more attention to attention: improving the performance of convolutional neural networks via attention transfer. In: International Conference on Learning Representations (ICLR) (2017)
8. Heo, B., Kim, J., Yun, S., Park, H., Kwak, N., Choi, J.Y.: A comprehensive overhaul of feature distillation. In: International Conference on Computer Vision (ICCV), pp. 1921–1930 (2019)
9. Ahn, S., Hu, S.X., Damianou, A., Lawrence, N.D., Dai, Z.: Variational information distillation for knowledge transfer. In: IEEE/CVF Conference on Computer Vision and Pattern Recognition (CVPR), pp. 9163–9171 (2019)
10. Xu, Y., Xu, C., Chen, X., Zhang, W., Xu, C., Wang, Y.: Kernel based progressive distillation for adder neural networks. Adv. Neural Inf. Process. Syst. **33**, 12322–12333 (2020)
11. Yim, J., Joo, D., Bae, J., Kim, J.: A gift from knowledge distillation: fast optimization, network minimization and transfer learning. In: IEEE/CVF Conference on Computer Vision and Pattern Recognition (CVPR), pp. 4133–4141 (2017)
12. Jin, Q., Ren, J., Woodford, O.J., Wang, J., Yuan, G., Wang, Y., Tulyakov, S.: Teachers do more than teach: compressing image-to-image models. In: IEEE/CVF Conference on Computer Vision and Pattern Recognition (CVPR), pp. 13600–13611 (2021)
13. Tung, F., Mori, G.: Similarity-preserving knowledge distillation. In: International Conference on Computer Vision (ICCV), pp. 1365–1374 (2019)
14. Peng, B., Jin, X., Liu, J., Li, D., Wu, Y., Liu, Y., Zhou, S., Zhang, Z.: Correlation congruence for knowledge distillation. In: International Conference on Computer Vision (ICCV), pp. 5007–5016 (2019)
15. Park, W., Kim, D., Lu, Y., Cho, M.: Relational knowledge distillation. In: IEEE/CVF Conference on Computer Vision and Pattern Recognition (CVPR), pp. 3967–3976 (2019)
16. Liu, Y., Chen, K., Liu, C., Qin, Z., Luo, Z., Wang, J.: Structured knowledge distillation for semantic segmentation. In: IEEE/CVF Conference on Computer Vision and Pattern Recognition (CVPR), pp. 2604–2613 (2019)
17. Li, Z., Jiang, R., Aarabi, P.: Semantic relation preserving knowledge distillation for image-to-image translation. In: European Conference on Computer Vision (ECCV), pp. 648–663. Springer (2020)
18. Dai, X., Jiang, Z., Wu, Z., Bao, Y., Wang, Z., Liu, S., Zhou, E.: General instance distillation for object detection. In: IEEE/CVF Conference on Computer Vision and Pattern Recognition (CVPR), pp. 7842–7851 (2021)
19. Srinivas, S., Fleuret, F.: Knowledge transfer with jacobian matching. arXiv preprint arXiv:1803.00443 (2018)
20. Lee, S.H., Kim, D.H., Song, B.C.: Self-supervised knowledge distillation using singular value decomposition. In: European Conference on Computer Vision (ECCV), pp. 335–350 (2018)

21. Hinton, G., Vinyals, O., Dean, J.: Distilling the knowledge in a neural network. In: Advances in Neural Information Processing Systems (NeurIPS) (2014)
22. Xu, Z., Hsu, Y-C., Huang, J.: Training shallow and thin networks for acceleration via knowledge distillation with conditional adversarial networks. arXiv preprint arXiv:1709.00513 (2017)
23. Ren, S., He, K., Girshick, R., Sun, J.: Faster r-cnn: towards real-time object detection with region proposal networks. In: Advances in Neural Information Processing Systems (NIPS), pp. 91–99 (2015)
24. Long, J., Shelhamer, E., Darrell, T.: Fully convolutional networks for semantic segmentation. In: IEEE/CVF Conference on Computer Vision and Pattern Recognition (CVPR), pp. 3431–3440 (2015)
25. Bansal, N., Chen, X., Wang, Z.: Can we gain more from orthogonality regularizations in training deep networks? Adv. Neural Inf. Process. Syst. **1**, 4261–4271 (2018)
26. He, K., Zhang, X., Ren, S., Sun, J.: Deep residual learning for image recognition. In: IEEE/CVF Conference on Computer Vision and Pattern Recognition (CVPR), pp. 770–778 (2016)
27. He, K., Zhang, X., Ren, S., Sun, J.: Identity mappings in deep residual networks. In: European Conference on Computer Vision (ECCV), pp. 630–645. Springer (2016)
28. Hu, J., Shen, L., Sun, G.: Squeeze-and-excitation networks. In: IEEE/CVF Conference on Computer Vision and Pattern Recognition (CVPR), pp. 7132–7141 (2018)
29. Xie, S., Girshick, R., Dollár, P., Tu, Z., He, K.: Aggregated residual transformations for deep neural networks. In: IEEE/CVF Conference on Computer Vision and Pattern Recognition (CVPR), pp. 5987–5995 (2017)
30. Howard, A.G., Zhu, M., Chen, B., Kalenichenko, D., Wang, W., Weyand, T., Andreetto, M., Adam, H.: Mobilenets: efficient convolutional neural networks for mobile vision applications. In: IEEE/CVF Conference on Computer Vision and Pattern Recognition (CVPR) (2017)
31. Sandler, M., Howard, A., Zhu, M., Zhmoginov, A., Chen, L-C.: Mobilenetv2: inverted residuals and linear bottlenecks. In: IEEE/CVF Conference on Computer Vision and Pattern Recognition (CVPR), pp. 4510–4520 (2018)
32. Zhang, X., Zhou, X., Lin, M., Sun, J.: Shufflenet: an extremely efficient convolutional neural network for mobile devices. In: IEEE/CVF Conference on Computer Vision and Pattern Recognition (CVPR), pp. 6848–6856 (2018)
33. Ma, N., Zhang, X., Zheng, H-T., Sun, J.: Shufflenet v2: practical guidelines for efficient cnn architecture design. In: European Conference on Computer Vision (ECCV), pp. 116–131 (2018)
34. Zagoruyko, S., Komodakis, N.: Wide residual networks. In: British Machine Vision Conference (BMVC) (2016)
35. Krizhevsky, A., Hinton, G.: Learning multiple layers of features from tiny images. Technical report, Citeseer (2009)
36. Deng, J., Dong, W., Socher, R., Li, L-J., Li, K., Fei-Fei, L.: Imagenet: a large-scale hierarchical image database. In: IEEE/CVF Conference on Computer Vision and Pattern Recognition (CVPR), pp. 248–255 (2009)
37. Li, G., Müller, M., Thabet, A., Ghanem, B.: Deepgcns: can gcns go as deep as cnns? arXiv preprint arXiv:1904.03751 (2019)
38. Wu, Z., Song, S., Khosla, A., Yu, F., Zhang, L., Tang, X., Xiao, J.: 3d shapenets: a deep representation for volumetric shapes. In: Proceedings of the IEEE Conference on Computer Vision and Pattern Recognition, pp. 1912–1920 (2015)
39. Zhang, Y., Xiang, T., Hospedales, T.M., Lu, H.: Deep mutual learning. In: IEEE/CVF Conference on Computer Vision and Pattern Recognition (CVPR), pp. 4320–4328 (2018)
40. Zhang, L., Song, J., Gao, A., Chen, J., Bao, C., Ma, K.: Be your own teacher: improve the performance of convolutional neural networks via self distillation. In: arXiv preprint:1905.08094 (2019)

References

41. Selvaraju, R.R., Cogswell, M., Das, A., Vedantam, R., Parikh, D., Batra, D.: Grad-cam: visual explanations from deep networks via gradient-based localization. In: Proceedings of the IEEE International Conference on Computer Vision, pp. 618–626 (2017)
42. Huang, G., Sun, Y., Liu, Z., Sedra, D., Weinberger, K.Q.: Deep networks with stochastic depth. In: European Conference on Computer Vision (ECCV), pp. 646–661 (2016)
43. Lee, C-Y., Xie, S., Gallagher, P., Zhang, Z., Tu, Z.: Deeply-supervised nets. In: International Conference on Artificial Intelligence and Statistics (AISTATS), pp. 562–570 (2015)
44. Wang, L., Lee, C-Y., Tu, Z., Lazebnik, S.: Training deeper convolutional networks with deep supervision. arXiv preprint arXiv:1505.02496 (2015)
45. Zhou, B., Khosla, A., Lapedriza, A., Oliva, A., Torralba, A.: Object detectors emerge in deep scene cnns. arXiv preprint arXiv:1412.6856 (2014)
46. Huang, G., Chen, D., Li, T., Wu, F., van der Maaten, L., Weinberger, K.Q.: Multi-scale dense networks for resource efficient image classification. In: International Conference on Learning Representations (ICLR) (2018)
47. Chen, T., Kornblith, S., Norouzi, M., Hinton, G.: A simple framework for contrastive learning of visual representations. arXiv preprint arXiv:2002.05709 (2020)
48. Chen, T., Kornblith, S., Swersky, K., Norouzi, M., Hinton, G.: Big self-supervised models are strong semi-supervised learners. arXiv preprint arXiv:2006.10029 (2020)
49. Khosla, P., Teterwak, P., Wang, C., Sarna, A., Tian, Y., Isola, P., Maschinot, A., Liu, C., Krishnan, D.: Supervised contrastive learning. arXiv preprint arXiv:2004.11362 (2020)
50. Chaitanya, K., Erdil, E., Karani, N., Konukoglu, E.: Contrastive learning of global and local features for medical image segmentation with limited annotations. arXiv preprint arXiv:2006.10511 (2020)
51. Xie, E., Ding, J., Wang, W., Zhan, X., Xu, H., Li, Z., Luo, P.: Detco: unsupervised contrastive learning for object detection. arXiv preprint arXiv:2102.04803 (2021)
52. Sun, D., Yao, A., Zhou, A., Zhao, H.: Deeply-supervised knowledge synergy. In: Proceedings of the IEEE/CVF Conference on Computer Vision and Pattern Recognition, pp. 6997–7006 (2019)
53. Li, D., Chen, Q.: Dynamic hierarchical mimicking towards consistent optimization objectives. In: Proceedings of the IEEE/CVF Conference on Computer Vision and Pattern Recognition, pp. 7642–7651 (2020)
54. Jaiswal, A., Babu, A.R., Zadeh, M.Z., Banerjee, D., Makedon, F.: A survey on contrastive self-supervised learning. Technologies **9**(1), 2 (2021)
55. Tian, Y., Krishnan, D., Isola, P.: Contrastive representation distillation. In: International Conference on Learning Representations (ICLR). OpenReview.net (2020)
56. Xu, G., Liu, Z., Li, X., Loy, C.C.: Knowledge distillation meets self-supervision. In: European Conference on Computer Vision (ECCV), pp. 588–604. Springer (2020)

Application of KD in High-Level Vision Tasks

Abstract Excellent breakthroughs have been achieved in various high-level computer vision tasks such as image recognition, object detection, and segmentation at the expense of growing computational costs. Recent efforts have been made to employ KD to solve this problem. Unfortunately, most previous KD methods in computer vision are designed for image classification and usually lead to trivial improvements in more challenging tasks. In this section, we delve into the design of KD for complex high-level vision by analyzing the key properties of these tasks, including detection and segmentation on images, point clouds, and multi-view images.

1 KD for 2D Object Detection and Instance Segmentation

We argue that the failure of KD on 2D object detection is caused by the following two issues: (1) the imbalance between foreground and background, and (2) lack of KD on the relation between different pixels (Fig. 1).

Imbalance Between Foreground and Background The background pixels in a to-be-detected image are often overwhelmingly more than the pixels of the foreground objects. However, only the pixels of foreground objects are actually useful for object detection. In previous KD, the student is usually trained to mimic the features of all pixels with the same priority. As a result, students have paid most of their attention to learning teacher knowledge on the background pixels, which suppresses student learning on features of the foreground objects. Hence, this imbalance has reduced the effectiveness of KD severely.

To address this issue, we propose *attention-guided distillation* which distills only the crucial foreground pixels. Extensive previous works show that the attention value of a pixel shows its importance [1, 2]. Based on this observation, attention-guided distillation adopts the map as the metric to decide whether a pixel belongs to the foreground objects. Then, KD is performed on only these foreground objects, instead of all the pixels.

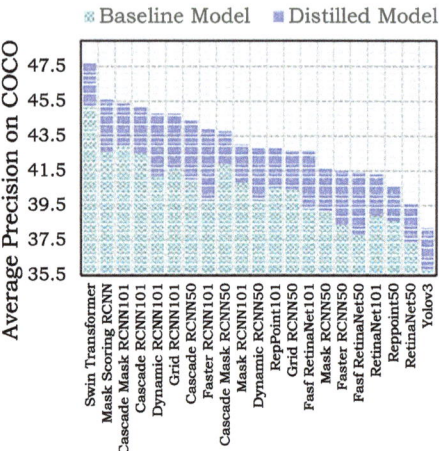

Fig. 1 The main results (mAP) of our method on MS COCO2017. Numbers after detectors' names indicate the depth of backbone networks

Lack of Distillation on Relational Information It is generally acknowledged that the relational information between different objects contains valuable information in object detection. Recently, lots of research has successfully improved the performance of detectors by enabling them to capture and make use of these relations such as non-local modules [3] and relation networks [4]. However, the existing object detection KD methods only distill the information of individual pixels but ignore the relation of different pixels.

To solve this issue, we propose non-local distillation, which aims to capture the relation information of students and teachers with non-local modules and then distill it from teachers to students. Since the non-local modules and attention mechanisms in our method are only required in the training period, they can be discarded in the inference period to avoid additional computation and storage costs.

Besides, we also study the relation between teachers and students in object detection and find that KD in object detection requires a high AP teacher, which is different from the conclusion in image classification where a high AP teacher may harm the performance of students [5, 6]. We hope these results are worth further contemplation of KD in tasks other than image classification.

1.1 Attention-Guided Distillation and Non-local Distillation

1.1.1 Overall Illustration

The details of our method are shown in Fig. 2. It is observed that our method is composed of two individual distillation methods—attention-guided distillation and non-local distillation. In attention-guided distillation, we first generate the spatial attention and channel attention of teachers and students by performing average

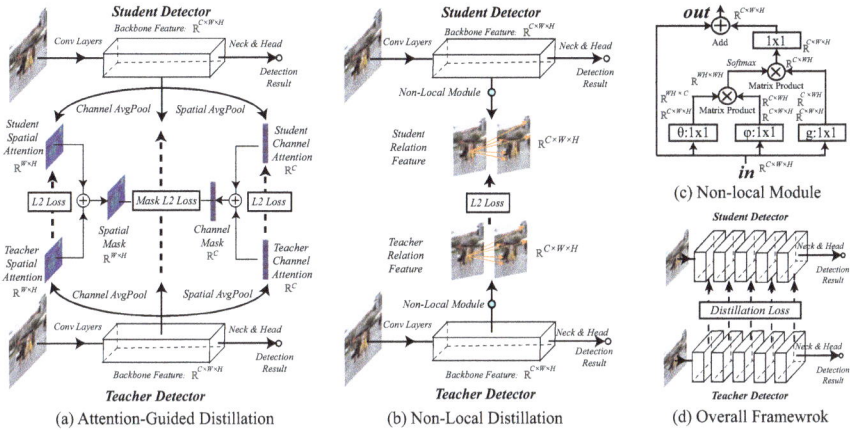

Fig. 2 Details of proposed method: (**a**) Attention-guided distillation generates the spatial and channel attention with average pooling in the channel dimension and the spatial dimension, respectively. Then, students are trained to learn teacher features in the pixels and channels with high attention value. Besides, students are encouraged to mimic the attention of teachers. (**b**) Non-local distillation captures the relation of pixels in an image with non-local modules. Then, the relation information of teachers is learned by students by minimizing L_2 norm loss. (**c**) The architecture of non-local modules. '1×1' is a convolution layer with a 1×1 kernel. (**d**) Distillation loss is applied to backbone features in different layers with various resolutions

pooling on the absolute value of features in the channel and spatial dimensions, respectively. Then, we normalize the spatial and channel attention of students and teachers with a temperature-parameterized softmax. After that, the normalized attention maps of teachers and students are added together and divided by 2, which finally forms the masks for attention-guided distillation. Note that each element in the masks ranges from 0 to 1 and shows the importance of different pixels and channels. When computing the feature distillation loss, the spatial and channel masks are utilized to reweight the feature loss in different pixels and channels, thus KD loss in the crucial pixels and channels can be highlighted and vice versa.

1.1.2 Formulation

Attention-guided Distillation We use $A \in \mathbb{R}^{C,H,W}$ to denote the feature of the backbone in an object detection model, where C, H, W denote its channel number, height, and width, respectively. Then, the generation of the spatial attention map and channel attention map is equivalent to finding the mapping function $\mathcal{G}^s : \mathbb{R}^{C,H,W} \to \mathbb{R}^{H,W}$ and $\mathcal{G}^c : \mathbb{R}^{C,H,W} \to \mathbb{R}^C$, respectively. Note that the superscripts s and c here are utilized to discriminate 'spatial' and 'channel'. Since the absolute value of each element in the feature implies its importance, we construct $\mathcal{G}^s$ by averaging the absolute values across the channel dimension and construct $\mathcal{G}^c$ by averaging the absolute values across the width and height dimensions, which can be formulated as

$$\mathcal{G}^c(A) = \frac{1}{HW} \sum_{H}^{i=1} \sum_{W}^{j=1} |A_{\cdot,i,j}| \quad \text{and} \quad \mathcal{G}^s(A) = \frac{1}{C} \sum_{C}^{k=1} |A_{k,\cdot,\cdot}|, \qquad (1)$$

where i, j, k denotes the i_{th}, j_{th}, k_{th} slice of A in the height, width, and channel dimensions, respectively. Then, the spatial attention mask M^s and the channel attention mask M^c in attention-guided distillation can be obtained by summing the attention maps from the teacher and the student, which can be formulated as

$$\begin{aligned} M^s &= HW \cdot \text{softmax}\left(\left(\mathcal{G}^s\left(A^S\right) + \mathcal{G}^s\left(A^T\right)\right)/T\right) \quad \text{and} \\ M^c &= C \cdot \text{softmax}\left(\left(\mathcal{G}^c\left(A^S\right) + \mathcal{G}^c\left(A^T\right)\right)/T\right). \end{aligned} \qquad (2)$$

The superscripts $\mathcal{S}$ and $\mathcal{T}$ here are used to discriminate students and teachers. T is a hyper-parameter in softmax introduced by Hinton et al. [7] to adjust the distribution of elements in attention masks (see Fig. 3). The attention-guided distillation loss $\mathcal{L}_{\text{AGD}}$ is composed of two sub-modules—attention transfer loss $\mathcal{L}_{\text{AT}}$ and attention-masked loss $\mathcal{L}_{\text{AM}}$. $\mathcal{L}_{\text{AT}}$ is utilized to encourage the student model to mimic the spatial and channel attention of the teacher model, which can be formulated as

$$\mathcal{L}_{\text{AT}} = \mathcal{L}_2(\mathcal{G}^s(A^S), \mathcal{G}^s(A^T)) + \mathcal{L}_2(\mathcal{G}^c(A^S), \mathcal{G}^c(A^T)). \qquad (3)$$

$\mathcal{L}_{\text{AM}}$ is utilized to encourage the student to mimic the features of teacher models by a $\mathcal{L}_2$ norm loss masked by M^s and M^c, which can be formulated as

$$\mathcal{L}_{\text{AM}} = \left(\sum_{k=1}^{C} \sum_{i=1}^{H} \sum_{j=1}^{W} (A_{k,i,j}^{\mathcal{T}} - A_{k,i,j}^{\mathcal{S}})^2 \cdot M_{i,j}^s \cdot M_k^c \right)^{\frac{1}{2}}. \qquad (4)$$

Non-local Distillation Non-local module [3] is an effective method to improve the performance of neural networks by capturing the global relation information. In this paragraph, we apply non-local modules to capture the relation between pixels in an

Fig. 3 Visualization and distribution of the spatial attention with different T (temperatures) in attention-guided knowledge distillation. With a smaller T, the pixels of high and low attention values are emphasized and suppressed more, respectively

Fig. 4 The relation between the mean average precision of students and teachers

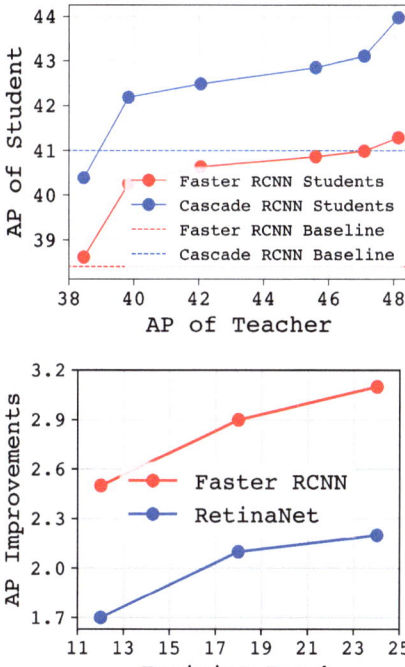

Fig. 5 The relation between the benefits of KD and the number of training epochs

image, which can be formulated as

$$r_{i,j} = \frac{1}{WH} \sum_{H}^{i'=1} \sum_{W}^{j'=1} f(A_{\cdot,i,j}, A_{\cdot,i',j'}) g(A_{\cdot,i',j'}), \quad (5)$$

where r denotes the obtained relation information. i, j are the spatial indexes of an output position whose response is to be computed. i', j' are the spatial indexes that enumerate all possible positions in an image. f is a pairwise function for computing the relation between two pixels and g is an unary function for computing the representation of an individual pixel. Now, we can introduce the proposed non-local distillation loss $\mathcal{L}_{\text{NLD}}$ as the $\mathcal{L}_2$ loss between the relation information of the students and teachers, which can be formulated as $\mathcal{L}_{\text{NLD}} = \mathcal{L}_2(r^S, r^T)$ (Figs. 4 and 5).

Overall Loss Function We introduce three hyper-parameters α, β, γ to balance different distillation loss. Then, the overall distillation loss can be formulated as

$$\mathcal{L}_{\text{Distill}}(A^T, A^S) = \underbrace{\alpha \cdot \mathcal{L}_{\text{AT}} + \beta \cdot \mathcal{L}_{\text{AM}}}_{\text{Attention-guided distillation}} + \underbrace{\gamma \cdot \mathcal{L}_{\text{NLD}}}_{\text{Non-local distillation}}. \quad (6)$$

The overall distillation loss is a model-agnostic loss, which can be added to the original training loss of any detection model directly. Hence, by denoting the original training loss of the detector (e.g., classification loss and regression loss) as $\mathcal{L}_{\text{Origin}}$, the overall training loss of a student detector $\mathcal{L}_{\text{Stdent}}$ can be written as

$$\mathcal{L}_{\text{Stdent}} = \mathcal{L}_{\text{Origin}} + \mathcal{L}_{\text{Distill}}. \tag{7}$$

Taking Faster RCNN as an example, $\mathcal{L}_{\text{origin}}$ can be formulated as

$$\mathcal{L}_{\text{Origin}}(\{p_i\}, \{t_i\}) = \frac{1}{N_{\text{cls}}} \sum_i \mathcal{L}_{\text{cls}}(p_i, p_i^*) + \lambda \frac{1}{N_{\text{reg}}} \sum_i p_i^* L_{\text{reg}}(t_i, t_i^*), \tag{8}$$

where i is the index of an anchor in a mini-batch and p_i is the predicted probability of anchor i being an object. The ground-truth label $p_i^* = 1$ when the anchor is positive, and $p_i^* = 0$ when the anchor is negative. t_i is a vector representing the 4 parameterized coordinates of the predicted bounding box. t_i^* is that of the ground-truth box assigned with a positive anchor. L_{cls} is the log loss for binary classification (object vs. not object). L_{cls} indicates the regression loss with smooth L1 loss. N_{cls} and N_{reg} are the numbers of samples in a mini-batch and the number of anchor localization, respectively, which are utilized to normalize the classification and regression loss, respectively. Then, the overall loss function of Faster RCNN students can be formulated as

$$\begin{aligned}\mathcal{L}_{\text{Stdent}} &= \mathcal{L}_{\text{Origin}} + \mathcal{L}_{\text{Distill}} \\ &= \frac{1}{N_{\text{cls}}} \sum_i \mathcal{L}_{\text{cls}}(p_i, p_i^*) + \lambda \frac{1}{N_{\text{reg}}} \sum_i p_i^* L_{\text{reg}}(t_i, t_i^*) \\ &+ \alpha \cdot \mathcal{L}_{\text{AT}} + \beta \cdot \mathcal{L}_{\text{AM}} + \gamma \cdot \mathcal{L}_{\text{NLD}}.\end{aligned} \tag{9}$$

1.2 Evaluation and Discussion

1.2.1 Experiment Settings

The proposed methods have been evaluated on MS COCO2017, which is a large-scale dataset that contains over 120k images spanning 80 categories [8]. Following the common practice [9, 10], we train detectors on COCO `train` split (around 118K images) and evaluate them on the `validation` split (5k images) with the official performance metrics [8] including AP (average precision), AP_{50}, AP_{75}, AP_S, AP_M, and AP_L. Besides, we also evaluate our method on Cityscapes [11], a dataset for semantic urban scene understanding, and COCO-C [12], a dataset with corrupted images to benchmark model robustness and domain generalization ability. Experiments have been conducted on four kinds of two-stage detectors including Faster RCNN [13], Cascade RCNN [14], Dynamic RCNN [15] and Grid RCNN [16], four kinds of one-stage detectors, including Yolov3 [17], SSD [18], RetinaNet [10] and Fsaf RetinaNet [19], and one anchor-free detector—RepPoints [20]. Besides, we also evaluate our method on instance segmentation with Mask RCNN [9], Cascade Mask RCNN [14], Mask Scoring RCNN [21] and Swin Transformer [22]. Eleven KD methods are adopted for comparison [23–33]. Mean average precision (mAP) is utilized as the performance metric.

1.2.2 Results on Detection and Instance Segmentation

In this subsection, we show the experimental results of detectors trained with and without our method on MS COCO2017 in Tables 1, 2, and 3, and compare our method with twelve previous KD methods in Table 6. Besides, we also evaluate our method on Cityscapes in Table 7. It is observed that: (i) Consistent and significant AP boost can be observed on all the nine kinds of detectors in Tables 2 and 1. On average, there are 3.1, 2.6, and 2.1 AP improvements on the two-stage, one-stage, and anchor-free detectors, respectively. (ii) With the proposed method, a student model with a ResNet50 backbone can outperform the same model with a ResNet101 backbone by 1.2 AP on average. (iii) On instance segmentation models in Table 3, there are 2.5 improvements on bounding box AP and 2.0 improvements on mask AP on average, indicating the proposed method can be utilized in not only object detection but also instance segmentation. (iv) Our method achieves 3.5 and 4.1 AP improvements on Faster RCNN with ViT-B-32 and ViT-B-16 backbones, respectively, indicating that our method is effective in both convolution networks and transformers. (v) Our method outperforms the other twelve KD methods by a clear margin. On Faster RCNN, it achieves 0.6 higher AP than the second-best distillation method. Besides, it is observed that the traditional prediction-based KD only achieves 0.5 AP improvements compared to the student without KD, indicating that traditional KD has limited performance on object detection. We argue that this is because prediction KD is only beneficial to the classification ability while unable to improve the ability of localization. (vi) There are 2.7 and 2.9 AP improvements on detectors with ResNet50 and ResNet101 backbones, respectively, indicating that deeper detectors benefit more from KD. (vii) The FPS-AP curves of detectors trained with and without KD are shown in Figs. 6 and 7, respectively, which indicate that the proposed KD method enables the neural network to be significantly accelerated and compressed with almost no drop and even improvements in mean average precision.

1.2.3 KD Improves Model Robustness

Besides accuracy and computational efficiency, another crucial metric on object detection is the robustness to various image corruption, such as noise, blur, and bad weathers [12, 34]. A robust detector is expected to process these corrupted images without additional data augmentation during training. Thus, a robust detector

Table 1 Experiments on MS COCO2017 with our method on two-stage detectors

Model	Backbone	FPS	Params	Distill	AP	AP_{50}	AP_{75}	AP_S	AP_M	AP_L
Faster RCNN	ResNet18	28.1	30.57	×	34.6	55.0	37.1	19.3	36.9	45.9
				✓	37.0+2.4	57.2+2.2	39.7+2.6	19.9+0.6	39.7+0.8	50.3+4.4
	ResNet50	18.1	43.57	×	38.4	59.0	42.0	21.5	42.1	50.3
				✓	41.5+3.1	62.2+3.2	45.1+3.1	23.5+2.0	45.0+2.9	55.3+5.0
	ResNet101	14.2	62.57	×	39.8	60.1	43.3	22.5	43.6	52.8
				✓	43.9+4.1	64.2+4.1	48.1+3.9	25.3+2.8	48.0+4.4	58.7+5.9
	ViT-B-32	11.8	104.49	×	30.9	50.5	31.7	9.7	33.7	51.5
				✓	34.4+3.5	54.9+4.4	34.7+3.0	11.9+2.2	37.5+3.8	56.0+4.5
	ViT-B-16	3.4	104.49	×	37.8	57.4	40.1	17.8	41.4	57.3
				✓	41.9+4.1	61.0+3.6	43.4+3.3	21.3+3.5	44.9+3.5	62.9+5.6
Cascade RCNN	ResNet50	15.4	71.22	×	41.0	59.4	44.4	22.7	44.4	54.3
				✓	44.4+3.4	62.7+3.3	48.3+3.9	24.8+2.1	48.0+3.6	59.3+5.0
	ResNet101	11.7	90.21	×	42.5	60.7	46.4	23.5	46.5	56.4
				✓	45.2+2.7	63.5+2.8	49.4+3.0	26.2+2.7	48.7+2.2	60.8+4.4
Dynamic RCNN	ResNet18	28.1	30.57	×	35.0	55.2	37.4	20.1	37.4	45.8
				✓	38.2+3.2	56.5+1.3	41.8+4.4	20.1+0.0	40.7+3.3	53.2+7.4
	ResNet50	18.1	43.57	×	39.8	58.3	43.2	23.0	42.8	52.4
				✓	42.8+3.0	61.2+2.9	47.0+3.8	23.9+0.9	46.2+3.4	57.7+5.3
	ResNet101	14.2	62.57	×	41.2	59.7	45.3	24.0	44.9	54.3
				✓	44.8+3.6	63.0+3.3	48.9+3.6	25.0+1.0	48.9+4.0	60.4+6.1
Grid RCNN	ResNet18	26.7	66.37	×	36.6	54.2	39.7	20.1	39.8	48.2
				✓	38.8+2.2	56.7+2.5	41.5+1.8	21.1+1.0	41.6+1.8	52.7+4.5
	ResNet50	14.0	66.37	×	40.4	58.4	43.6	22.8	43.9	53.3
				✓	42.6+2.2	61.1+2.7	46.1+2.5	24.2+1.4	46.6+2.7	55.8+2.5
	ResNet101	11.0	85.36	×	41.6	59.8	45.0	23.7	45.7	54.7
				✓	44.8+3.2	63.6+3.8	48.9+3.9	26.5+2.8	48.9+3.2	59.6+1.9

Table 2 Experiments on MS COCO2017 with our method on one-stage detectors

Model	Backbone	FPS	Params	Distill	AP	AP$_{50}$	AP$_{75}$	AP$_S$	AP$_M$	AP$_L$
RetinaNet	RegNet-800M	22.4	19.27	×	35.6	54.7	37.7	19.7	39.0	47.8
				✓	38.4+2.8	57.4+3.3	40.7+3.0	21.4+1.7	42.0+3.0	52.3+4.5
	ResNet18	25.8	23.30	×	33.4	51.8	35.1	16.9	35.6	44.9
				✓	35.9+2.5	54.4+3.3	38.0+2.9	17.9+1.0	39.1+3.5	49.4+4.5
	ResNet50	17.7	37.74	×	37.4	56.7	39.6	20.0	40.7	49.7
				✓	39.6+2.2	58.8+2.1	42.1+2.5	22.7+2.7	43.3+2.6	52.5+2.8
	ResNet101	13.5	56.74	×	38.9	58.0	41.5	21.0	42.8	52.4
				✓	41.3+2.4	60.8+2.8	44.3+2.8	22.7+1.7	46.0+3.2	55.2+2.8
Fsaf RetinaNet	ResNet50	20.0	36.19	×	37.8	56.8	39.8	20.4	41.1	48.8
				✓	41.4+3.6	61.0+3.2	44.2+4.4	23.1+2.7	45.2+4.1	55.2+6.4
	ResNet101	15.0	55.19	×	39.3	58.6	42.1	22.1	43.4	51.2
				✓	42.6+3.3	62.0+3.4	45.5+3.4	24.5+2.4	47.0+2.6	56.2+5.0
RepPoints	ResNet50	18.2	36.62	×	38.6	59.6	41.6	22.5	42.2	50.4
				✓	40.6+2.0	61.7+2.1	43.8+2.2	23.4+0.9	44.6+2.4	53.0+2.6
	ResNet101	13.2	55.62	×	40.5	61.3	43.5	23.4	44.7	53.2
				✓	42.7+2.2	63.7+2.4	46.4+2.9	24.9+1.5	47.2+2.5	56.4+3.2
Yolo v3	DarkNet53	42.2	61.95	×	33.4	56.3	35.2	19.5	36.4	43.6
				✓	35.8+2.4	58.2+1.9	38.1+2.9	21.2+1.7	39.0+2.6	45.6+2.0
SSD	VGG16	26.1	38.08	×	29.4	49.3	31.0	11.7	34.1	44.9
				✓	31.2+1.8	52.1+2.8	32.8+1.8	12.6+0.9	37.4+3.3	46.2+1.3

Table 3 Experiments on MS COCO2017 with our method on instance segmentation

Model	Backbone	Params	FPS	Distill	Bounding box AP					Mask AP				
					AP	AP_S	AP_M	AP_L		AP	AP_S	AP_M	AP_L	
Mask RCNN	ResNet50	44.17	17.4	×	39.2	22.9	42.6	51.2		35.4	19.1	38.6	48.4	
				✓	41.7+2.5	23.4+0.5	45.3+2.7	55.8+4.6		37.4+2.0	19.7+0.6	40.5+1.9	52.1+3.7	
	ResNet101	63.16	13.5	×	40.8	23.0	45.0	54.1		36.6	19.2	40.2	50.5	
				✓	43.0+2.2	24.7+1.7	47.2+2.2	57.1+3.0		38.7+2.1	20.7+1.5	42.3+2.1	53.3+2.8	
Cascade mask RCNN	ResNet50	77.10	16.1	×	41.9	23.2	44.9	55.9		36.5	18.9	39.2	50.7	
				✓	43.8+1.9	24.9+1.7	47.2+2.3	58.4+2.5		38.0+1.5	20.2+1.3	40.9+1.7	52.8+2.1	
	ResNet101	96.09	13.1	×	42.9	24.4	46.5	57.0		37.3	19.7	40.6	51.5	
				✓	45.4+2.5	26.3+1.9	49.0+2.5	60.9+3.9		39.6+2.3	21.3+2.6	42.8+2.2	55.0+3.5	
Mask scoring RCNN	ResNet50	60.51	18.0	×	38.8	21.7	41.9	51.8		36.3	18.8	39.3	50.8	
				✓	41.5+2.7	24.3+2.6	45.5+3.6	53.8+2.0		38.5+2.2	20.7+1.9	42.0+2.7	52.3+1.5	
	ResNet101	79.40	15.0	×	42.6	24.4	46.2	56.6		38.1	20.0	41.5	53.5	
				✓	45.6+3.0	28.4+4.0	49.0+2.8	58.3+1.7		39.7+1.6	20.6+0.6	42.6+1.1	56.0+2.5	
Swin transformer	Swin-T	69.11	10.4	×	42.7	26.5	45.9	56.6		39.3	20.5	41.8	57.8	
				✓	45.2+2.5	27.6+1.1	48.9+3.0	58.5+1.9		41.6+2.3	22.9+2.4	44.8+3.0	59.4+1.6	

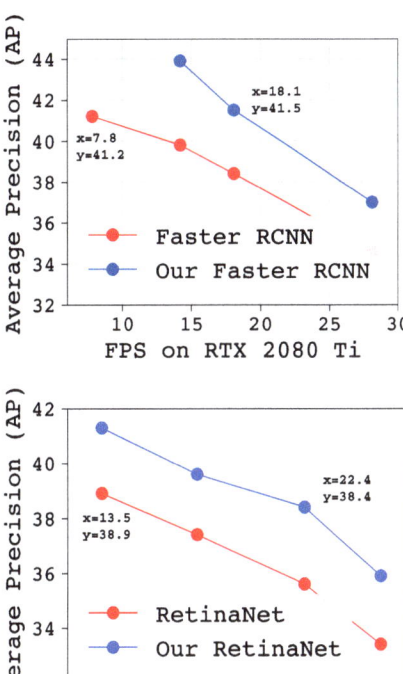

Fig. 6 KD on Faster RCNN with different backbones (ResNet18/50/101 and RegNet800M)

Fig. 7 KD on RetinaNet with different backbones (ResNet18/50/101 and RegNet800M)

can also be considered a detector with better domain generalization [35]. In this subsection, we follow Claudio et al. to evaluate the robustness of detectors trained with and without KD on COCO-C [12]. COCO-C is an evaluation dataset built from the validation set of COCO by adding four types of image corruption, including noise, blur, weather, and digital corruption. Each type of corruption is further composed of several fine-grained corruption. Table 4 has compared the mAP of Faster RCNN trained with and without KD on images with corruption. It is observed that the distilled detector achieves consistently higher mAP in all kinds of corruption, indicating that KD can improve the robustness and domain generalization ability of object detection.

1.2.4 Ablation Study

Ablation Study on KD Loss Table 5 shows the ablation study of attention-guided distillation ($\mathcal{L}_{AT}$ and $\mathcal{L}_{AM}$) and non-local distillation ($\mathcal{L}_{NLD}$). It is observed that: (i) Attention-guided distillation and non-local distillation lead to 2.8 and 1.4 AP improvements, respectively. (ii) $\mathcal{L}_{AT}$ and $\mathcal{L}_{AM}$ lead to 1.2 and 2.4 AP improvements respectively, indicating that most of the benefits of attention-guided distillation are obtained from the feature loss masked by the attention maps ($\mathcal{L}_{AM}$). (iii) There

Table 4 Experimental results (mAP) of Faster RCNN with ResNet50 Backbone on COCO2017 with different types of image corruption

Distill	Noise corruption			Blur corruption				Weather corruption				Digital corruption			
	Gaussian	Shot	Impulse	Defocus	Glass	Motion	Zoom	Snow	Frost	Fog	Bright	Contrast	Elastic	Pixelate	Jpeg
×	16.8	16.8	13.4	17.6	10.9	16.4	7.4	17.6	22.1	30.8	33.6	22.4	21.2	14.2	15.4
✓	19.9+3.1	20.1+3.3	16.5+3.1	20.1+2.5	12.6+1.7	18.2+1.8	8.3+0.9	19.4+1.8	24.2+2.1	33.7+2.9	36.4+2.8	24.2+1.8	23.9+2.7	16.2+2.0	18.1+2.7

Table 5 Ablation study of the three distillation loss in our method. Experiments are conducted with Faster RCNN students with ResNet50 backbones on MS COCO2017

Loss	$\mathcal{L}_{AT}$	×	✓	×	×	✓	✓
	$\mathcal{L}_{AM}$	×	×	✓	×	✓	✓
	$\mathcal{L}_{NLD}$	×	×	×	✓	×	✓
Result	AP	38.4	39.6	40.8	39.8	41.2	**41.5**
	AP_S	21.5	22.7	22.8	22.7	23.0	**23.5**
	AP_M	42.1	42.9	44.3	43.1	44.6	**45.0**
	AP_L	50.3	52.5	54.3	52.3	55.3	**55.3**

Numbers in bold indicate the highest results

Table 6 Comparison between our method and other distillation methods on Faster RCNN with ResNet50 backbones. Some results are missing because their origin papers do not report them

KD method	AP	AP_{50}	AP_{75}	AP_S	AP_M	AP_L
Without KD	38.4	59.0	42.0	21.5	42.1	50.3
Prediction KD [7]	38.9	59.6	42.3	21.0	42.8	52.4
Adriana et al. [23]	39.6	60.1	43.3	22.5	42.8	52.2
Kang et al.† [24]	40.9	–	–	24.5	44.0	52.0
Sun et al.† [25]	40.1	–	–	23.0	43.6	53.0
Chen et al.[26]	38.7	59.0	42.1	22.0	41.9	51.0
Wang et al.[27]	39.1	59.8	42.8	22.2	42.9	51.1
Li et al. [28]	39.6	60.1	43.3	22.5	42.8	52.2
Heo et al.[29]	38.9	60.1	42.6	21.8	42.7	50.7
Guo et al. [30]	40.9	–	–	23.6	44.8	53.3
Du et al. [31]	39.5	60.1	43.3	22.3	43.6	51.7
Zhang et al. [32]	39.2	–	–	–	–	–
Dai et al. [33]	40.2	60.7	43.8	22.7	44.0	53.2
Our method	**41.5**	**62.2**	**45.1**	**23.5**	**45.0**	**55.3**

Results marked by † are from their original papers. Numbers in bold indicate the highest results

are 3.1 AP improvements with the combination of attention-guided distillation and non-local distillation. These observations indicate that each distillation loss in our method has its effectiveness, and they can be utilized together to achieve better performance (Tables 6 and 7).

Ablation Study on Attention Types Different from previous attention-based KD methods, the attention-guided distillation in our method uses not only spatial attention but also channel attention. In this subsection, we have conducted an ablation study on the two kinds of attention with Faster RCNN (ResNet50 backbone) on MS COCO2017 to show their individual effectiveness. As shown in Table 8, spatial attention and channel attention lead to 2.6 and 2.3 AP improvements, respectively. In contrast, the combination of the two kinds of attention leads to 2.8 AP improvements. These results indicate that both spatial and channel attention have their individual effectiveness, and they can be utilized together to achieve better performance.

Table 7 Experimental results on Cityscapes

Model	Backbone	Distill	Box AP	Mask AP
Faster RCNN	ResNet50	×	40.3	–
		✓	43.5+3.2	–
Mask RCNN	ResNet50	×	41.0	35.8
		✓	43.0+2.0	37.5+1.7

Table 8 Ablation study on spatial attention and channel attention

Attention type	Spatial	×	✓	×	✓
	Channel	×	×	✓	✓
Result	AP	38.4	41.0	40.7	**41.2**
	AP_S	21.5	22.7	22.9	**23.0**
	AP_M	42.1	44.7	44.1	**44.6**
	AP_L	50.3	54.2	54.1	**55.3**

Numbers in bold indicate the highest results

1.2.5 KD Benefits More from Longer Training Time

In this subsection, we study how the training time influences the effectiveness of KD. Experimental results on Faster RCNN and RetinaNet with 12, 18, and 24 epochs of training time are shown in Fig. 5. It is observed that when the training time increases, the mAP improvements from KD on the two detectors increase significantly. For instance, the mAP improvements with 24 training epochs are 24% and 29% higher than the mAP improvements with 12 epochs on Faster RCNN and RetinaNet respectively, indicating that KD benefits from long training time. We suggest that this is because compared with the supervision in the ground truth, the knowledge from teachers has a much higher dimension and a larger variance. Hence, a longer training time is required for the detectors to converge.

1.2.6 Analysis of the Benefits of KD

Qualitative Analysis Figure 8 shows the comparison of detection results between detectors trained with and without KD. It is observed that: (i) KD improves the detection ability of small objects. For instance, in Fig. 8a–c, the distilled e the handbag, and the person in the car, respectively. (ii) KD enables detectors to generate better bounding boxes. For instance, in Fig. 8d, e, the baseline model generates multiple bounding boxes for the boat and the train while the distilled model avoids these errors. (iii) KD enables detectors to classify better. For example, in Fig. 8j, the baseline model misclassifies the woman's hand as a cat, while the distilled model does not have this problem. (iv) KD improves the ability to detect dense objects. In Fig. 8h, the distilled model can detect many more carrots on the plate than the baseline model.

Fig. 8 Qualitative analysis of MS COCO2017 with Faster RCNN (ResNet50 backbone) trained with and without KD. (**a**)–(**k**) indicate the visualization results of different images

1.2.7 Relation Between Students and Teachers

An Accurate Teacher is Usually a Good Teacher There is sufficient research focusing on the relation between students and teachers. Mirzadeh et al. and Cho et al. [5, 6] show that a teacher with higher accuracy may not be the better teacher for KD, and sometimes a teacher with too high accuracy may harm the performance of students. Besides, Hossein et al. [36] and Li et al. [37] show that the same model and even a model with lower accuracy than the student can be utilized as the teacher for KD. However, all their experiments are conducted on image classification. In this subsection, we study whether these observations still hold in the task of object detection. As shown in Fig. 4, we conduct experiments on Faster RCNN and Cascade RCNN students (ResNet50 backbones) with teacher models of different AP. It is observed that: (i) In all of our experiments, the student with a higher AP teacher always achieves higher AP. The Pearson correlation coefficients between the AP of students and teachers on Faster RCNN and Cascade RCNN are 0.86 and 0.96, respectively, indicating a strong positive correlation. (ii) When the teacher has lower or the same AP as the student, there are very limited and even negative improvements with KD, indicating that an inaccurate teacher may harm the performance of students (Figs. 9 and 10).

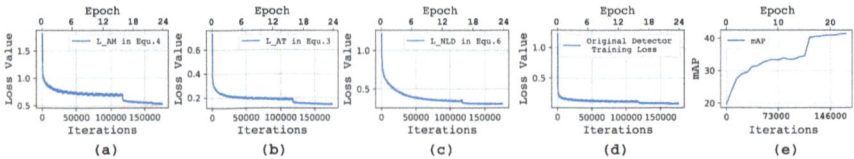

Fig. 9 The curves of different loss and mAP during training of distilled Faster RCNN with a ResNet50 backbone on MS COCO2017. (**a**)–(**c**) are curves of KD loss. (**d**) is the original training loss of Faster RCNN. Note that there are significant mAP improvements and loss reduction at the 16_{th} epoch because the learning rate decays at this time. (**e**) The mAP of detectors in the validation set during training

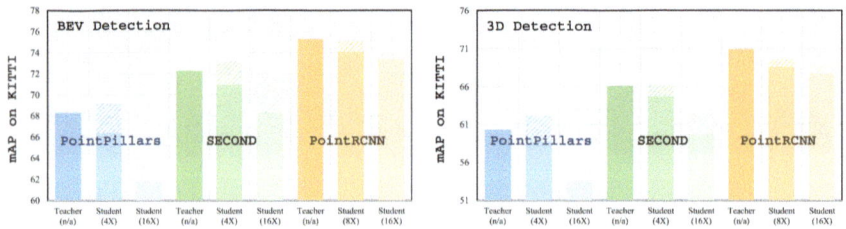

Fig. 10 Experimental results (mAP of the moderate difficulty) of our methods on 4×, 8×, and 16× compressed students on KITTI. The area of the *dashed lines* indicates the benefits of KD

2 KD for Point Cloud-based 3D Object Detection

Compared with images, point clouds have their properties: (i) Point clouds inherently lack topological information, which makes recovering the local topology information crucial for the visual tasks [38–40]. (ii) Different from images which have a regular structure, point clouds are irregularly and sparsely distributed in the metric space [41, 42]. These differences between images and point clouds have hindered the image-based KD methods from achieving satisfactory performance on point clouds and also raised the requirement to design specific KD methods for point clouds. Recently, a few methods have been proposed to apply KD to 3D detection [43, 44]. However, most of these methods focus on the choice of student-teacher in a multi-modal setting, e.g., teaching point clouds-based student detectors with an image-based teacher or vice versa, and still ignore the peculiar properties of point clouds. To address this problem, we propose a structured KD framework named PointDistiller, which involves *local distillation* to distill teacher knowledge in the local geometric structure of point clouds, and *reweighted learning* strategy to handle the sparsity of point clouds by highlighting student learning on the crucial voxels.

Local Distillation Sufficient recent studies show that capturing and making use of the semantic information in the local geometric structure of point clouds has a crucial impact on the representation learning of point clouds [45, 46]. Hence, instead

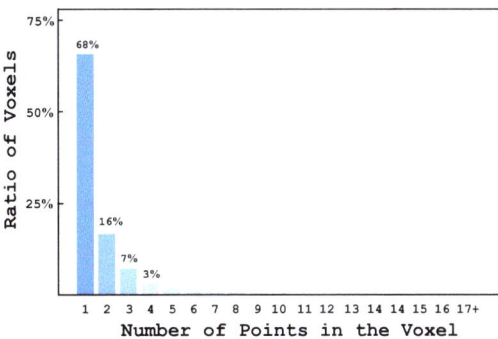

Fig. 11 Distribution of voxels with different numbers of points inside. Voxels with no points are not included here

of directly distilling the backbone feature of teacher detectors to student detectors, we propose local distillation, which firstly clusters the local neighboring voxels or points with KNN (K-Nearest Neighbours), then encodes the semantic information in local geometric structure with dynamic graph convolutional layers [46], and finally distills them from teachers to students. Hence, the student detectors can inherit the teacher's ability to understand the local geometric information of point clouds and achieve better detection performance.

Reweighted Learning Strategy One of the mainstream methods for processing point clouds is to convert them into volumetric voxels and then encode them as regular data. However, due to the sparsity and the noise in point clouds, most of these voxels contain only a single point. For instance, as shown in Fig. 11, on the KITTI dataset, about 68% of the voxels in point clouds contain only one point, which has a high probability of being a noise point. Hence, the representative features in these single-point voxels have relatively lower importance in KD compared with the voxels which contain multiple points (Fig. 12). Motivated by this observation, we propose a reweighted learning strategy, which highlights student learning on the voxels with multiple points by giving them larger learning weights. Besides, the similar idea can also be easily extended to raw point-based detectors to highlight KD on the points with more considerable influence on the prediction (Fig. 13).

2.1 Local Distillation and Reweighted Learning Strategy

2.1.1 Preliminaries

Given a set of point clouds $\mathcal{X} = \{x_1, x_2, \ldots, x_n\}$ and the corresponding label set $\mathcal{Y} = \{y_1, y_2, \ldots, y_m\}$, the object detector can be formulated as $\mathcal{F} = f \circ g$, where f is the feature encoding layer to extract representation features from inputs and g is the detection head for prediction. Then, the representation feature on the sample x can be written as $f(x) \in \mathbb{R}^{n \times C}$, where n indicates the number of voxels for voxel-based detectors or the number of points for raw point-based detectors. C indicates

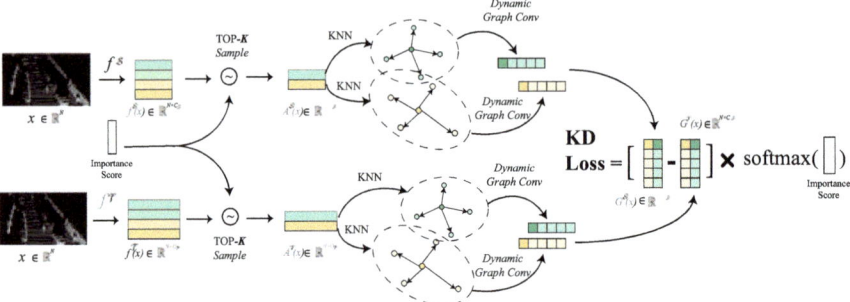

Fig. 12 The overview of our method. f^T and f^S: the feature encoding layers in the teacher and student detectors. A^T and A^S: features of the sampled to-be-distilled voxels or points with top-N largest importance score. C_T and C_S: the number of channels for features of the teacher and the student detectors. $\mathcal{G}_T$ and $\mathcal{G}_S$: the graph features of the teacher and student detectors. Based on the pre-defined importance score, our method samples the relatively more crucial N voxels or points from the whole point cloud, extracts their local geometric structure with dynamic graph convolution, and then distills them in a reweighted manner

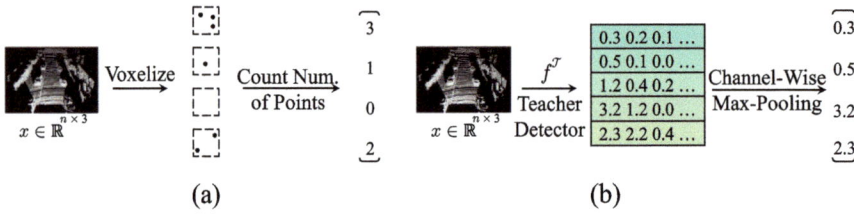

Fig. 13 The computation of the importance score for voxel-based and raw point-based detectors. The importance scores are later utilized to determine which voxel or point is utilized for distillation and how they contribute to the distillation loss. (**a**) For voxels-based detectors. (**b**) For raw points-based detectors

the number of channels. Besides, for voxel-based detectors, we define $v_{ij}(x) = 1$ if the j-th point of x belongs to the i-voxel. Then, the number of points in the i-th voxel can be denoted as $\sum_j v_{ij}(x)$. We distinguish the student detector and the teacher detector with scripts $\mathcal{S}$ and $\mathcal{T}$, respectively.

2.1.2 Methodology

Sampling Top-N To-be-distilled Voxels (Points) As discussed in previous sections, since the point clouds are overwhelmingly sparse while the voxels are usually equally spaced, most of the voxels only contain very few and even single points. Thus, these single-point voxels have much less value to be learned by students in KD. Even in raw point-based detectors, there usually exist some points that are relatively more crucial and some points which are not meaningful (e.g., the noise points). Thus, instead of distilling all the voxels or points in point clouds, we propose to distill the voxels or points which are more valuable for KD. Concretely, for voxel-based detectors, we define the importance score of i-th voxel as $\sum_j v_{ij}(x)$, which indicates the number of points inside it. For point-based detectors, motivated by previous works that localize the crucial pixels in images with attention, we define the importance score for i-th point as its permutation-invariant maximal value along the channel dimension, which can be formulated as $\max(f(x)[i])$. Based on the importance score, we can sample the top-N significant voxels or points for KD based on the importance score computed from $f^\mathcal{T}(x)$. For simplicity in writing, we denote the selected student and teacher features in top-N important voxels or points as $A^\mathcal{T}(x) \in \mathbb{R}^{N \times C_\mathcal{T}}$ and $A^\mathcal{S}(x) \in \mathbb{R}^{N \times C_\mathcal{S}}$, respectively, where $C_\mathcal{S}$ and $C_\mathcal{T}$ indicate the number of channels in student and teacher features, respectively.

Extracting Local Geometric Information As pointed out by abundant previous works, the local geometric information has a crucial influence on the performance of point cloud detectors [45, 46]. Thus, instead of directly distilling the representative feature, we propose *local distillation* which extracts the local geometric information of point clouds with dynamic graph convolution layers and distills it to the student detector. Concretely, denoting $z_i = A(x)[i]$ as the feature of the i-th voxel or point for distillation, we can build a graph based on this voxel or point and its K neighboring voxels or points clustered by KNN (K-Nearest Neighbours). By denoting the features of z_i and its $K-1$ neighbors as $z_{i,1}$ and $\mathcal{N}_i = \{z_{i,2}, z_{i,3}, \ldots, z_{i,K}\}$ respectively, motivated by previous methods [46, 47], we firstly update the feature of each voxel (or point) in this graph by concatenating them with the global centroid voxel (or point) feature $z_{i,1}$, which can be formulated as $\hat{z}_{i,j} = \text{cat}([z_{i,1}, z_{i,j}])$ for all $z_{i,j} \in \mathcal{N}_i$. Then, we apply a dynamic graph convolution as the aggregation operation upon them, which can be formulated as $\mathcal{G}_i = \gamma(\hat{z}_{i,1}, \ldots, \hat{z}_{i,K})$, where γ is the aggregation operator. Following previous graph-based point cloud networks, we set γ as a nonlinear layer with ReLU activation and batch normalization. Then the training objective of local distillation can be formulated as

$$\arg\min_{\theta_S, \theta_\gamma} \mathbb{E}_x \left[\frac{1}{N} \sum_{i=1}^{N} \left\| \mathcal{G}_i^\mathcal{S}(x) - \mathcal{G}_i^\mathcal{T}(x) \right\| \right], \tag{10}$$

where θ_S indicates the parameters of student encoding layer $f^\mathcal{S}$. $\theta_\gamma = [\theta_{\gamma^S}, \theta_{\gamma^\mathcal{T}}]$ indicates the parameters of dynamic graph convolution layers for the student and teacher detectors. Note that these layers are trained with the student simultaneously and can be discarded during inference.

2.1.3 Reweighting KD Loss

Usually, compared with the teacher detector, the student detector has much fewer parameters, implying inferior learning capacity. Thus, it is challenging for the student detector to inherit teacher knowledge in all points or voxels. As discussed above, different voxels and points in point cloud object detection have different values in KD. Thus, we propose to reweight the learning weight of each voxel or point based on the importance score introduced in previous paragraphs. Denote the learning weight for the N voxels for distillation as $\phi \in \mathbb{R}^N$. Similar to the importance score defined during sampling, we define the learning weight of each graph as the maximal value on the corresponding features after a softmax function, which can be formulated as $\phi = \text{softmax}\left(\max(G^T(x))/\tau\right)$, where τ is the temperature hyper-parameter in the softmax function. For voxel-based methods, we define ϕ as the number of points in the voxel after a softmax function, which can be formulated as $\phi_i = \text{softmax}\left(\sum_j v_{i,j}/\tau\right)$. Then, with the reweighting strategy, the objective of KD can be formulated as

$$\arg\min_{\theta_S, \theta_\gamma} \mathbb{E}_x \left[\frac{1}{N} \sum_{i=1}^{N} \phi_i \cdot \left\| \mathcal{G}_i^S(x) - \mathcal{G}_i^{T(x)} \right\| \right]. \tag{11}$$

As shown in the above loss function, with a higher ϕ_i, the KD loss between student and teacher features at the i-th graph will have a more extensive influence on the overall loss, and thus student learning on the i-th graph can be highlighted. As a result, the proposed reweighting strategy allows the student detector to pay more attention to learning teacher knowledge in the relatively more crucial voxel graphs (point graphs). Moreover, Eq. (11) also implies that our method is a feature-based KD method that is not correlated with the architecture of detectors and the label set $\mathcal{Y}$. Hence, it can be directly added to the original training loss of all kinds of 3D object detectors for model compression.

2.2 Evaluation and Discussion

2.2.1 Experiment Setting

We have evaluated our method in both voxel-based object detectors, including PointPillars [48], SECOND [49] and CenterPoint [50], and the raw point-based object detector including PointRCNN [51]. Most experiments are conducted on KITTI [52], which consist of samples that have both lidar point clouds and images. Our models are trained with only the lidar point clouds. For KITTI, we report the average precision calculated by 40 sampling recall positions for BEV (Bird's Eye View) object detection and 3D object detection on the *validation* split.

2.2.2 Experimental Results

Table 9 shows the performance of detectors trained with and without our method for BEV detection and 3D detection, respectively. It is observed that: (i) Significant

2 KD for Point Cloud-based 3D Object Detection

Table 9 Experimental results of our method for BEV (Bird-Eye-View) object detection. **F** and **P** indicate the number of float operations (/G) and parameters (/M) of the detector, respectively. **mAP** indicates the mean average precision of moderate difficulty

Model	F	P	KD	Car			Pedestrians			Cyclists			mAP
				Easy	Moderate	Hard	Easy	Moderate	Hard	Easy	Moderate	Hard	
PointPillars	34.3	4.8	×	94.3	88.1	83.6	57.9	51.8	47.6	86.5	65.0	61.1	68.3
	9.0	1.3	×	92.4	88.2	83.6	53.0	47.9	44.1	81.8	63.1	59.0	66.4
	9.0	1.3	✓	**93.1**	**89.0**	**86.3**	**59.8**	**52.8**	**48.2**	**83.8**	**65.8**	**62.0**	**69.2**
	2.5	0.3	×	91.3	84.8	82.2	50.1	44.4	41.6	74.2	56.1	52.5	61.8
	2.5	0.3	✓	**92.5**	**85.2**	81.9	**50.8**	**45.8**	**42.5**	**77.2**	**59.5**	**55.6**	**63.5**
SECOND	69.8	5.3	×	93.1	88.9	85.9	64.9	58.1	51.9	84.3	69.9	65.7	72.3
	17.8	1.4	×	93.1	86.6	85.7	64.7	57.8	52.8	84.1	68.5	64.5	71.0
	17.8	1.4	✓	**93.2**	**88.6**	**86.0**	**65.1**	**58.1**	**53.1**	**87.4**	**72.9**	**68.5**	**73.2**
	4.6	0.4	×	95.0	86.2	83.3	61.6	54.9	49.2	80.9	63.6	59.6	68.3
	4.6	0.4	✓	**95.4**	**88.3**	**83.7**	**64.5**	**57.6**	**52.2**	**85.2**	**68.8**	**64.4**	**71.6**
PointRCNN	104.9	4.1	×	95.0	86.7	84.3	69.8	64.5	58.1	92.8	74.6	70.4	75.3
	13.7	0.5	×	**93.5**	**85.9**	**83.5**	71.6	65.4	59.1	91.1	71.0	67.2	74.1
	13.7	0.5	✓	93.3	85.7	**83.5**	**74.0**	**67.2**	**60.5**	**94.6**	**72.3**	**67.9**	**75.1**
	7.1	0.3	×	**95.8**	**85.4**	81.7	**72.9**	**65.5**	**58.6**	91.8	69.3	65.9	73.4
	7.1	0.3	✓	95.2	84.3	**81.7**	72.6	64.8	57.7	**92.6**	**72.9**	**68.5**	**74.0**

Numbers in bold indicate the highest results

average precision improvements on all kinds of detectors and all compression ratios for both BEV and 3D detection. On average, 2.4 and 1.0 moderate mAP improvements can be observed for the voxel and raw point-based detectors, respectively. On BEV and 3D detection, 1.9 and 1.9 moderate mAP improvements can be obtained, respectively. (ii) On the BEV detection of PointPillars and SECOND detectors, the 4× compressed and accelerated students trained with our method outperform their teachers by 0.9 and 0.9 mAP, respectively. On the 3D detection of PointPillars and SECOND detectors, the 4× compressed and accelerated students trained with our method outperform their teachers by 1.8 and 0.1 mAP, respectively. (iii) Consistent average precision boosts can be observed in the detection results of all difficulties. For instance, on BEV detection of PointPillars students, 2.4, 2.3, and 2.3 mAP improvements can be observed for easy, moderate, and hard difficulties, respectively. These observations demonstrate that our method can successfully transfer teacher knowledge to the student detectors. (iv) Consistent average precision boosts can be observed in the detection results of all categories. For instance, on moderate BEV detection of PointPillars students, 0.6, 3.2, and 3.1 mAP improvements can be obtained on cars, pedestrians, and cyclists, respectively. (v) On PointRCNN, on average 1.3 and 1.2 moderate mAP improvements can be observed on BEV and 3D detection, respectively, indicating that our method is also effective for raw point-based detectors (Table 10).

PointDistiller is mainly composed of two components, including the reweighted learning strategy (RL) and local distillation (LD). Ablation studies with 4× compressed PointPillars students on KITTI are shown in Table 11. It is observed that: (i) 2.0 and 1.9 mAP improvements can be obtained by only using the reweighted learning strategy to distill the backbone features on BEV detection and 3D detection, respectively. (ii) 2.3 and 2.5 mAP boosts can be gained by using local distillation without reweighted learning on BEV detection and 3D detection, respectively. (iii) By combining the two methods together, 0.5 and 0.9 further mAP improvements can be achieved on BEV detection and 3D detection, respectively. These observations indicate that each module in PointDistiller has its individual effectiveness and their merits are orthogonal (Table 12).

2.2.3 Visualization Analysis

Visualization on Importance Score In the reweighted learning strategy, the importance scores of each voxel or point are utilized to determine whether it should be distilled. The visualization of the importance scores in PointPillars is shown in Fig. 14. It is observed that they successfully localize the foreground objects (e.g., cars and pedestrians) and the hard-negative objects (e.g., walls), indicating that the importance score in our method is able to find the voxels or points which are relatively more important.

Visualization of Detection Results We visualize the detection results of the student model trained with and without our method for comparison. Note that

Table 10 Experimental results of our method for 3D object detection. **F** and **P** indicate the number of float operations (/G) and parameters (/M) of the detector, respectively. **mAP** indicates the mean average precision of moderate difficulty

Model	F	P	KD	Car Easy	Car Moderate	Car Hard	Pedestrians Easy	Pedestrians Moderate	Pedestrians Hard	Cyclists Easy	Cyclists Moderate	Cyclists Hard	mAP
PointPillars	34.3	4.8	×	87.3	75.9	71.1	52.0	45.9	41.4	78.6	59.2	55.8	60.3
	9.0	1.3	×	87.4	75.9	71.0	48.2	43.0	38.7	74.1	57.2	53.3	58.7
	9.0	1.3	✓	**88.1**	**76.9**	**73.8**	**54.6**	**47.5**	**42.3**	**80.3**	**62.0**	**58.8**	**62.1**
SECOND	2.5	0.3	×	83.1	69.8	65.4	44.0	38.7	35.3	70.9	52.1	48.7	53.5
	2.5	0.3	✓	**83.7**	**69.8**	65.3	**45.3**	**40.3**	**36.5**	**72.7**	**54.7**	**51.1**	**54.9**
	69.8	5.3	×	88.6	79.3	75.7	60.1	53.2	47.0	79.8	65.7	61.6	66.1
	17.8	1.4	×	89.2	77.4	74.0	58.8	51.3	45.5	80.5	65.4	61.3	64.7
	17.8	1.4	✓	88.9	76.9	73.6	**60.0**	**53.0**	**47.4**	**83.2**	**68.6**	**64.2**	**66.2**
	4.6	0.4	×	86.3	72.6	66.0	53.6	47.8	41.8	76.7	58.7	55.1	59.7
	4.6	0.4	✓	**87.0**	**73.3**	**68.1**	**57.0**	**51.0**	**45.4**	**81.0**	**63.5**	**59.3**	**62.6**
PointRCNN	104.9	4.1	×	92.1	80.1	77.4	66.8	60.3	54.3	92.1	72.3	67.8	70.9
	13.7	0.5	×	89.8	76.8	72.7	67.9	60.9	54.0	88.1	68.0	64.4	68.6
	13.7	0.5	✓	**91.4**	75.6	**72.9**	**70.1**	**63.5**	**56.1**	**92.0**	**69.8**	**65.4**	**69.6**
	7.1	0.3	×	89.8	75.3	70.7	68.7	60.7	53.4	91.1	67.2	63.9	67.7
	7.1	0.3	✓	89.6	**75.6**	**72.6**	**69.4**	**61.0**	**53.5**	91.0	**70.2**	**65.5**	**69.0**

Numbers in bold indicate the highest results

Table 11 Ablation study on 4× compressed PointPillars. LD and RL indicate local distillation and the reweighted learning strategy, respectively. mAP is measured on the moderate difficulty

		BEV detection											3D detection											
		Car			Pedestrians			Cyclists			mAP		Car			Pedestrians			Cyclists			mAP
LD	RL	Easy	Moderate	Hard	Easy	Moderate	Hard	Easy	Moderate	Hard			Easy	Moderate	Hard	Easy	Moderate	Hard	Easy	Moderate	Hard	
×	×	92.4	88.2	83.6	53.0	47.9	44.1	81.8	63.1	59.0	66.4		87.4	75.9	71.0	48.2	43.0	38.7	74.1	57.2	53.3	58.7
✓	×	92.7	88.2	83.7	58.2	51.0	47.0	84.3	66.9	63.1	68.7		87.6	76.0	71.5	52.6	45.9	40.7	79.8	61.6	58.0	61.2
×	✓	93.1	88.5	85.7	55.6	49.6	45.7	84.2	67.3	62.9	68.4		87.8	76.5	72.0	49.4	43.7	39.4	78.7	61.5	57.5	60.6
✓	✓	93.1	89.0	86.3	59.8	52.8	48.2	83.8	65.8	62.0	69.2		88.1	76.9	73.8	54.6	47.5	42.3	80.3	62.0	58.8	62.1

Numbers in bold indicate the highest results

2 KD for Point Cloud-based 3D Object Detection

Table 12 Student-teacher settings in our experiments

Model	FPS	Params	2D backbone	BEV query	Decoder depth
Student-1	14.5	40.45	ResNet50	(150, 150)	3
Teacher-1	10.2	56.57	ResNet101	(150, 150)	3
Student-2	14.5	40.45	ResNet50	(150, 150)	3
Teacher-2	5.3	201.20	ResNeXt-Large	(150, 150)	3
Student-3	5.2	47.56	ResNet50	(200, 200)	6
Teacher-3	3.5	65.93	ResNet101	(200, 200)	6

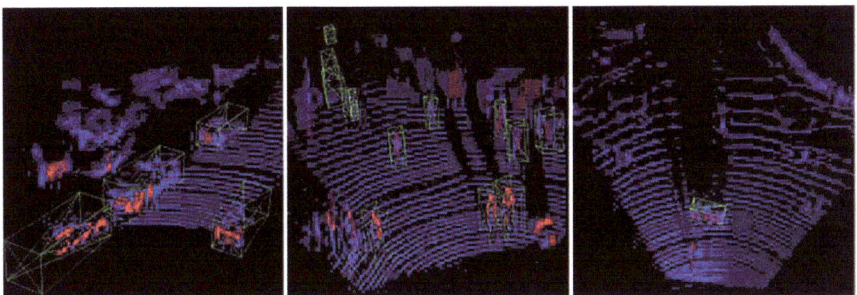

Fig. 14 Visualization on importance scores for PointPillars. Red points indicate the voxels with high importance scores

Fig. 15 Comparison between the detection results of students trained with and without KD. *Green and blue boxes* indicate the bounding boxes from prediction and ground-truths, respectively. *Red dots* are the points inside the predicted bounding boxes

both student models are 4× compressed PointPillars trained on KITTI. The green and blue boxes indicate the boxes of the model prediction and the ground truth, respectively. As shown in Fig. 15, the student model without KD tends to have much more false positive (FP) predictions. In contrast, this excessive FP problem is alleviated in the students trained with our method. This observation is consistent with our experimental results that the distilled PointPillars have 3.4 mAP improvements (Fig. 16).

Fig. 16 Experimental results on nuScenes

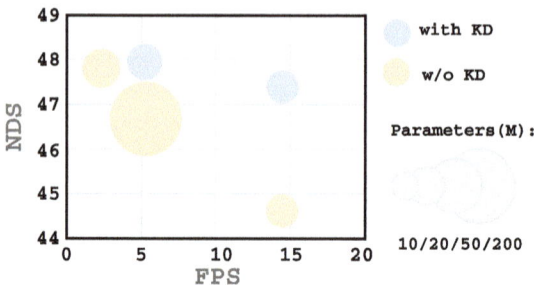

3 KD for Multi-View Images based 3D Object Detection

Recently, bird's-eye-view (BEV) based multi-camera perception frameworks have greatly narrowed the performance gap with LiDAR-based methods for 3D object detection tasks [53–56]. Such vision-centric BEV frameworks usually involve two stages: single view feature extraction using backbone networks (convnets [57] or transformers [58]), and information fusion across multiple camera views and multiple timestamps using transformers [54, 59, 60] or the lift-splat-shoot paradigm [53, 61, 62]. However, such performance improvements are achieved with a hefty computation overhead. For instance, the 120M parameters in BEVDet [61] require more than 4 TFlops computation, which is almost 20× larger and 10× slower than CenterPoint [50], a state-of-the-art LiDAR-based 3D detector. Practical applications such as self-driving vehicles, usually have limited computation budget but rather strict latency and accuracy requirements. Deployment of such visual BEV models onto edge devices requires a delicate balance between low computation cost and high detection accuracy. Compared with neural network pruning [63] and quantization [64, 65], KD [7, 66] is more suited for striking such a balance.

While KD has demonstrated great success in various 2D computer vision tasks, such as classification [67], object detection [26, 28, 68], semantic segmentation [69, 70], and image generation [71–74], the application of KD on 3D computer vision, especially the camera-based multi-view 3D detection, has not been well-studied. However, it is also brought to our attention that simply applying traditional KD methods to 3D vision tasks usually leads to limited performance gains. To address the aforementioned problems, this paper proposes a novel KD framework for visual BEV detection models. We start with analyzing the challenges in the multi-view 3D detection task and then propose the corresponding solution.

Information Fusion from Multiple Positions In multi-view 3D detection, the detector takes input from multiple cameras across different timestamps to identify objects. Hence, the student should be able to learn not only the information from single images but also how to fuse and leverage the information from multiple spatial/temporal positions. To tackle this challenge, we propose spatial-temporal distillation, which improves student performance by allowing it to learn the semantic correspondence between inputs in different spatial (i.e., view) and temporal positions from their teachers. Moreover, we also propose BEV response distillation, which aims to distill teacher responses to different positions/pillars in the BEV feature map, which contains high-level information on object localization.

Discrepancies Between the Inputs BEV 3D detectors usually employ a DETR-like architecture, which utilizes self-attention and cross-attention layers for information fusion [55, 75]. Different from traditional convolutional detectors, the input information of DETR-style detectors contains not only images but also trainable queries and positional encodings. Without explicit constraints, student and teacher models could have learned different positional encodings and queries after training. KD will be hindered by such discrepancies [76]. To address this problem, we propose a weight-inheriting scheme that fixes the positional encodings and BEV queries of the student model to the corresponding values in the teacher detector. In this way, the student detector will benefit from the pre-trained weights of the teacher detector (Fig. 17).

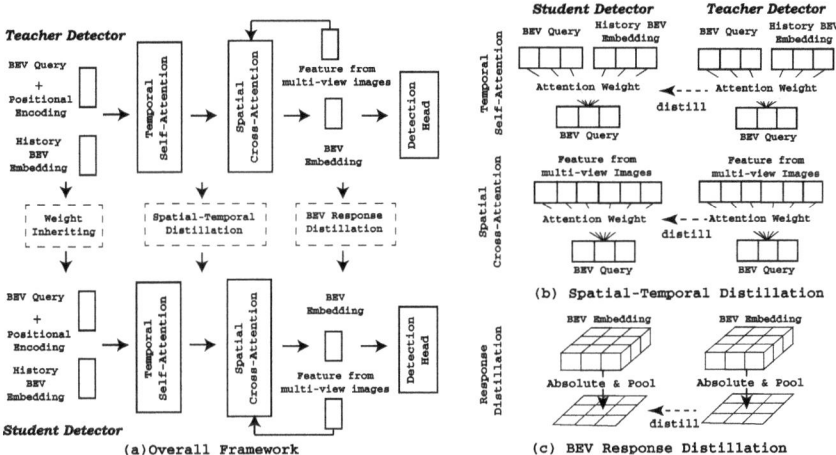

Fig. 17 The overall framework and details of our method. (**a**) The proposed KD methods mainly include weight-inheriting, spatial-temporal distillation, and BEV response distillation. Weight-inheriting fixes the parameters of BEV queries and positional encoding to their value in the pre-trained teacher detector during the whole training period to guarantee that students and teachers have the same inputs. (**b**) Spatial-temporal distillation aims to improve student performance on information fusion of images from multiple views and timestamps by transferring teacher knowledge in the attention weights in the temporal self-attention and spatial cross-attention layers. (**c**) BEV response distillation first computes the response of different positions in the BEV map and then distills it to the students

3.1 Distilling Crucial Knowledge in Multi-view Images

3.1.1 Preliminary

Without loss of generality, we conduct our experiments on top of the BEVFormer, which is a performant and representative multi-view 3D object detection architecture. BEVFormer consists of four stages, including feature extraction from single images, temporal information fusion, spatial information fusion, and prediction.

(I) Feature Extraction of Single Images In multi-view 3D detection, at timestamp t, the input image set can be denoted as $\mathcal{X}^{(t)} = \{x_1^{(t)}, x_2^{(t)}, \ldots, x_v^{(t)}\}$, where v denotes the number of views. BEVFormer firstly encodes the feature of every single image with a convolutional 2D backbone f_{2D}, which can be formulated as $F^{(t)} = f_{2D}(\mathcal{X}^{(t)})$. These features are then fed into spatial cross-attention in Stage III for fusion.

(II) Temporal Information Fusion Temporal self-attention is utilized to fuse the information between the current input images and the historical images. The input of temporal self-attention layers includes the predefined trainable BEV queries with positional encoding and the previous BEV embedding at timestamp $t-1$, which can be formulated as Q^{BEV} and $E_{BEV}^{(t-1)}$, respectively. Then, the computation of temporal self-attention can be written as

$$\begin{aligned} E_{BEV}^{\prime(t)} &= \text{TSA}\left(Q_p^{BEV}, \{Q^{BEV}, E_{BEV}^{(t-1)}\}\right) \\ &= \sum_{V \in \{Q^{BEV}, E_{BEV}^{(t-1)}\}} \text{DeformAttn}(Q_p^{BEV}, p, V), \end{aligned} \quad (12)$$

where DeformAttn indicates the deformable attention layers [77] and Q_p^{BEV} denotes the BEV query located at the position p. TSA and $E_{BEV}^{\prime(t)}$ indicate temporal self-attention and its outputs, respectively.

(III) Spatial Information Fusion In the stage of spatial information fusion, BEVFormer samples N_{ref} 3D reference points from each pillar, and then projects them to 2D views. Then, spatial cross-attention is utilized to fuse the BEV embedding from temporal information fusion with the reference points, which can be formulated as

$$E_{BEV}^{(t)} = \frac{1}{|v_{hit}|} \sum_{i \in v_{hit}} \sum_{j=1}^{N_{ref}} \text{DeformAttn}\left(E_{BEV}^{\prime(t)}, \mathcal{P}(p, i, j), F^{(t)}\right), \quad (13)$$

where v_{hit} indicates the number of views that contain the projection of the 3D reference points. $\mathcal{P}(p, i, j)$ is the projection function to get the j-th reference point on the i-th view image. $F^{(t)}$ indicates the feature of single images from Stage I.

(IV) Prediction In this stage, BEVFormer predicts the positions, dimensions, headings, and categories of objects based on the two inputs, including the output of spatial cross-attention and a set of object queries, which can be denoted as Q^{Object} and $E_{\text{BEV}}^{(t)}$, respectively. Its computation can be formulated as

$$\text{B, P} = \text{Detection Head}(E_{\text{BEV}}^{(t)}, Q^{\text{Object}}), \quad (14)$$

where "B" and "P" indicate the predicted bounding boxes and the corresponding probability distribution.

3.1.2 Structured KD on Multi-view Images

In this subsection, we introduce the proposed KD based on the above four stages in BEVFormer. Note that the Stage I (2D convolutional feature extraction) and Stage IV (prediction) in BEVFormer share quite some similarities with common 2D detectors. Successful attempts have been made to apply KD onto these stages [26, 68]. We mainly focus on the Stage II and Stage III, which are critical for multi-view 3D detection but rarely explored for KD. In particular, our method can be divided into the following three folds.

3.1.3 Spatial-Temporal KD

In Stage II and Stage III, BEVFormer first integrates the BEV queries with the BEV embeddings at the previous timestamp for temporal information fusion and then fuses the information from different image views for spatial information fusion. Deformable attention layers are utilized during the two processes. Recall that the computation of attention weights in deformable attention layers is obtained by a linear projection over queries followed by a softmax function, which can be formulated as

$$\mathcal{A}(\mathbf{Q}) = \text{softmax}(\mathbf{WQ}), \quad (15)$$

where $\mathbf{Q}$ and $\mathbf{W}$ indicate the queries and the trainable parameters in the linear projection layer, respectively. In temporal self-attention, $\mathbf{Q}$ indicates the BEV query Q^{BEV}. And the obtained attention weights are utilized to fuse information from Q^{BEV} and the historical BEV embedding $E_{\text{BEV}}^{(t-1)}$. Hence, the attention weights here show the temporal relation between the information of the current inputs and the previous input. By distilling them, the student is allowed to learn how to fuse temporal information from the teacher detector. In spatial cross-attention, $\mathbf{Q}$ indicates the output of temporal self-attention $E'^{(t)}_{\text{BEV}}$. The obtained attention weights are utilized to fuse the information from the reference points in the multi-view images. Hence, distilling the attention weights here enables the student to learn how to fuse spatial information from the teacher detector. Concretely, we can denote the attention weights in temporal self-attention and temporal self-attention as $\mathbf{A}^{\text{temporal}}$ and $\mathbf{A}^{\text{spatial}}$, respectively, which can be formulated as

$$\mathbf{A}^{\text{temporal}} = \mathcal{A}(Q^{\text{BEV}}), \text{ and } \quad \mathbf{A}^{\text{spatial}} = \mathcal{A}(E'^{(t)}_{\text{BEV}}), \text{ respectively.} \quad (16)$$

Then, by distinguishing the student and teacher detector with the scripts $\mathcal{S}$ and $\mathcal{T}$ respectively, the proposed spatial-temporal attention can be formulated as

$$\mathcal{L}_{\text{spatial-temp}} = \|\mathbf{A}^{\text{temporal}}_{\mathcal{S}} - \mathbf{A}^{\text{temporal}}_{\mathcal{T}}\|^2 + \|\mathbf{A}^{\text{spatial}}_{\mathcal{S}} - \mathbf{A}^{\text{spatial}}_{\mathcal{T}}\|^2. \quad (17)$$

3.1.4 BEV Response Distillation

Besides distilling teacher knowledge on the fusion of the information from different timestamps and views, we propose BEV response distillation to distill teacher responses to different object queries, which correspond to different pillars in 3D space. In this section, we define the BEV response as the average score across the channel dimension on the absolute value of BEV embedding, which can be written as

$$\mathcal{R}(E_{\text{BEV}(i,j)}) = \sum_{j=1}^{C} \frac{1}{C} |E_{\text{BEV}(i,j)}|, \quad (18)$$

where C denotes the number of channels. The scripts (i, j) denotes the value on the i_{th} BEV query (i.e., pillar) of the j_{th} channel. As pointed out by abundant research [1, 68, 78], the response of features demonstrates the importance of their corresponding spatial positions. Hence, by distilling the BEV response from the teacher, the student model can better correlate between the learned semantic features and the potential object spatial occupancies. L2 loss is adopted for BEV response distillation:

$$\mathcal{L}_{\text{response}} = \|\mathcal{R}(E^{\mathcal{S}}_{\text{BEV}}) - \mathcal{R}(E^{\mathcal{T}}_{\text{BEV}})\|^2, \quad (19)$$

where $\mathcal{S}$ and $\mathcal{T}$ denote the student detector and the teacher detector, respectively. Based on the above notations, the overall training loss of the detector $\mathcal{L}$ becomes:

$$\mathcal{L} = \mathcal{L}_{\text{original}} + \lambda \cdot (\mathcal{L}_{\text{spatial-temp}} + \mathcal{L}_{\text{response}}), \quad (20)$$

where $\mathcal{L}_{\text{original}}$ indicates the original training loss of BEVFormer. λ is a hyperparameter to balance the magnitudes of KD loss.

3.1.5 Weight-Inheriting

Convnet-based detectors usually only require images as input. However modern transformer-based detection models require additional learned queries and positional encodings as input. The teacher and the student model tend to have different query and positional encoding values after training converges. Intuitively, KD works by aligning the output of the student with the teacher, given the same input. Such a paradigm is likely to fail for transformer-based detectors, as the teacher and student can have different learned queries and position encodings. The discrepancies between the transformer inputs must be resolved to make the underlying assumptions of KD hold. Hence, we propose a weight-inheriting scheme that fixes the value of the BEV queries and positional encoding in the students with their values from the teacher detector *during the whole training period*. Hence, the student detector can have consistent inputs with its teacher detector. Surprisingly, we find that simply performing this weight-inheriting scheme can make a significant difference in the effectiveness of KD.

3.2 Evaluation and Discussion

3.2.1 Experiment Results

Experimental results of our method and eight previous KD methods in three different student-teacher settings are shown in Table 13. It is observed that: (i) On average, 2.16 mAP and 2.27 NDS improvements can be observed with our method in the three student-teacher settings, which are 1.26 mAP and 0.80 NDS higher than the second-best KD methods. (ii) In all three student-teacher settings, our method leads to performance improvements in terms of most of the performance metrics, including mAP, NDS, mATE, mATE, mASE, mAOE, mAVE, and mAAE, indicating that our method benefits students in estimating the translation, scale, orientation, velocity, and attributes of the objects. (iii) The performance of our method in different categories is shown in Table 14. It is observed that our method leads to consistent improvements in most of the categories. (iv) The first student achieves 0.67 higher mAP than the second student, indicating that our method benefits from a strong teacher.

4 Brief Summary

In this chapter, we introduce the application of KD in high-level vision tasks, including image-based 2D object detection and instance segmentation and point cloud-based 3D object detection. In these works, we follow the setting of building students and teachers in original KD and mainly study the second fundamental problem, (i.e. what kind of knowledge should be distilled). For example, in image-based 2D object detection, observing the fact the foreground pixels are much fewer than the background, we propose to localize the foreground with attention and then highlight student learning on these foreground pixels. In point cloud-based 3D

Table 13 Comparison with other KD methods on the nuScenes [79] dataset with BEVFormer. Note that a higher mAP and NDS, as well as a lower ATE, ASE, AOE, and AAE indicate better performance. Params: the number of parameters (M). FPS: Frame per second

Backbone	FPS	Params	KD method	mAP(↑)	NDS(↑)	mATE(↓)	mASE(↓)	mAOE(↓)	mAVE(↓)	mAAE(↓)
ResNet101	10.2	56.57	Teacher w/o KD	36.31	47.49	69.21	28.16	46.08	43.87	19.32
ResNet50	14.5	40.45	Student w/o KD	33.56	44.61	71.41	28.65	54.17	46.44	21.03
			+ Hinton et al. [7]	33.57	45.23	71.17	28.50	49.04	46.52	20.33
			+ Zagoruyko et al. [1]	33.68	45.69	70.13	27.74	47.87	45.45	20.26
			+ Heo et al. [29]	33.87	45.82	69.92	27.79	47.78	45.55	20.09
			+ Park et al. [80]	33.77	45.87	70.88	27.78	48.18	43.47	19.83
			+ Pung et al. [81]	34.01	45.36	71.21	28.06	50.49	45.77	20.88
			+ Ahn et al. [82]	34.11	46.36	70.69	28.02	46.16	42.09	20.04
			+ Zhang et al. [68]	34.25	46.34	70.84	28.44	47.06	41.68	19.82
			+ Guo et al. [30]	34.10	46.22	70.39	28.39	46.75	42.52	20.22
			+ **Ours**	**34.91**	**46.87**	**69.77**	**28.07**	**46.31**	**42.23**	**19.43**
ResNeXt-Large	5.3	201.2	Teacher w/o KD	37.69	46.67	70.44	28.52	56.89	45.81	20.12
ResNet50	14.5	40.45	Student w/o KD	33.56	44.61	71.41	28.65	54.17	46.44	21.03
			+ Hinton et al. [7]	33.84	45.68	72.72	28.16	46.54	44.50	20.48
			+ Zagoruyko et al. [1]	34.10	46.26	70.99	28.24	46.12	42.45	20.05
			+ Heo et al. [29]	34.30	46.50	70.36	27.94	44.78	43.06	20.39
			+ Park et al. [80]	33.98	46.40	71.82	28.07	45.84	39.86	20.24
			+ Pung et al. [81]	34.23	46.23	70.05	28.32	47.33	43.13	20.04
			+ Ahn et al. [82]	34.16	46.25	70.37	28.08	46.43	42.73	20.66
			+ Zhang et al. [68]	34.56	46.61	70.11	28.01	46.00	42.39	20.14
			+ Guo et al. [30]	34.35	46.06	69.92	27.79	47.78	45.55	20.09
			+ **Ours**	**35.58**	**47.39**	**68.97**	**28.25**	**48.06**	**39.79**	**18.93**

4 Brief Summary

ResNet101	3.5	65.93	Teacher w/o KD	41.01	51.88	67.45	27.36	34.92	37.57	18.97
ResNet50	5.2	47.56	Student w/o KD	35.77	46.74	73.61	28.26	45.85	43.79	19.94
			+ Hinton et al. [7]	35.89	46.93	73.45	**28.02**	45.46	43.66	19.58
			+ Zagoruyko et al. [1]	35.98	46.98	73.30	28.22	45.32	43.68	19.60
			+ Heo et al. [29]	36.23	47.16	73.09	28.18	45.28	43.34	19.69
			+ Park et al. [80]	36.30	47.18	72.94	28.17	45.48	43.43	19.64
			+ Pung et al. [81]	36.42	47.26	72.96	28.23	45.48	43.37	19.51
			+ Ahn et al. [82]	36.38	47.20	73.02	28.25	45.51	43.50	19.60
			+ Zhang et al. [68]	36.64	47.38	73.12	28.15	**45.28**	43.11	19.53
			+ Guo et al. [30]	36.77	47.40	73.14	28.25	45.34	43.43	19.74
			+ Ours	**38.88**	**48.52**	**71.53**	28.24	47.34	**42.91**	**19.17**

Numbers in bold indicate the highest results

Table 14 Average precision in different classes on nuScenes. "KD" indicates whether our method is applied. Experiments of the three groups are conducted with student-teacher settings in Table 12

KD	Car	Truck	Bus	Trailer	Con.Veh.	Pedest.	Motor.	Bicycle	Barrier	Tra.Cone
×	54.3	26.0	32.3	8.9	7.4	41.8	31.8	28.2	53.8	51.0
✓	55.1	27.4	34.2	10.1	6.8	43.4	34.2	31.1	53.9	52.9
×	54.3	26.0	32.3	8.9	7.4	41.8	31.8	28.2	53.8	51.0
✓	56.5	29.3	37.5	13.3	10.3	45.6	34.4	34.4	43.8	50.8
×	55.8	28.7	35.0	9.7	6.5	46.6	37.5	37.3	54.6	46.0
✓	58.7	33.1	36.2	12.8	10.1	47.4	40.4	40.8	57.6	51.9

object detection, motivated by the sparsity and noise in point clouds, we propose to highlight student learning on the dense voxels that have more points inside. In summary, these works demonstrate that different information has different values in KD, which further supports our findings in chapter "Student and Teacher Models in KD".

References

1. Zagoruyko, S., Komodakis, N.: Paying more attention to attention: improving the performance of convolutional neural networks via attention transfer. In: International Conference on Learning Representations (ICLR) (2017)
2. Zhou, B., Khosla, A., Lapedriza, A., Oliva, A., Torralba, A.: Learning deep features for discriminative localization. In: IEEE/CVF Conference on Computer Vision and Pattern Recognition (CVPR) (2016)
3. Wang, X., Girshick, R., Gupta, A., He, K.: Non-local neural networks. In: IEEE/CVF Conference on Computer Vision and Pattern Recognition (CVPR), pp. 7794–7803 (2018)
4. Hu, H., Gu, J., Zhang, Z., Dai, J., Wei, Y.: Relation networks for object detection. In: IEEE/CVF Conference on Computer Vision and Pattern Recognition (CVPR), pp. 3588–3597 (2018)
5. Mirzadeh, S-I., Farajtabar, M., Li, A., Ghasemzadeh, H.: Improved knowledge distillation via teacher assistant: bridging the gap between student and teacher. arXiv preprint arXiv:1902.03393 (2019)
6. Cho, J.H., Hariharan, B.: On the efficacy of knowledge distillation. In: International Conference on Computer Vision (ICCV) (2019)
7. Hinton, G., Vinyals, O., Dean, J.: Distilling the knowledge in a neural network. In: Advances in Neural Information Processing Systems (NeurIPS) (2014)
8. Lin, T-Y., Maire, M., Belongie, S., Hays, J., Perona, P., Ramanan, D., Dollár, P., Zitnick, C.L.: Microsoft coco: common objects in context. In: European Conference on Computer Vision (ECCV), pp. 740–755. Springer (2014)
9. He, K., Gkioxari, G., Dollar, P., Girshick, R.: Mask r-cnn. In: International Conference on Computer Vision (ICCV) (2017)
10. Lin, T-Y., Goyal, P., Girshick, R., He, K., Dollár, P.: Focal loss for dense object detection. In: International Conference on Computer Vision (ICCV) (2017)
11. Cordts, M., Omran, M., Ramos, S., Rehfeld, T., Enzweiler, M., Benenson, R., Franke, U., Roth, S., Schiele, B.: The cityscapes dataset for semantic urban scene understanding. In: IEEE/CVF Conference on Computer Vision and Pattern Recognition (CVPR) (2016)

References

12. Michaelis, C., Mitzkus, B., Geirhos, R., Rusak, E., Bringmann, O., Ecker, A.S., Bethge, M., Brendel, W.: Benchmarking robustness in object detection: Autonomous driving when winter is coming. arXiv:1907.07484, pp. 1–8 (2019)
13. Ren, S., He, K., Girshick, R., Sun, J.: Faster r-cnn: Towards real-time object detection with region proposal networks. In: Advances in Neural Information Processing Systems (NIPS), pp. 91–99 (2015)
14. Cai, Z., Vasconcelos, N.: Cascade R-CNN: high quality object detection and instance segmentation. IEEE Trans. Pattern Anal. Mach. Intell. **43**(5), 1483–1498 (2021). https://doi.org/10.1109/TPAMI.2019.2956516
15. Zhang, H., Chang, H., Ma, B., Wang, N., Chen, X.: Dynamic R-CNN: Towards high quality object detection via dynamic training. arXiv preprint arXiv:2004.06002 (2020)
16. Lu, X., Li, B., Yue, Y., Li, Q., Yan, J.: Grid r-cnn. In: IEEE/CVF Conference on Computer Vision and Pattern Recognition (CVPR) (2019)
17. Redmon, J., Farhadi, A.: Yolov3: An incremental improvement (2018). https://doi.org/10.48550/arXiv.1804.02767
18. Liu, W., Anguelov, D., Erhan, D., Szegedy, C., Reed, S., Fu, C-Y., Berg, A.C.: Ssd: Single shot multibox detector. In: European Conference on Computer Vision (ECCV), pp. 21–37. Springer, Cham (2016)
19. Zhu, C., He, Y., Savvides, M.: Feature selective anchor-free module for single-shot object detection. In: IEEE/CVF Conference on Computer Vision and Pattern Recognition (CVPR), pp. 840–849 (2019)
20. Yang, Z., Liu, S., Hu, H., Wang, L., Lin, S.: Reppoints: Point set representation for object detection. In: The IEEE International Conference on Computer Vision (ICCV) (2019)
21. Huang, Z., Huang, L., Gong, Y., Huang, C., Wang, X.: Mask scoring r-cnn. In: CVPR, pp. 6409–6418 (2019)
22. Liu, Z., Lin, Y., Cao, Y., Hu, H., Wei, Y., Zhang, Z., Lin, S., Guo, B.: Swin transformer: hierarchical vision transformer using shifted windows, pp. 10012–10022 (2021)
23. Romero, A., Ballas, N., Kahou, S.E., Chassang, A., Gatta, C., Bengio, Y.: Fitnets: Hints for thin deep nets. In: International Conference on Learning Representations (ICLR) (2015)
24. Kang, Z., Zhang, P., Zhang, X., Sun, J., Zheng, N.: Instance-conditional knowledge distillation for object detection. Adv. Neural Inform. Process. Syst. 34 (2021)
25. Sun, R., Tang, F., Zhang, X., Xiong, H., Tian, Q.: Distilling object detectors with task adaptive regularization. arXiv preprint arXiv:2006.13108, pp. 1–8 (2020)
26. Chen, G., Choi, W., Yu, X., Han, T., Chandraker, M.: Learning efficient object detection models with knowledge distillation. In: Advances in Neural Information Processing Systems (NIPS), pp. 742–751 (2017)
27. Wang, T., Yuan, L., Zhang, X., Feng, J.: Distilling object detectors with fine-grained feature imitation. In: IEEE/CVF Conference on Computer Vision and Pattern Recognition (CVPR), pp. 4933–4942 (2019)
28. Li, Q., Jin, S., Yan, J.: Mimicking very efficient network for object detection. In: IEEE/CVF Conference on Computer Vision and Pattern Recognition (CVPR), pp. 6356–6364 (2017)
29. Heo, B., Kim, J., Yun, S., Park, H., Kwak, N., Choi, J.Y.: A comprehensive overhaul of feature distillation. In: International Conference on Computer Vision (ICCV), pp. 1921–1930 (2019)
30. Guo, J., Han, K., Wang, Y., Wu, H., Chen, X., Xu, C., Xu, C.: Distilling object detectors via decoupled features. In: IEEE/CVF Conference on Computer Vision and Pattern Recognition (CVPR), pp. 2154–2164. Computer Vision Foundation / IEEE (2021)
31. Du, Z., Zhang, R., Chang, M., Zhang, X., Liu, S., Chen, T., Chen, Y.: Distilling object detectors with feature richness. In: NeurIPS, pp. 5213–5224 (2021)
32. Zhang, P., Kang, Z., Yang, T., Zhang, X., Zheng, N., Sun, J.: Lgd: label-guided self-distillation for object detection. Proc. AAAI Conf. Artif. Intell **36**(3), 3309–3317 (2022)
33. Dai, X., Jiang, Z., Wu, Z., Bao, Y., Wang, Z., Liu, S., Zhou, E.: General instance distillation for object detection. In: IEEE/CVF Conference on Computer Vision and Pattern Recognition (CVPR), pp. 7842–7851 (2021)

34. Hendrycks, D., Dietterich, T.: Benchmarking neural network robustness to common corruptions and perturbations. In: International Conference on Learning Representations (ICLR) (2019)
35. Wang, J., Lan, C., Liu, C., Ouyang, Y., Qin, T.: Generalizing to unseen domains: a survey on domain generalization. In: Proceedings of the Thirtieth International Joint Conference on Artificial Intelligence, IJCAI 2021, Virtual Event / Montreal, Canada, 19-27 August 2021, pp. 4627–4635. ijcai.org (2021)
36. Mobahi, H., Farajtabar, M., Bartlett, P.L.: Self-distillation amplifies regularization in hilbert space. arXiv preprint arXiv:2002.05715 (2020)
37. Yuan, L., Tay, F.E.H., Li, G., Wang, T., Feng, J.: Revisit knowledge distillation: a teacher-free framework. arXiv preprint arXiv:1909.11723 (2019)
38. Wu, W., Qi, Z., Li, F.: Pointconv: Deep convolutional networks on 3d point clouds. In: IEEE/CVF Conference on Computer Vision and Pattern Recognition (CVPR), pp. 9621–9630. Computer Vision Foundation / IEEE (2019)
39. Ma, X., Qin, C., You, H., Ran, H., Fu, Y.: Rethinking network design and local geometry in point cloud: A simple residual mlp framework. In: International Conference on Learning Representations (ICLR) (2021)
40. Li, G., Mueller, M., Qian, G., DelgadilloPerez, I.C., Abualshour, A., Thabet, A.K., Ghanem, B.: Deepgcns: Making gcns go as deep as cnns. IEEE Trans. Pattern Anal. Mach. Intell. 1–1 (2021)
41. Graham, B.: Sparse 3d convolutional neural networks. In: British Machine Vision Conference (BMVC), pp. 150.1–150.9. BMVA Press (2015)
42. Fan, L., Pang, Z., Zhang, T., Wang, Y-X., Zhao, H., Wang, F., Wang, N., Zhang, Z.: Embracing single stride 3d object detector with sparse transformer. In: IEEE/CVF Conference on Computer Vision and Pattern Recognition (CVPR) (2022)
43. Sautier, C., Puy, G., Gidaris, S., Boulch, A., Bursuc, A., Marlet, R.: Image-to-lidar self-supervised distillation for autonomous driving data. In: IEEE/CVF Conference on Computer Vision and Pattern Recognition (CVPR) (2022)
44. Guo, X., Shi, S., Wang, X., Li, H.: Liga-stereo: Learning lidar geometry aware representations for stereo-based 3d detector. In: International Conference on Computer Vision (ICCV), pp. 3133–3143. IEEE (2021)
45. Qi, C.R., Yi, L., Su, H., Guibas, L.J.: Pointnet++: deep hierarchical feature learning on point sets in a metric space. In: Advances in Neural Information Processing Systems (NIPS), p. 30 (2017)
46. Wang, Y., Sun, Y., Liu, Z., Sarma, S.E., Bronstein, M.M., Solomon, J.M.: Dynamic graph cnn for learning on point clouds. ACM Trans. Graph. **38**(5), 1–12 (2019)
47. Qi, C.R., Su, H., Mo, K., Guibas, L.J.: Pointnet: deep learning on point sets for 3d classification and segmentation. In: IEEE/CVF Conference on Computer Vision and Pattern Recognition (CVPR), pp. 652–660 (2017)
48. Lang, A.H., Vora, S., Caesar, H., Zhou, L., Yang, J., Beijbom, O.: Pointpillars: Fast encoders for object detection from point clouds. In: IEEE/CVF Conference on Computer Vision and Pattern Recognition (CVPR), pp. 12697–12705 (2019)
49. Yan, Y., Mao, Y., Li, B.: Second: Sparsely embedded convolutional detection. Sensors **18**(10), 3337 (2018)
50. Yin, T., Zhou, X., Krahenbuhl, P.: Center-based 3d object detection and tracking. In: Proceedings of the IEEE/CVF conference on computer vision and pattern recognition, pp. 11784–11793 (2021)
51. Shi, S., Wang, X., Li, H.: Pointrcnn: 3d object proposal generation and detection from point cloud. In: IEEE/CVF Conference on Computer Vision and Pattern Recognition (CVPR), pp. 770–779 (2019)
52. Geiger, A., Lenz, P., Stiller, C., Urtasun, R.: Vision meets robotics: the kitti dataset. Int. J. Robot. Res. **32**(11), 1231–1237 (2013)
53. Li, Y., Ge, Z., Yu, G., Yang, J., Wang, Z., Shi, Y., Sun, J., Li, Z.: Bevdepth: acquisition of reliable depth for multi-view 3d object detection. arXiv preprint arXiv:2206.10092 (2022)

54. Li, Z., Wang, W., Li, H., Xie, E., Sima, C., Lu, T., Yu, Q., Dai, J.: Bevformer: learning bird's-eye-view representation from multi-camera images via spatiotemporal transformers. arXiv preprint arXiv:2203.17270 (2022)
55. Wang, Y., Guizilini, V.C., Zhang, T., Wang, Y., Zhao, H., Solomon, J.: Detr3d: 3d object detection from multi-view images via 3d-to-2d queries. In: Conference on Robot Learning, pp. 180–191. PMLR (2022)
56. Wang, T., Zhu, X., Pang, J., Lin, D.: Fcos3d: fully convolutional one-stage monocular 3d object detection. In: Proceedings of the IEEE/CVF International Conference on Computer Vision, pp. 913–922 (2021)
57. Liu, Z., Mao, H., Wu, C-Y., Feichtenhofer, C., Darrell, T., Xie, S.: A convnet for the 2020s. In: Proceedings of the IEEE/CVF Conference on Computer Vision and Pattern Recognition, pp. 11976–11986 (2022)
58. Vaswani, A., Shazeer, N., Parmar, N., Uszkoreit, J., Jones, L., Gomez, A.N., Kaiser, Ł., Polosukhin, I.: Attention is all you need. In: Advances in Neural Information Process Systems (NIPS), pp. 5998–6008 (2017)
59. Liu, Y., Wang, T., Zhang, X., Sun, J.: Petr: position embedding transformation for multi-view 3d object detection. arXiv preprint arXiv:2203.05625 (2022)
60. Liu, Y., Yan, J., Jia, F., Li, S., Gao, Q., Wang, T., Zhang, X., Sun, J.: Petrv2: a unified framework for 3d perception from multi-camera images. arXiv preprint arXiv:2206.01256 (2022)
61. Huang, J., Huang, G., Zhu, Z., Du, D.: Bevdet: high-performance multi-camera 3d object detection in bird-eye-view. arXiv preprint arXiv:2112.11790 (2021)
62. Huang, J., Huang, G.: Bevdet4d: exploit temporal cues in multi-camera 3d object detection. arXiv preprint arXiv:2203.17054 (2022)
63. Han, S., Mao, H., Dally, W.J.: Deep compression: compressing deep neural networks with pruning, trained quantization and huffman coding. In: International Conference on Learning Representations (ICLR) (2016)
64. Zhou, A., Yao, A., Guo, Y., Xu, L., Chen, Y.: Incremental network quantization: towards lossless cnns with low-precision weights. arXiv preprint arXiv:1702.03044 (2017)
65. Choi, J., Wang, Z., Venkataramani, S., Chuang, P.I., Srinivasan, V., Gopalakrishnan, K.: PACT: parameterized clipping activation for quantized neural networks. CoRR. abs/1805.06085 (2018)
66. Buciluǎ, C., Caruana, R., Niculescu-Mizil, A.: Model compression. In: ACM SIGKDD International Conference on Knowledge Discovery and Data Mining (KDD), pp. 535–541. ACM (2006)
67. Zhang, L., Song, J., Gao, A., Chen, J., Bao, C., Ma, K.: Be your own teacher: improve the performance of convolutional neural networks via self distillation. arXiv preprint:1905.08094 (2019)
68. Zhang, L., Ma, K.: Improve object detection with feature-based knowledge distillation: towards accurate and efficient detectors. In: International Conference on Learning Representations (ICLR) (2021)
69. Liu, Y., Chen, K., Liu, C., Qin, Z., Luo, Z., Wang, J.: Structured knowledge distillation for semantic segmentation. In: IEEE/CVF Conference on Computer Vision and Pattern Recognition (CVPR), pp. 2604–2613 (2019)
70. He, T., Shen, C., Tian, Z., Gong, D., Sun, C., Yan, Y.: Knowledge adaptation for efficient semantic segmentation. In: Proceedings of the IEEE/CVF Conference on Computer Vision and Pattern Recognition, pp. 578–587 (2019)
71. Li, Z., Jiang, R., Aarabi, P.: Semantic relation preserving knowledge distillation for image-to-image translation. In: European Conference on Computer Vision (ECCV), pp. 648–663. Springer (2020)
72. Ren, Y., Wu, J., Xiao, X., Yang, J.: Online multi-granularity distillation for GAN compression. In: International Conference on Computer Vision (ICCV), pp. 6773–6783. IEEE (2021)
73. Chen, H., Wang, Y., Shu, H., Wen, C., Xu, C., Shi, B., Xu, C., Xu, C.: Distilling portable generative adversarial networks for image translation. In: AAAI Conference on Artificial Intelligence (AAAI), vol. 34, pp. 3585–3592 (2020)

74. Zhang, L., Chen, X., Tu, X., Wan, P., Xu, N., Ma, K.: Wavelet knowledge distillation: towards efficient image-to-image translation. In: IEEE/CVF Conference on Computer Vision and Pattern Recognition (CVPR) (2022)
75. Carion, N., Massa, F., Synnaeve, G., Usunier, N., Kirillov, A., Zagoruyko, S.: End-to-end object detection with transformers. In: European Conference on Computer Vision (ECCV), vol. 12346, pp. 213–229. Springer (2020)
76. Beyer, L., Zhai, X., Royer, A., Markeeva, L., Anil, R., Kolesnikov, A.: Knowledge distillation: a good teacher is patient and consistent. In: Proceedings of the IEEE/CVF Conference on Computer Vision and Pattern Recognition, pp. 10925–10934 (2022)
77. Zhu, X., Su, W., Lu, L., Li, B., Wang, X., Dai, J.: Deformable detr: deformable transformers for end-to-end object detection. arXiv preprint arXiv:2010.04159 (2020)
78. Zhang, L., Chen, X., Dong, R., Ma, K.: Region-aware knowledge distillation for efficient image-to-image translation. arXiv preprint arXiv:2205.12451 (2022)
79. Caesar, H., Bankiti, V., Lang, A.H., Vora, S., Liong, V.E., Xu, Q., Krishnan, A., Pan, Y., Baldan, G., Beijbom, O.: Nuscenes: a multimodal dataset for autonomous driving. In: IEEE/CVF Conference on Computer Vision and Pattern Recognition (CVPR), pp. 11618–11628. Computer Vision Foundation / IEEE (2020)
80. Park, W., Kim, D., Lu, Y., Cho, M.: Relational knowledge distillation. In: IEEE/CVF Conference on Computer Vision and Pattern Recognition (CVPR), pp. 3967–3976 (2019)
81. Tung, F., Mori, G.: Similarity-preserving knowledge distillation. In: International Conference on Computer Vision (ICCV), pp. 1365–1374 (2019)
82. Ahn, S., Hu, S.X., Damianou, A., Lawrence, N.D., Dai, Z.: Variational information distillation for knowledge transfer. In: IEEE/CVF Conference on Computer Vision and Pattern Recognition (CVPR), pp. 9163–9171 (2019)

Application of KD in Low-Level Vision Tasks

Abstract Recent advances in GANs and diffusion models have enhanced capabilities for low-level vision tasks like image generation and image-to-image translation, yet their computational intensity impedes deployment on resource-limited devices. While KD shows promise in high-level vision tasks, adapting it to pixel-wise generative tasks remains challenging. This chapter establishes a framework addressing these fundamental limitations through distillation mechanisms adapted to the unique characteristics of generative models in low-level vision tasks, aiming to bridge the efficiency-fidelity gap in real-world applications.

Tremendous progress has been achieved with generative adversarial networks (GANs) and diffusion models in generating high-fidelity, high-resolution, and photo-realistic images and videos with both paired and unpaired datasets [1–10]. The excellent performance of GANs and diffusion models has promoted their application in various real-world applications, such as image style transfer [11, 12], super-resolution [13], and text-to-image generation [10]. Compared with other tasks such as image classification and object detection, low-level vision is more complex since it has a much larger output space. As a consequence, existing GANs and diffusion models always have high computational demands and a large number of parameters, which leads to inefficient inference and intolerant memory footprint, and limits their usage in resource-constrained platforms. Following previous methods on classification [14], object detection [15], semantic segmentation [16] and action recognition [17], some recent research has tried to apply KD to low-level vision models directly. Unfortunately, most of them obtain very limited and even negative effects [18, 19]. In this section, we delve into the design of KD for low-level computer vision tasks on GANs and diffusion models. Based on the findings in chapters "Student and Teacher Models in KD" and "Distilled Knowledge in KD", we analyze this problem from the perspective of "how to build the student model and the teacher model" and "what kind of knowledge should be distilled" based on the properties of low-level vision, GANs, and diffusion models. These works have formed a structured system of KD for low-level vision tasks.

1 Wavelet KD for Image-to-Image Translation

Why does KD not work well on GAN? In this section, we first study this question from a frequency perspective with the following experiment. Firstly, discrete wavelet transformation (DWT) is utilized to decompose the generated images and the ground truth images into different frequency bands. Then, we compute the normalized L_1-norm distance on each frequency band respectively. As shown in Fig. 1, all the GANs achieve very low error on the low-frequency band but fail in the generation on high-frequency bands, which is consistent with the observation that images generated by GANs do not have good details. Compared with the large GAN, the tiny GAN achieves comparable performance on the low-frequency band but much worse performance on high-frequency bands. These two observations demonstrate that more attention should be paid to the high frequency during GAN compression.

However, naive KD in GANs application directly minimizes the difference between the images generated by students and teachers and ignores the priority of high frequency. Motivated by these observations, we propose wavelet KD, which highlights students learning on the high frequency in KD. As shown in Fig. 2, we

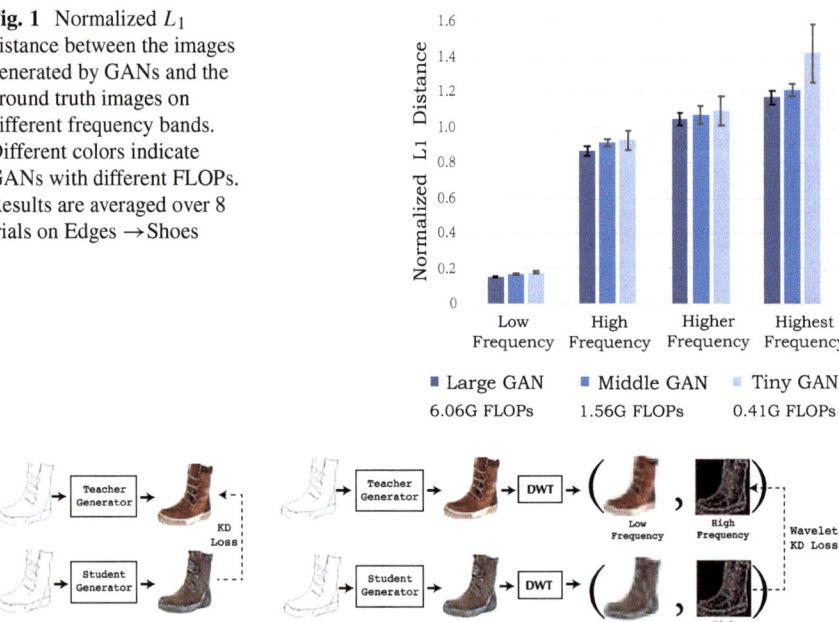

Fig. 1 Normalized L_1 distance between the images generated by GANs and the ground truth images on different frequency bands. Different colors indicate GANs with different FLOPs. Results are averaged over 8 trials on Edges →Shoes

Fig. 2 Comparison between KD [20] (**a**) and the proposed wavelet KD (**b**) on Edges →Shoes. Wavelet KD first applies discrete wavelet transformation (DWT) to the generated images and then minimizes the difference only on high-frequency bands

first apply a discrete wavelet transformation to decompose the images generated by teachers and students into different frequency bands and then only minimize the L_1 loss on the high-frequency bands. Abundant experiments demonstrate the effectiveness of our method both quantitatively and qualitatively. Additionally, studies on the relation between discriminators and generators in model compression have also been introduced, showing that the compression of discriminators can significantly promote the performance of compressed generators.

1.1 Distilling High-Frequency Information in Images

1.1.1 Wavelet Analysis

Given a function ψ, let $\mathcal{X}(\psi)$ be the collection of the dilations and shift of ψ:

$$\mathcal{X}(\psi) = \{\psi_{jk} = 2^{-j/2}\psi(2^{-j}x - k) | \ j, k \in \mathbb{Z}\}, \tag{1}$$

where ψ is the orthogonal wavelet if $\mathcal{X}(\psi)$ forms a basis in $\mathcal{L}_2$ spaces. Discrete wavelet transformation (DWT) is a mathematical tool for pyramidal image decomposition. With DWT, each image can be decomposed into four bands, including LL, LH, HL, and HH, where LL indicates the low-frequency band and the others are high-frequency bands. The LL band can be further decomposed by DWT into LL2, LH2, HL2 HH2 and so on. By denoting DWT as $\Psi(\cdot)$, then the high-frequency and the low-frequency bands of an image x can be written as $\Psi^H(x)$ and $\Psi^L(x)$, respectively. More specifically, in this section, we apply 3-level discrete wavelet transformation in all the experiments. $\Psi^L(x)$ indicates LL3 band. $\Psi^H(x) = \{$ HL3, LH3, HH3, HL2, LH2, HH2, HL1, LH1, HH1$\}$.

1.1.2 KD for Image-to-Image Translation

Revisiting KD for Classification At the beginning of this subsection, we revisit the formulation of KD on classification [20]. Given a set of training samples $\mathcal{X} = \{x_1, x_2, \ldots, x_n\}$ and their labels $\mathcal{Y} = \{y_1, y_2, \ldots, y_n\}$, denoting the networks of the student and the teacher as f_s and f_t, the loss function of the student can be formulated as $\mathcal{L}_{Student} = \alpha \cdot \mathcal{L}_{CE} + (1 - \alpha) \cdot \mathcal{L}_{KD}$, where $\mathcal{L}_{CE}$ indicates the cross-entropy loss between the prediction $f(x)$ and its label y. $\alpha \in (0, 1]$ is a hyper-parameter to balance two loss items, and $\mathcal{L}_{KD}$ indicates the KD loss.

On classification tasks, $\mathcal{L}_{KD}$ can be formulated as

$$\mathcal{L}_{KD} = \frac{1}{n} \sum_{i}^{n} \mathcal{KL}\left(\text{softmax}\left(\frac{f_t(x_i)}{\tau}\right), \text{softmax}\left(\frac{f_s(x_i)}{\tau}\right)\right), \tag{2}$$

where $\mathcal{KL}$ indicates the Kullback-Leibler divergence, which measures the distance between the categorical probability distributions of students and teachers. τ is the temperature hyper-parameter in the softmax function.

KD for Image-to-Image Translation On the task of image-to-image translation, since the prediction result $f(x_i)$ is the value of pixels instead of a categorical probability distribution, KL divergence can not be utilized to measure the difference between students and teachers. A naive alternative is to replace KL divergence with the L_1-norm distance between the generated images from students and teachers. Then, we can extend Hinton KD for image-to-image translation, whose loss function can be formulated as

$$\mathcal{L}_{\text{KD}} = \frac{1}{n} \sum_i^n \|(f_t(x_i) - f_s(x_i)\|_1. \tag{3}$$

1.1.3 Wavelet KD

Based on the above notations, we can introduce the proposed wavelet KD, which only minimizes the difference in the high frequency between students and teachers. Its loss function $\mathcal{L}_{\text{WKD}}$ can be formulated as

$$\mathcal{L}_{\text{WKD}} = \frac{1}{n} \sum_i^n \|(\Psi^H \circ f_t)(x_i) - (\Psi^H \circ f_s)(x_i)\|_1. \tag{4}$$

On unpaired image-to-image translation models such as CycleGAN, there are sometimes two generators for the two translation directions. In this case, the proposed wavelet KD loss can be applied to the two directions simultaneously. The overall training loss can be formulated as $\mathcal{L}_{\text{overall}} = \mathcal{L}_{\text{origin}} + \alpha \cdot \mathcal{L}_{\text{WKD}}$, where $\mathcal{L}_{\text{origin}}$ indicates the original training loss of different models, such as the adversarial learning loss and the recycling loss. α is the hyper-parameter to balance the two loss functions.

1.2 Evaluation and Discussion

1.2.1 Experiment Setting

Experiments are mainly conducted with three models including Pix2Pix [4], CycleGAN [5] and Pix2PixHD [21]. Our teacher is the original model with the setting from their released codes. The student model has the same architecture and depth but fewer channels (*ngf=32/24/16*) compared with its teacher. Quantitative experiments have been conducted on Horse →Zebra, Edges →Shoes. Besides, we also conduct qualitative experiments on Winter →Summer, Summer →Winter,

Apple →Orange, Photo →Monet, Facades and Maps [22, 23]. Following previous works [24], we adopt *Fréchet Inception Distance (FID)* and mIoU as the performance metrics on Cityscapes and the other datasets. A lower FID indicates that the generated images have better quality.

1.2.2 Quantitative Results

The quantitative experiment results on paired and unpaired image-to-image translation are shown in Tables 1 and 2, respectively. It is observed that: (**a**) Directly applying the native KD (Eq. (3)) to GANs sometimes leads to performance degradation. For instance, there are 1.91 and 0.67 FID increments (performance degradation) on Edges →Shoes with Pix2pix and Pix2PixHD, respectively. (**b**) In contrast, our method achieves consistent and significant performance improvements on all the datasets and models, which outperforms the other GAN KD methods by a clear margin, e.g. 3.78 FID lower than the second-best method on CycleGAN, on average. (**c**) On Horse →Zebra and Zebra →Horse, the student models trained with our method achieve almost the same FID with the teacher model, which indicates $7.08\times$ compression and $6.80\times$ acceleration with almost no performance degradation. (**d**) Compared with the students trained without KD, the distilled students usually not only achieve lower FID but also tend to have lower FID standard deviation, which shows that KD may stabilize the training of GANs. (**e**) Our method and previous feature KD methods can be utilized together, which further leads to a 0.63 FID reduction on CycleGAN on average.

1.2.3 Qualitative Results

The qualitative results of CycleGAN on Horse →Zebra (a–d) and Pix2Pix on Edges →Shoes (e–h) are shown in Fig. 3. It is observed that: (**a**) On Horse →Zebra, the baseline model can not transform the whole body of horses to zebras (e.g. Fig. 3a–c). Besides, the generated stripes of zebras are chaotic and unnatural (e.g. Fig. 3d). This problem also exists in the other KD methods (e.g. Fig. 3c). In contrast, the images generated by the distilled students don't have these issues. (**b**) On Edges →Shoes, the generated images from the students trained with KD have much better color and details (e.g. shoestrings in Fig. 3f and g). In Fig. 3f, the distilled students have successfully generated the highlights on the shoes, which makes the images more realistic (Fig. 4).

1.2.4 Influence from Discriminators

Usually, in real-world GAN applications, only the generators are required to be deployed in devices, while the discriminators are always discarded at this time. As a result, most of the previous works only perform compression on generators but

Table 1 Experiment results on paired image-to-image translation on Edges → Shoes with Pix2Pix and Pix2PixHD. A lower FID indicates better performance. Δ indicates the performance improvements compared with the original student. Each result is averaged over 8 trials

Pix2PixHD

#Params (M)	FLOPs (G)	Method	Metric FID ↓	Δ ↑
45.59	48.36	Teacher	41.59±0.42	–
1.61	1.89	Origin student	44.64±0.54	–
28.32×	25.59×	Hinton et al. [20]	45.31±0.63	−0.67
		Zagoruyko et al. [25]	44.21±0.72	0.43
		Li and Lin et al. [18]	44.03±0.41	0.61
		Li and Jiang et al. [19]	43.90±0.36	0.74
		Jin et al. [24]	43.97±0.17	0.67
		Ahn et al. [26]	44.53±0.48	0.11
		Ours	**42.53±0.29**	**2.11**

Pix2Pix

#Params (M)	FLOPs (G)	Method	Metric FID ↓	Δ ↑
54.41	6.06	Teacher	59.70±0.91	–
13.61	1.56	Origin Student	85.06±0.98	–
4.00×	3.88×	Hinton et al. [20]	86.97±3.49	−1.91
		Zagoruyko et al. [25]	84.25±2.08	0.81
		Li and Lin et al. [18]	83.63±3.12	1.43
		Li and Jiang et al. [19]	84.01±2.31	1.05
		Jin et al. [24]	84.39±3.62	0.67
		Ahn et al. [26]	84.92±0.78	0.14
		Ours	**80.13±2.18**	**4.93**

Numbers in bold indicates the best results

1 Wavelet KD for Image-to-Image Translation

Table 2 Experiment results on unpaired image-to-image translation on Horse →Zebra and Zebra →Horse with CycleGAN. A lower FID is better. Δ indicates the performance improvements compared with the original student. Each result is averaged over 8 trials

Horse →Zebra						Zebra →Horse					
#Params (M)	FLOPs (G)	Method	Metric			#Params (M)	FLOPs (G)	Method	Metric		
			FID ↓	Δ ↑					FID ↓	Δ ↑	
11.38	49.64	Teacher	61.34±4.35	–		11.38	49.64	Teacher	138.07±4.01	–	
0.72	3.35	Origin Student	85.04±6.88	–		0.72	3.35	Origin Student	152.67±9.63	–	
15.81×	14.82×	Hinton et al. [20]	84.08±3.78	0.96		15.81×	14.82×	Hinton et al. [20]	148.64±1.62	4.03	
		Zagoruyko et al. [25]	81.24±2.01	3.80				Zagoruyko et al. [25]	148.92±1.20	3.75	
		Li and Lin et al. [18]	83.97±5.01	1.07				Li and Lin et al. [18]	151.32±2.31	1.35	
		Li and Jiang et al. [19]	81.74±4.65	3.30				Li and Jiang et al. [19]	151.09±3.67	1.58	
		Jin et al. [24]	82.37±8.56	2.67				Jin et al. [24]	149.73±3.94	2.94	
		Ahn et al. [26]	82.91±2.41	2.13				Ahn et al. [26]	150.31±3.55	2.36	
		Ours	**77.04±3.52**	**8.00**				**Ours**	**146.01±1.86**	**6.66**	
		Ours + Li and Lin et al.	**76.40±3.17**	**8.64**				**Ours + Li and Lin et al.**	**145.96±1.92**	**6.71**	
1.61	7.29	Origin Student	70.54±9.63	–		1.61	7.29	Origin Student	141.86±1.57	–	
7.08×	6.80×	Hinton et al. [20]	70.35±3.27	0.19		7.08×	6.80×	Hinton et al. [20]	142.03±1.61	−0.17	
		Zagoruyko et al. [25]	67.51±4.57	3.03				Zagoruyko et al. [25]	141.23±1.88	0.63	
		Li and Lin et al. [18]	68.58±4.31	1.96				Li and Lin et al. [18]	141.32±1.27	0.54	
		Li and Jiang et al. [19]	68.94±2.98	1.60				Li and Jiang et al. [19]	151.09±3.67	1.58	
		Jin et al. [24]	67.31±3.01	3.23				Jin et al. [24]	140.98±1.41	0.88	
		Ahn et al. [26]	69.32±5.89	1.22				Ahn et al. [26]	141.50±2.51	0.36	
		Ours	**61.65±4.73**	**8.89**				**Ours**	**138.84±1.47**	**3.02**	
		Ours + Li and Lin et al.	**60.13±4.08**	**10.41**				**Ours + Li and Lin et al.**	**138.52±0.95**	**3.34**	

Numbers in bold indicates the best results

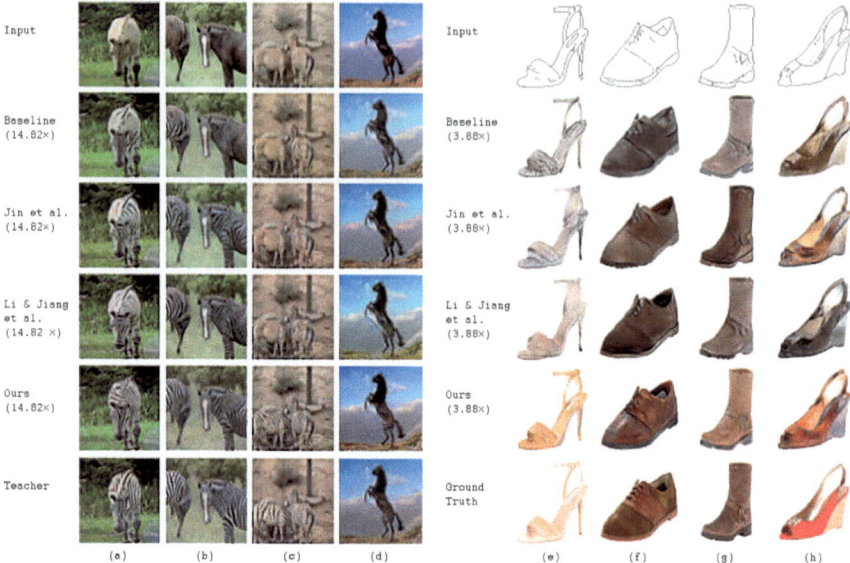

Fig. 3 Qualitative results on Horse →Zebra with CycleGAN (**a**)–(**d**) and Edges →Shoes with Pix2Pix (**e**)–(**h**). Numbers in the brackets indicate the acceleration ratio compared with their teachers. "Baseline" indicates the students trained without KD

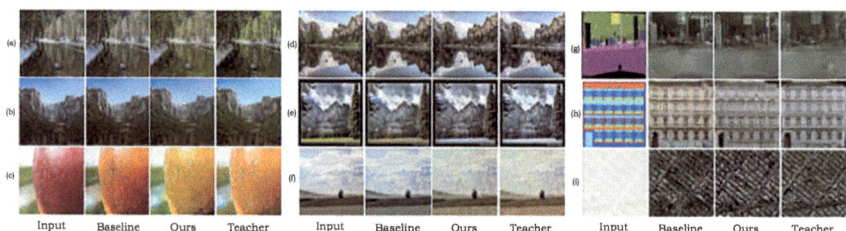

Fig. 4 Qualitative experiments on the other datasets: Winter →Summer (**a**)–(**b**), Summer →Winter (**d**)–(**e**), Apple →Orange (**c**), Photo →Monet (**f**), Cityscapes (**g**), Facades (**h**) and Maps (**i**)

ignore what should be done on discriminators. However, since the discriminator directly influences the training loss of generators, it has a crucial impact on the performance of generators. In this subsection, we study how the capacity of the discriminators influences generators. Figure 5 shows the training loss of generators and discriminators for four CycleGANs with discriminators of different sizes. In all the subfigures, the generators are $15.81\times$ compressed and trained with wavelet KD. In subfigure (d), the discriminator has its original size. In subfigure (a–c), the discriminators are compressed by $15.39\times$, $4.01\times$, and $1.78\times$, respectively. Besides, their corresponding FIDs are shown in Fig. 6. When the generator is compressed but the discriminator is not compressed (subfigure d), the loss of the generator is much higher and the loss of the discriminator is much lower. This observation

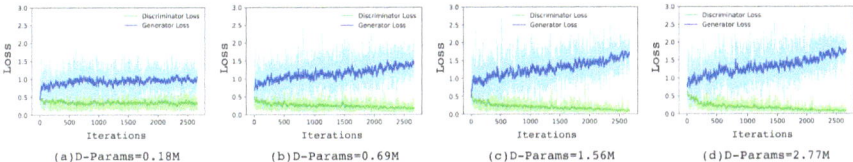

(a) D-Params=0.18M   (b) D-Params=0.69M   (c) D-Params=1.56M   (d) D-Params=2.77M

Fig. 5 The discriminator loss and the generator loss during the training period. In all the subfigures, the generators are 15.81× compressed. In (**d**), the discriminator has its original size. In (**a**)–(**c**), the discriminators are compressed by 15.39, 4.01, and 1.78 times, respectively. The FID of these four experiments is shown in Fig. 6

Fig. 6 Experiments on the distilled CycleGAN with discriminators of different sizes from Fig. 5. A lower FID is better

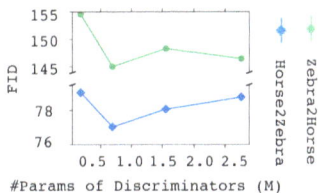

indicates that when the discriminator has a much larger size than the generator, it achieves overwhelming success in its competition with generators. Thus, the balance between discriminators and generators is broken, making it difficult for the generators to learn useful information from the adversarial loss. (**ii**) The distilled generator achieves the best performance when the discriminator is 4.01× compressed (0.69 M). Both a discriminator that is too small and a discriminator that is too large lead to performance degradation on generators, indicating that the imbalance between discriminators and generators in adversarial learning harms the training of generators.

Based on these observations, we can conclude that although discriminators are not utilized in the application, they are still required to be properly compressed to maintain the balance between them and generators in adversarial learning, which further benefits the training of generators.

2 Region-aware KD for Image-to-Image Translation

In this section, we first argue that most previous KD methods ignore the *spatial redundancy* in I2IT, which results in their failure. More specifically, in I2IT, usually, only a few regions of the images are actually required to be translated. For example, in the Horse →Zebra task, only the regions of horses need to be translated while the regions of the background should be preserved. Even in some tasks where the whole image is required to be translated, there are some relatively more crucial regions. However, previous KD methods directly employ the student to mimic teacher's features in all the regions with the same priority while ignoring the spatial redundancy. which further leads to their unsatisfactory performance. Since students

Fig. 7 Visualization of the attention results on the Zebra →Horse translation. It is observed that the attention module in ReKo can localize the objects to be translated (zebras) without annotations

have much fewer parameters than their teachers, they are usually not able to learn all the knowledge from teachers. Thus, in KD, the student should pay more attention to the teacher knowledge in the crucial regions instead of learning all the regions with the same priority. Unfortunately, different from the other vision tasks such as object detection, there are no annotations on crucial regions in I2IT, especially unpaired I2IT. Thus, it is still difficult to localize and make good use of these crucial regions. To tackle this challenge, we introduce Region-aware Knowledge Distillation (ReKo), which mainly consists of the following two steps.

Firstly, ReKo localizes the crucial regions in an image with a parameter-free attention module and then only distills teacher features in these crucial regions. As discussed in previous works [15, 25, 27], the attention value in a region shows its importance. The region with a higher attention value usually has more influence on the prediction of the neural network and thus should be considered a more important region. Hence, we define the importance of a region as its attention value, which is further utilized to decide whether teacher features in this region should be distilled to the student. Visualization results of this attention module are shown in Fig. 7. It is observed that this method successfully localizes the regions of horses while filtering the regions of background.

Secondly, ReKo adopts a patch-wise contrastive learning framework to optimize KD. Instead of distilling teacher knowledge to students by directly minimizing the L_2-norm distance between their features, we propose to adopt a contrastive learning framework for optimization. Tian et al. firstly show that on image classification, KD can be performed with contrastive learning to maximize the mutual information between students and teachers [14]. However, their method requires a huge memory bank to contain massive negative samples, which is not applicable for I2IT. To address this issue, we propose to apply patch-wise contrastive learning framework [28] for KD, which regards student features and teacher features in the same patch as a positive pair and the other features as negative pairs. During the distillation period, by optimizing these pairs with InfoNCE loss [29], the similarity between student and teacher features in the same region is improved, and thus teacher knowledge is distilled to the student (Fig. 8).

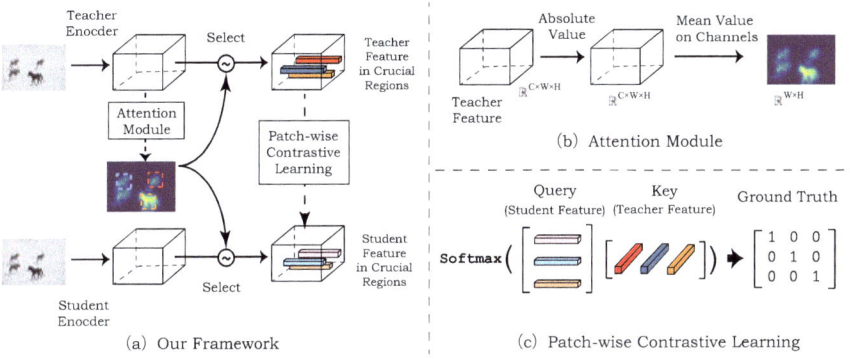

Fig. 8 The overview of region-aware KD (best viewed in color). It mainly consists of two steps. **Step-1**: Find the crucial regions in the image to be translated by applying the attention module to teacher features. Note that the attention module is composed of an absolute value operation and an average operation on the channel dimension. Then, K regions with the K largest attention values are selected as the crucial regions (here $K=3$). **Step-2**: Perform KD in these crucial regions with patch-wise contrastive learning. Student features and teacher features in the same region (such as *pink square box* and *red square box*) are considered a positive pair and the others (such as *blue square box* and *red square box*) are regarded as negative pairs. All these pairs are optimized in a contrastive learning framework with InfoNCE loss, which regards the student features as queries and teacher features as the keys. (**a**) Our framework. (**b**) Patch-wise contrastive learning

2.1 Distilling Knowledge in Crucial Regions

2.1.1 Preliminaries

Given two sets of images $\mathcal{X}$ and $\mathcal{Y}$, I2IT aims to find a mapping function $\mathcal{F}$ which maps the images from $\mathcal{X}$ to $\mathcal{Y}$. Usually, $\mathcal{F}$ can be divided into an encoder $\mathcal{E}$ to encode the intermediate features, and a decoder $\mathcal{D}$ which decodes the intermediate features into the images. Given an image x, then its intermediate feature can be formulated as $\mathcal{E}(x) \in \mathbb{R}^{W \times H \times C}$ where C, W and H denote the number of channels, width, and height, respectively. For convenience, we reshape $\mathcal{E}(x)$ into $\mathbb{R}^{WH \times C}$, where $\mathcal{E}(x)[i]$ indicates the feature of the i-th region. Then, the corresponding index set of regions can be formulated as $\mathcal{I} = \{1, 2, 3, \ldots, WH\}$.

2.1.2 Patch-wise Contrastive Learning for KD

In this section, we adopt a noise contrastive estimation framework [29] to maximize the mutual information between the features of students and teachers. Given a query v, a positive key v^+ and a set of negative keys $\{v_1^-, v_2^-, \ldots, v_N^-\}$, the InfoNCE loss can be formulated as

$$L_{\text{InfoNCE}}(v, v^+, v^-) = -\log\left[\frac{\exp(v \cdot v^+/\tau)}{\exp(v \cdot v^+/\tau) + \sum_{n=1}^{N}\exp(v \cdot v_i^-/\tau)}\right], \quad (5)$$

where τ is a temperature hyper-parameter. By regarding the features of students and teachers at the same region (patch) as positive pairs and the other features as the negative pairs, we can extend InforNCE to a patch-wise contrastive distillation framework. By distinguishing the student model and the teacher model with the scripts $\mathcal{S}$ and $\mathcal{T}$, respectively, its loss function can be formulated as

$$L_{\text{RegionDistill}} = \mathbb{E}_{x \sim \mathcal{X}} \sum_{i \in I} L_{\text{InfoNCE}}(v, v^+, v^-) \qquad (6)$$

where the student feature at the i-th patch $v = \mathcal{E}^\mathcal{S}(x)[i]$ is the query, the teacher feature at the i-th patch $v^+ = \mathcal{E}^\mathcal{T}(x)[i]$ is the positive key, and the teacher features at the patches except the i-th patch $v^- = \{\mathcal{E}^\mathcal{T}[j] \mid j \in I, j \neq i\}$ is the set of negative keys. During KD, the similarity between the query and the positive key (student and teacher features in the same region) is maximized and the similarity between the query and the negative queries (student and teacher features in different regions) is minimized. Thus, the knowledge in teacher features can be distilled to the student.

Parameter-free Attention Module It is generally acknowledged that the attention value of each pixel shows its importance [15]. In this section, we define the attention value of a region as its absolute mean value across the channel dimension, which can be formulated as $\mathcal{A}: \mathbb{R}^{c \times wh} \xrightarrow{\text{absolute}} \mathbb{R}^{c \times wh} \xrightarrow{\text{mean on channel}} \mathbb{R}^{wh}$. Note that since the absolute operation and the mean computation operation do not have any trainable parameters, they can be directly applied to any neural network to find the desired importance score.

KD on Crucial Regions Given a teacher feature, $\mathcal{E}^\mathcal{T}(x)$, its attention map can be denoted as $\mathcal{A}(\mathcal{F}_{\text{enc}}^\mathcal{T})(x)$. Then, we select K regions with the K largest attention values as the crucial regions. Denote the index set of regions as I_K, the proposed region-aware KD can be formulated as

$$L_{\text{ReKo}} = \mathbb{E}_{x \sim \mathcal{X}} \sum_{i \in I_K} L_{\text{InfoNCE}}(v, v^+, v^-), \qquad (7)$$

where $v = \mathcal{E}^\mathcal{S}(x)[i]$ is the query, i-th patch $v^+ = \mathcal{E}^\mathcal{T}(x)[i]$ is the positive key, and $v^- = \{\mathcal{E}^\mathcal{T}[j] \mid j \in I, j \neq i\}$ is the set of negative keys. It is observed that the main difference between $L_{\text{RegionDis}}$ and L_{ReKo} is that L_{ReKo} applies KD only to the K crucial regions found by $\mathcal{A}$ instead of all the regions. Based on the above formulation, we can introduce the overall training loss of students as

$$L_{\text{Student}} = \alpha \cdot L_{\text{ReKo}} + L_{\text{Origin}}, \qquad (8)$$

where L_{Origin} is the original training loss of I2IT models.

2.2 Evaluation and Discussion

2.2.1 Experimental Result

Quantitative Result Quantitative experimental results of ReKo and the other nine KD methods on Horse →Zebra and Edge →Shoe are shown in Tables 3 and 4, respectively. Besides, quantitative results of our method with the students pruned with the methods from Li et al. [18] and Jin et al. [24] are shown in Table bənʊɪq:dɐɪ. We mainly have the following observations: (i) ReKo leads to consistent and significant performance improvements (FID reduction) on all kinds of datasets and models. On average, it leads to 9.2 and 4.85 FID reduction on unpaired and paired I2IT tasks, respectively. (ii) ReKo outperforms the other eight kinds of I2IT KD methods by a large margin. For instance, on Horse →Zebra, it outperforms the second-best method by 3.7 FID, on average. (iii) Not all KD methods work well on GAN for I2IT. Directly applying the naïve Hinton KD [20] leads to limited and sometimes even negative effects. For instance, it leads to a 1.91 FID increment (performance drop) on the Pix2Pix student for Edge →Shoe. (iv) Compared with paired I2IT, there are more performance improvements on unpaired I2IT with ReKo. This observation may be caused by the fact that there is less labeled supervision in unpaired I2IT. Thus the knowledge from teachers is more helpful. (v) A high ratio of acceleration and compression can be achieved by replacing the teacher model with the distilled student model. For example, ReKo leads to 7.08× compression and 6.80× acceleration on CycleGAN students. Besides, the compressed students outperform their teachers by 1.33 and 1.04 FID on Horse →Zebra and Zebra →Horse, respectively. (vi) As shown in Table 4, our method can also be combined with previous methods. For instance, 6.07 and 6.03 FID reduction can be observed on Edge →Shoe with Pix2Pix by combining the techniques of Ren et al. and Li et al., respectively.

Qualitative Result Qualitative results on Horse →Zebra and the other datasetsare shown in Figs. 9 and 10, respectively. It is observed that: (i) The student model trained without KD can not always translate the whole body of horses and zebras. In contrast, the student model trained with ReKo does not have this issue. Moreover, on Horse →Zebra, the student model trained by ReKo sometimes outperforms its teacher on the effect of removing the stripes in zebras. (ii) As shown in Fig. 10, ReKo also leads to consistent and significant image quality improvements on all of them. Specifically, on the tasks in which all the images should be translated, such as Summer →Winter, Cityscapes, and Map →Aerial, ReKo still leads to significant improvements in the generated images.

Table 3 Experimental results on unpaired I2IT on Horse →Zebra and Zebra →Horse with CycleGAN. A lower FID is better. Δ indicates the performance improvements compared with the original student. Each result is averaged from 8 trials

Horse →Zebra					Zebra →Horse				
#Params (M)	FLOPs (G)	Method	Metric FID ↓	Δ ↑	#Params (M)	FLOPs (G)	Method	Metric FID ↓	Δ ↑
11.38	49.64	Teacher	61.34±4.35	–	11.38	49.64	Teacher	138.07±4.01	–
0.72	3.35	Origin Student	85.04±6.88	–	0.72	3.35	Origin Student	152.67±9.63	–
15.81×	14.82×	Hinton et al. [20]	84.08±3.78	0.96	15.81×	14.82×	Hinton et al. [20]	148.64±1.62	4.03
		Zagoruyko et al. [25]	81.24±2.01	3.80			Zagoruyko et al. [25]	148.92±1.20	3.75
		Li and Lin et al. [18]	83.97±5.01	1.07			Li and Lin et al. [18]	151.32±2.31	1.35
		Li and Jiang et al. [19]	81.74±4.65	3.30			Li and Jiang et al. [19]	151.09±3.67	1.58
		Jin et al. [24]	82.37±8.56	2.67			Jin et al. [24]	149.73±3.94	2.94
		Ahn et al. [26]	82.91±2.41	2.13			Ahn et al. [26]	150.31±3.55	2.36
		Ren et al. [30]	77.31±6.41	7.73			Ren et al. [30]	147.34±2.98	5.23
		Li et al. [31]	79.29±7.31	5.75			Li et al. [31]	148.30±1.53	4.27
		Zhang et al. [32]	77.04±3.52	8.00			Zhang et al. [32]	146.01±1.80	6.66
		ReKo (Ours)	**71.21±6.17**	**13.83**			**ReKo (Ours)**	**142.58±4.27**	**10.09**
1.61	7.29	Origin Student	70.54±9.63	–	1.61	7.29	Origin Student	141.86±1.57	–
7.08×	6.80×	Hinton et al. [20]	70.35±3.27	0.19	7.08×	6.80×	Hinton et al. [20]	142.03±1.61	−0.17
		Zagoruyko et al. [25]	67.51±4.57	3.03			Zagoruyko et al. [25]	141.23±1.27	0.63
		Li and Lin et al. [18]	68.58±4.31	1.96			Li and Lin et al. [18]	141.32±1.27	0.54
		Li and Jiang et al. [19]	68.94±2.98	1.60			Li and Jiang et al. [19]	151.09±3.67	1.58
		Jin et al. [24]	67.31±3.01	3.23			Jin et al. [24]	140.98±1.41	0.88
		Ahn et al. [26]	69.32±5.89	1.22			Ahn et al. [26]	141.50±2.51	0.36
		Ren et al. [30]	64.78±5.21	5.76			Ren et al. [30]	140.87±2.03	0.99
		Li et al. [31]	66.85±6.17	3.69			Li et al. [31]	140.92±2.31	0.94
		Zhang et al. [32]	61.65±4.73	8.89			Zhang et al. [32]	138.84±1.47	3.02
		ReKo (Ours)	**60.01±5.22**	**10.53**			**ReKo (Ours)**	**137.03±3.03**	**4.83**

Numbers in bold indicates the best results

Table 4 Experimental results on paired I2IT on Edge →Shoe with Pix2Pix and Pix2PixHD. A lower FID is better performance. Δ indicates the performance improvements compared with the original student trained without KD. Each result is averaged over 8 trials

Pix2PixHD					Pix2Pix			
#Params (M)	FLOPs (G)	Method	Metric FID ↓	Δ ↑	#Params (M)	FLOPs (G)	Method	Metric FID ↓	Δ ↑
45.59	48.36	Teacher	41.59±0.42	–	54.41	6.06	Teacher	59.70±0.91	–
1.61	1.89	Origin Student	44.64±0.54	–	13.61	1.56	Origin Student	85.06±0.98	–
28.32×	25.59×	Hinton et al. [20]	45.31±0.63	−0.67	4.00×	3.88×	Hinton et al. [20]	86.97±3.49	−1.91
		Zagoruyko et al. [25]	44.21±0.72	0.43			Zagoruyko et al. [25]	84.25±2.08	0.81
		Li and Lin et al. [18]	44.03±0.41	0.61			Li and Lin et al. [18]	83.63±3.12	1.43
		Li and Jiang et al. [19]	43.90±0.36	0.74			Li and Jiang et al. [19]	84.01±2.31	1.05
		Jin et al. [24]	43.97±0.17	0.67			Jin et al. [24]	84.39±3.62	0.67
		Ahn et al. [26]	44.53±0.48	0.11			Ahn et al. [26]	84.92±0.78	0.14
		Ren et al. [30]	42.98±0.34	1.66			Ren et al. [30]	80.31±2.59	4.75
		Li et al. [31]	43.21±0.35	0.29			Li et al. [31]	81.24±3.74	3.82
		Zhang et al. [32]	42.53±0.29	2.11			Zhang et al. [32]	80.13±2.18	4.93
		ReKo (Ours)	**42.31±0.17**	**2.33**			**ReKo (Ours)**	**77.69±3.14**	**7.37**
		ReKo + Ren et al. [30]	41.25±0.54	3.39			ReKo + Ren et al. [30]	74.24±2.48	10.85
		ReKo + Li et al. [31]	41.88±0.53	2.76			ReKo + Li et al. [31]	75.21±3.15	9.85

Numbers in bold indicates the best results

Fig. 9 Qualitative results on Horse →Zebra and Zebra →Horse with 15.81× compressed students. (**a**) Horse → Zebra. (**b**) Zebra → Horse

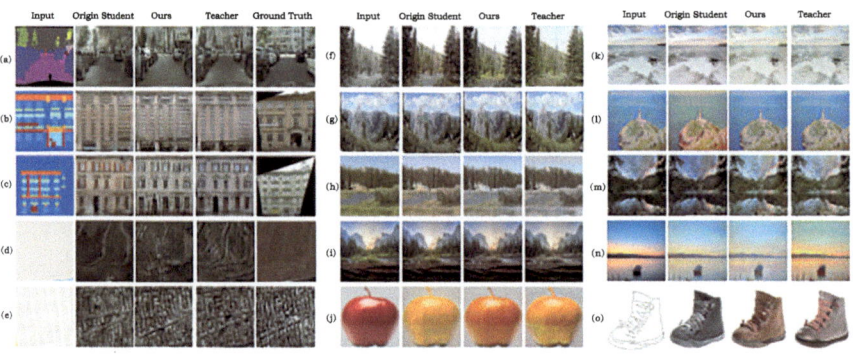

Fig. 10 Qualitative experiments on the other datasets: Cityscapes (**a**), Facades (**b**)–(**c**), Maps →. Aerial Photos (**d**)–(**e**), Edge →. Shoe (o) with Pix2Pix for paired I2IT and Winter →. Summer (**f**)–(**g**), Summer →. Winter (**h**)–(**i**), Apple →. Orange (**j**), Photo →. Monet (**k**)–(**l**), Photo →. Vangogh (**m–n**) for unpaired I2IT. Pix2Pix students on Cityscapes, Edge →Shoe, and the other datasets are 4.00×, 4.00×, and 28.32× compressed, respectively. CycleGAN students are 15.81× compressed

3 KD for Diffusion-based Image Generation

A significant difference between diffusion models and previous generative models is that diffusion models iteratively perform inference via a UNet over multiple timesteps. While this property potentially enhances their representational learning capabilities, it also introduces substantial computational overhead, resulting in increased latency. This challenge has limited the deployment of diffusion models on edge devices and in interactive applications. The computational cost of diffusion models, denoted as C_{all}, can be roughly approximated as $C_{all} = T \times C_{UNet}$, where T represents the number of sampling steps, and C_{UNet} signifies the computational expense of inferring a UNet once. To accelerate diffusion models, numerous recent studies have attempted to reduce the value of T by implementing improved sampling techniques [33] and step distillation methods [34, 35]. Nevertheless, the methods to reduce C_{UNet} have not received extensive attention.

In the original KD, a single student model and a single teacher model are input with the same data, and the student is trained to give a similar output to the teacher model. By directly applying traditional KD to diffusion models, a single student diffusion model should be trained to mimic a single teacher diffusion model at all timesteps. For simplicity, we refer to this type of knowledge distillation as "one-to-one knowledge distillation" (O2OKD). Regrettably, our experimental findings reveal that O2OKD leads to unsatisfactory performance. To understand the underlying cause, we examine the behavior of diffusion models at different timesteps as follows.

① **The Diffusion Model Exhibits Different Input Distributions across Different Timesteps** The standard formulation of the diffusion model represents the image distribution at various timesteps as Gaussian distributions with varying means and variances [9]. As the timestep t increases from 0 to its upper limit T, the means and variances of the images x_t progressively converge to **0** and **I**, respectively. Notably, since the images at timestep t serve as the input for the diffusion model at timestep $t-1$, this indicates variations in the input distribution of the diffusion model.

② **The Diffusion Model Exhibits Varying Feature Distributions at Different Timesteps** As illustrated in Fig. 11 and discussed in prior studies [36, 37], diffusion models display different feature distributions at different timesteps. With the progression of timesteps from 0 to its maximum value, the activation range gradually reduces, leading to increased challenges in feature-based knowledge distillation.

③ **The Diffusion Model Generates Different Kinds of Information at Different Timesteps** As discussed in previous works [38], diffusion models tend to generate basic content at larger (noisier) timesteps while generating detailed information at smaller timesteps.

The above observations indicate that an ideal diffusion model should be capable of handling different input distributions, feature distributions, and the generation of different kinds of information. While this is feasible for the original teacher diffusion model, which contains an ample number of parameters, ensuring sufficient

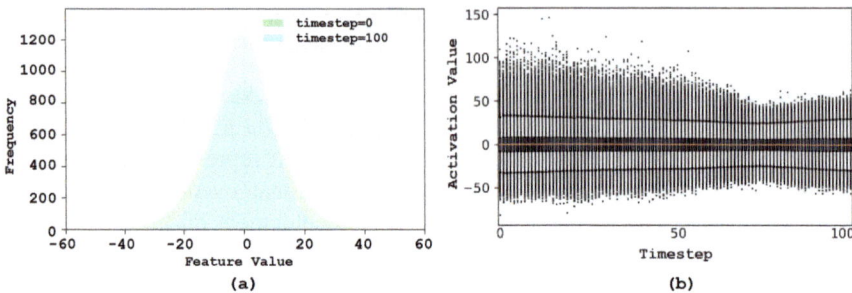

Fig. 11 Feature visualization of pre-trained diffusion models on CIFAR10. The maximal timestep T here is 100. (**a**) Visualization of the feature distribution at timesteps of 0 and 100. (**b**) The box plot of feature distribution at all the timesteps

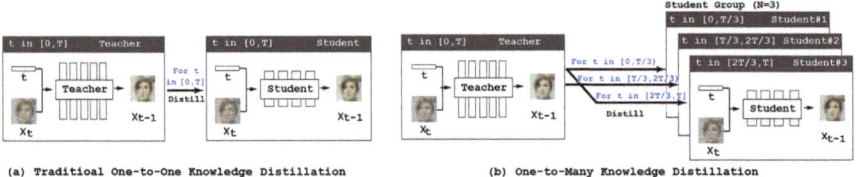

Fig. 12 Comparison between traditional one-to-one knowledge distillation and the proposed one-to-many knowledge distillation with three students ($N = 3$) in their training period. T indicates the largest timestep. (**a**) Traditional one-to-one knowledge distillation. (**b**) One-to-many knowledge distillation

learning capacity, it poses a formidable challenge for the student diffusion model, which has limited parameters. The student model's struggle to match its teacher in handling these complexities ultimately results in the failure of one-to-one knowledge distillation on diffusion models.

Fortunately, we can also derive the following observation from Fig. 11b: The transition in distributions within diffusion models at different timesteps occurs gradually, rather than abruptly. This implies that adjacent timesteps exhibit similar distributions. Consequently, it becomes possible to divide the task of learning teacher knowledge across all timesteps into multiple subtasks, each focused on learning teacher knowledge within a subset of neighboring timesteps. Given the similarity in the distributions among adjacent timesteps, it becomes notably easier for a small student model to tackle these sub-tasks in comparison to the original task.

In light of these insights, we propose "one-to-many knowledge distillation" (O2MKD), which aims to distill knowledge from a single teacher model into a group of $N(N > 1)$ students. As illustrated in Fig. 12, during the training phase, each student primarily focuses on learning teacher knowledge within a subset of neighboring timesteps. As shown in Fig. 13, in the inference phase, each student is exclusively deployed within its designated timesteps. For instance, denoting the number of teacher timesteps as T, the i_{th} student is exclusively trained to

3 KD for Diffusion-based Image Generation   109

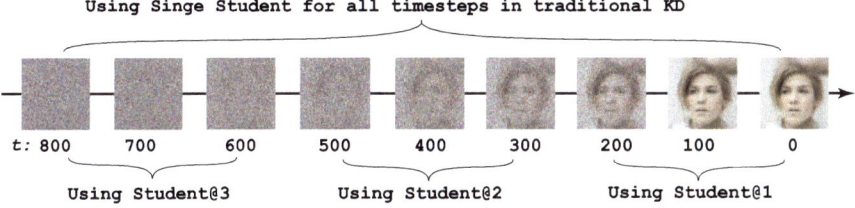

Fig. 13 Comparison between traditional one-to-one knowledge distillation and our O2MKD with three students ($N = 3$) in the sampling period. t indicates the timestep

acquire teacher knowledge and utilized for sampling during timesteps $t \in [(i-1)T/N, iT/N]$ in both training and sampling phases. All students within the group collaborate to generate high-quality images similar to their respective teachers while preserving the same acceleration ratio as one-to-one knowledge distillation. In O2MKD, since each student is solely responsible for learning the teacher in a subset of timesteps, the learning complexity for each student is significantly reduced. This results in superior image fidelity compared to traditional knowledge distillation.

3.1 From One Teacher to Multiple Students

3.1.1 Preliminary

By denoting the data distribution as $p_{\text{data}}(x)$, a diffusion model $\hat{x}_\theta$ with parameters θ is trained to minimize the weighted mean square error:

$$\mathbb{E}_{t \sim U[0,T], x \sim p_{\text{data}}(x), z_t \sim q(z_t|x)}[\omega(\lambda_t) \|\hat{x}_\theta(z_t) - x\|_2^2], \tag{9}$$

where $\lambda_t = \log[\sigma_t^2/\theta_t^2]$ indicates the signal-to-noise ratio and α_t and σ_t indicate the noise scheduling functions. $q(z_t|x) = \mathcal{N}(z_t; \alpha_t x, \sigma_t^2 \mathbf{I})$ and $\omega(\lambda_t)$ is a pre-specified weighting function.

3.1.2 Predication-based KD

For simplicity, we denote $f_t = \hat{x}_{\theta_t}$ and $f_s = \hat{x}_{\theta_s}$ as the teacher model and the student model, respectively, where θ_t and θ_s denote their parameters, respectively. In naive prediction-based knowledge distillation, the student model f_s is trained to mimic the generation result of the teacher model f_t, which can be formulated as

$$\mathbb{E}_{t \sim U[0,T], x \sim p_{\text{data}}(x), z_t \sim q(z_t|x)}[\omega(\lambda_t) \|f_t(z_t) - x\|_2^2 + \lambda_{\text{kd}} \|f_t(z_t) - f_s(z_t)\|_2^2], \tag{10}$$

where λ_{kd} is a hyper-parameter to balance the original training loss (i.e., the first term) and the knowledge distillation loss (i.e., the second term). In this formulation, the student model is trained to mimic the prediction results of the teacher diffusion for all timesteps $t \sim U[0, T]$.

3.1.3 One-to-Many KD

In the aforementioned knowledge distillation, the teacher model is distilled to a single student model. In contrast, our O2MKD, we distill the teacher model into a group of N students, which can be denoted as $\mathcal{F}_s = \{f_{s1}, f_{s2}, \cdots, f_{sN}\}$. During training, the i_{th} student is trained to mimic teacher knowledge at timesteps from $(i-1)T/N$ to iT/N. Then, in the sampling period, each image is generated by sequentially inferring $f_{sN}, f_{sN-1}, \cdots, f_{s1}$ at the corresponding timesteps. Intuitively, the training loss of f_{si} can be formulated as

$$\mathbb{E}_{t \sim U[(i-1)T/N, iT/N], x \sim p_{\text{data}}(x), z_t \sim q(z_t|x)} \\ \times [\omega(\lambda_t) \| f_t(z_t) - x \|_2^2 + \lambda_{kd} \| f_t(z_t) - f_s(z_t) \|_2^2], \quad (11)$$

Trade-off with p In Eq. (11), student f_{si} is exclusively trained to acquire knowledge within its designated timestep period. However, over-specializing the student to a specific range of time steps makes the student unable to benefit from the information at the other timesteps, thereby harming its performance. To achieve a balance between model convergence and acquiring knowledge for specific time steps, we introduce the following strategy. For each training iteration, the i_{th} student has the possibility of p to be trained with $t \sim U[(i-1)T/N, iT/N]$ with Eq. (11), indicating knowledge distillation for the specific timesteps. Otherwise, it has possibility of $(1-p)$ to be trained with $t \sim U[0, T]$ as the following formulation

$$\mathbb{E}_{t \sim U[0,T], x \sim p_{\text{data}}(x), z_t \sim q(z_t|x)} [\omega(\lambda_t) \| f_t(z_t) - x \|_2^2 + \lambda_{kd} \| f_t(z_t) - f_s(z_t) \|_2^2], \quad (12)$$

which indicates knowledge distillation at all the timesteps. With a larger p, each student is trained to learn more on its designated timesteps. When p becomes 0, O2MKD degenerates into the common one-to-one knowledge distillation. Another important hyper-parameter in O2MKD is the number N of students in the student group. With a larger N, each student is trained and sampled for fewer timesteps and a lower FID can be obtained. However, a larger N also increases the memory consumption since more students should be loaded on GPUs.

3.2 Evaluation and Discussion

Models and Datasets We primarily evaluate our methods on DDPM using datasets that include CIFAR10 [39], CelebA-HQ [40], and LSUN Church [41]. For CIFAR10, each model is trained for 200 K iterations with a batch size of 128. On LSUN Church and CelebA, each model undergoes training for 1 million iterations with a batch size of 8. The teacher models employed in our experiments follow the original settings of DDPM, which are available in the huggingface repository.

3.2.1 Quantitative and Qualitative Results

The quantitative results of our O2MKD on CIFAR10 and other datasets are presented in Tables 5 and 6, respectively. Our observations are as follows: (1) On CIFAR10, O2MKD results in a $1.8\times$ acceleration with only a 0.18 FID improvement. On average, the students trained with O2MKD exhibit a 2.57 lower FID compared to students trained without knowledge distillation, demonstrating its effectiveness. (2) Applying O2MKD in conjunction with the four knowledge distillation methods yields a 1.46 FID reduction compared to applying these methods in the traditional one-to-one knowledge distillation framework, indicating the generalization ability of our approach across various knowledge distillation methods. (3) Using more students (i.e., a larger N), the FID can be further reduced. For instance, on CIFAR10, using eight students leads to greater FID reduction compared to using four students on Student-1 and Student-2, respectively, demonstrating that the effectiveness of our method can be further enhanced by employing more students. (4) O2MKD consistently reduces FID on more challenging datasets and tasks. On average, O2MKD leads to a 24.12 and 14.82 FID reduction when compared to students trained without knowledge distillation on LSUN Church and CelebA-HQ, respectively. (5) Using multiple students in traditional O2MKD results in higher memory usage compared to using a single student in the traditional one-to-one knowledge distillation. This is because even though all the students are utilized successively, the GPU still needs to pre-load all the parameters of the student models during inference. From another point of view, the memory consumption of O2MKD remains significantly lower than that of the teacher model (i.e., the model before compression). A qualitative comparison between the students trained with and without O2MKD on LSUN Church is shown in Fig. 14. it is evident that our approach surpasses the student baseline concerning the rationality, chromatic attributes, lucidity, and aesthetic qualities of the images.

Table 5 Experimental results on CIFAR10. "B" indicates the batchsize

Model	Throughput	MACs (G)	Memory Footprint (M)			KD method	FID
			@B=100	@B=400	@B=700		
Teacher	10.71	6.1	1684	4868	7982	Training without KD	4.19
Student-1	21.56	3.3	926	3316	5706	Training without KD	5.84
						+ Hinton et al. KD	5.36
						+ Zagoruyko et al. KD	5.51
						+ Tian et al. KD	5.44
						+ Tung et al. KD	5.32
			1231	3621	6011	+ Ours ($N = 4$) & Hinton et al. KD	4.73
						+ Ours ($N = 4$) & Zagoruyko et al. KD	4.81
						+ Ours ($N = 4$) & Tian et al. KD	4.75
						+ Ours ($N = 4$) & Tung et al. KD	4.62
			1536	3926	6316	+ Ours ($N = 8$) & Hinton et al. KD	4.58
						+ Ours ($N = 8$) & Zagoruyko et al. KD	4.61
						+ Ours ($N = 8$) & Tian et al. KD	4.58
						+ Ours ($N = 8$) & Tung et al. KD	4.34
Student-2	39.69	1.4	605	2199	3793	Training without KD	10.2
						+ Hinton et al. KD	8.48
						+ Zagoruyko et al. KD	8.53
						+ Tian et al. KD	8.31
						+ Tung et al. KD	8.35
			710	2302	3894	+ Ours ($N = 4$) & Hinton et al. KD	6.42
						+ Ours ($N = 4$) & Zagoruyko et al. KD	6.59
						+ Ours ($N = 4$) & Tian et al. KD	6.41
						+ Ours ($N = 4$) & Tung et al. KD	6.40
			848	2442	4036	+ Ours ($N = 8$) & Hinton et al. KD	6.28
						+ Ours ($N = 8$) & Zagoruyko et al. KD	6.18
						+ Ours ($N = 8$) & Tian et al. KD	6.15
						+ Ours ($N = 8$) & Tung et al. KD	5.86

3 KD for Diffusion-based Image Generation   113

Table 6 Experimental results on LSUN Church and CelebA-HQ. "B" indicates the batchsize

Dataset	Model	Throughput	MACs (G)	Memory Footprint (M)			KD Method	FID
				@B=10	@B=15	@B=20		
LSUN Church	Teacher	1.47	248.68	3987	5595	7203	Training without KD	10.60
	Student	3.21	119.20	2914	4121	5329	Training without KD	35.86
							+ Hinton et al. KD	27.32
							+ Zagoruyko et al. KD	28.22
							+ Tian et al. KD	26.80
							+ Tung et al. KD	24.09
				3654	4868	6081	+ Ours ($N=4$) & Hinton et al. KD	14.72
							+ Ours ($N=4$) & Zagoruyko et al. KD	15.40
							+ Ours ($N=4$) & Tian et al. KD	13.60
							+ Ours ($N=4$) & Tung et al. KD	11.74
CelebA-HQ	Teacher	1.47	248.68	3987	5595	7203	Training without KD	6.80
	Student	3.52	121.80	2909	4117	5326	Training without KD	22.45
							+ Hinton et al. KD	13.55
							+ Zagoruyko et al. KD	15.36
							+ Tian et al. KD	15.35
							+ Tung et al. KD	13.36
				3872	5080	6288	+ Ours ($N=4$) & Hinton et al. KD	8.92
							+ Ours ($N=4$) & Zagoruyko et al. KD	9.21
							+ Ours ($N=4$) & Tian et al. KD	9.56
							+ Ours ($N=4$) & Tung et al. KD	7.62

Fig. 14 Qualitative comparison between the student trained without knowledge distillation and the student trained with our method on LSUN Church. DDIM with 50 steps is utilized for sampling

4 Brief Summary

In this chapter, we introduce the application of KD in low-level vision tasks, including GAN-based image-to-image translation and diffusion-based image generation. In these works, we mainly design KD methods tailored to them from the two fundamental problems introduced in chapters "Student and Teacher Models in KD" and "Distilled Knowledge in KD". For instance, we propose to distill the knowledge from a single teacher diffusion model into multiple student diffusion models as a new framework of building students and teachers. On GANs, we propose to highlight student learning on the high-frequency information from teachers. These works have formed a systemic methodology for the application of KD in complex real-world tasks.

References

1. Shaham, T.R., Dekel, T., Michaeli, T.: Singan: learning a generative model from a single natural image. In: International Conference on Computer Vision (ICCV), pp. 4570–4580 (2019)
2. Brock, A., Donahue, J., Simonyan, K.: Large scale gan training for high fidelity natural image synthesis. arXiv preprint arXiv:1809.11096 (2018)
3. Goodfellow, I., Pouget-Abadie, J., Mirza, M., Xu, B., Warde-Farley, D., Ozair, S., Courville, A., Bengio, Y.: Generative adversarial nets. In: Advances in Neural Information Processing Systems (NIPS), p. 27 (2014)
4. Isola, P., Zhu, J-Y., Zhou, T., Efros, A.A.: Image-to-image translation with conditional adversarial networks. In: IEEE/CVF Conference on Computer Vision and Pattern Recognition (CVPR), pp. 1125–1134 (2017)
5. Zhu, J-Y., Park, T., Isola, P., Efros, A.A.: Unpaired image-to-image translation using cycle-consistent adversarial networks. In: International Conference on Computer Vision (ICCV), pp. 2223–2232 (2017)

6. Li, X., Zhang, S., Hu, J., Cao, L., Hong, X., Mao, X., Huang, F., Wu, Y., Ji, R.: Image-to-image translation via hierarchical style disentanglement. In: IEEE/CVF Conference on Computer Vision and Pattern Recognition (CVPR), pp. 8639–8648. Computer Vision Foundation / IEEE (2021)
7. Jeong, S., Kim, Y., Lee, E., Sohn, K.: Memory-guided unsupervised image-to-image translation. In: IEEE Conference on Computer Vision and Pattern Recognition, CVPR 2021, virtual, 19-25 June 2021, pp. 6558–6567. Computer Vision Foundation / IEEE (2021)
8. Richardson, E., Alaluf, Y., Patashnik, O., Nitzan, Y., Azar, Y., Shapiro, S., Cohen-Or, D.: Encoding in style: a stylegan encoder for image-to-image translation. In: IEEE/CVF Conference on Computer Vision and Pattern Recognition (CVPR), pp. 2287–2296. Computer Vision Foundation / IEEE (2021)
9. Ho, J., Jain, A., Abbeel, P.: Denoising diffusion probabilistic models. Adv. Neural Inf. Proces. Syst. **33**, 6840–6851 (2020)
10. Rombach, R., Blattmann, A., Lorenz, D., Esser, P., Ommer, B.: High-resolution image synthesis with latent diffusion models. In: Proceedings of the IEEE/CVF conference on computer vision and pattern recognition, pp. 10684–10695 (2022)
11. Karras, T., Laine, S., Aila, T.: A style-based generator architecture for generative adversarial networks. In: IEEE/CVF Conference on Computer Vision and Pattern Recognition (CVPR), pp. 4401–4410 (2019)
12. Karras, T., Laine, S., Aittala, M., Hellsten, J., Lehtinen, J., Aila, T.: Analyzing and improving the image quality of stylegan. In: IEEE/CVF Conference on Computer Vision and Pattern Recognition (CVPR), pp. 8110–8119 (2020)
13. Ledig, C., Theis, L., Huszár, F., Caballero, J., Cunningham, A., Acosta, A., Aitken, A., Tejani, A., Totz, J., Wang, Z., et al.: Photo-realistic single image super-resolution using a generative adversarial network. In: IEEE/CVF Conference on Computer Vision and Pattern Recognition (CVPR), pp. 4681–4690 (2017)
14. Tian, Y., Krishnan, D., Isola, P.: Contrastive representation distillation. In: International Conference on Learning Representations (ICLR). OpenReview.net (2020)
15. Zhang, L., Ma, K.: Improve object detection with feature-based knowledge distillation: towards accurate and efficient detectors. In: International Conference on Learning Representations (ICLR) (2021)
16. Liu, Y., Chen, K., Liu, C., Qin, Z., Luo, Z., Wang, J.: Structured knowledge distillation for semantic segmentation. In: IEEE/CVF Conference on Computer Vision and Pattern Recognition (CVPR), pp. 2604–2613 (2019)
17. Liu, M., Chen, X., Zhang, Y., Li, Y., Rehg, J.M.: Attention distillation for learning video representations. In: British Machine Vision Conference (BMVC) (2020)
18. Li, M., Lin, J., Ding, Y., Liu, Z., Zhu, J-Y., Han, S.: Gan compression: efficient architectures for interactive conditional gans. In: IEEE/CVF Conference on Computer Vision and Pattern Recognition (CVPR), pp. 5284–5294 (2020)
19. Li, Z., Jiang, R., Aarabi, P.: Semantic relation preserving knowledge distillation for image-to-image translation. In: European Conference on Computer Vision (ECCV), pp. 648–663. Springer (2020)
20. Hinton, G., Vinyals, O., Dean, J.: Distilling the knowledge in a neural network. In: Advances in Neural Information Processing Systems (NeurIPS) (2014)
21. Wang, T-C., Liu, M-Y., Zhu, J-Y., Tao, A., Kautz, J., Catanzaro, B.: High-resolution image synthesis and semantic manipulation with conditional gans. In: IEEE/CVF Conference on Computer Vision and Pattern Recognition (CVPR), pp. 8798–8807 (2018)
22. Zhu, J-Y., Park, T., Isola, P., Efros, A.A.: Pix2pix datasets. http://efrosgans.eecs.berkeley.edu/cyclegan/datasets
23. Isola, P., Zhu, J-Y., Zhou, T., Efros, A.A.: Pix2pix datasets. http://efrosgans.eecs.berkeley.edu/pix2pix/datasets/
24. Jin, Q., Ren, J., Woodford, O.J., Wang, J., Yuan, G., Wang, Y., Tulyakov, S.: Teachers do more than teach: compressing image-to-image models. In: IEEE/CVF Conference on Computer Vision and Pattern Recognition (CVPR), pp. 13600–13611 (2021)

25. Zagoruyko, S., Komodakis, N.: Paying more attention to attention: improving the performance of convolutional neural networks via attention transfer. In: International Conference on Learning Representations (ICLR) (2017)
26. Ahn, S., Hu, S.X., Damianou, A., Lawrence, N.D., Dai, Z.: Variational information distillation for knowledge transfer. In: IEEE/CVF Conference on Computer Vision and Pattern Recognition (CVPR), pp. 9163–9171 (2019)
27. Zhou, B., Khosla, A., Lapedriza, A., Oliva, A., Torralba, A.: Learning deep features for discriminative localization. In: IEEE/CVF Conference on Computer Vision and Pattern Recognition (CVPR) (2016)
28. Park, T., Efros, A.A., Zhang, R., Zhu, J-Y.: Contrastive learning for unpaired image-to-image translation. In: European Conference on Computer Vision (ECCV), pp. 319–345. Springer (2020)
29. van den Oord, A., Li, Y., Vinyals, O.: Representation learning with contrastive predictive coding. arXiv preprint arXiv:1807.03748 (2018)
30. Ren, Y., Wu, J., Xiao, X., Yang, J.: Online multi-granularity distillation for GAN compression. In: International Conference on Computer Vision (ICCV), pp. 6773–6783. IEEE (2021)
31. Li, S., Wu, J., Xiao, X., Chao, F., Mao, X., Ji, R.: Revisiting discriminator in GAN compression: a generator-discriminator cooperative compression scheme. In: Advances in Neural Information Processing Systems (NeurIPS), pp. 28560–28572 (2021)
32. Zhang, L., Chen, X., Tu, X., Wan, P., Xu, N., Ma, K.: Wavelet knowledge distillation: towards efficient image-to-image translation. In: IEEE/CVF Conference on Computer Vision and Pattern Recognition (CVPR) (2022)
33. Song, J., Meng, C., Ermon, S.: Denoising diffusion implicit models. arXiv preprint arXiv:2010.02502 (2020)
34. Meng, C., Rombach, R., Gao, R., Kingma, D., Ermon, S., Ho, J., Salimans, T.: On distillation of guided diffusion models. In: Proceedings of the IEEE/CVF Conference on Computer Vision and Pattern Recognition, pp. 14297–14306 (2023)
35. Salimans, T., Ho, J.: Progressive distillation for fast sampling of diffusion models. arXiv preprint arXiv:2202.00512 (2022)
36. Li, X., Lian, L., Liu, Y., Yang, H., Dong, Z., Kang, D., Zhang, S., Keutzer, K.: Q-diffusion: quantizing diffusion models. arXiv preprint arXiv:2302.04304 (2023)
37. Shang, Y., Yuan, Z., Xie, B., Wu, B., Yan, Y.: Post-training quantization on diffusion models. In: Proceedings of the IEEE/CVF Conference on Computer Vision and Pattern Recognition, pp. 1972–1981 (2023)
38. Fang, G., Ma, X., Wang, X.: Structural pruning for diffusion models. arXiv preprint arXiv:2305.10924 (2023)
39. Krizhevsky, A., Hinton, G.: Learning multiple layers of features from tiny images. Technical report, Citeseer (2009)
40. Karras, T., Aila, T., Laine, S., Lehtinen, J.: Progressive growing of gans for improved quality, stability, and variation. arXiv preprint arXiv:1710.10196 (2017)
41. Yu, F., Seff, A., Zhang, Y., Song, S., Funkhouser, T., Xiao, J.: Lsun: construction of a large-scale image dataset using deep learning with humans in the loop. arXiv preprint arXiv:1506.03365 (2015)

Application of KD Beyond Model Compression

Abstract In previous chapters, we introduced research works that employ KD to compress and accelerate neural networks. In these works, the teacher models are usually defined as the models that have more parameters while the student models are defined as the models that are more lightweight and efficient. In this setting, when the knowledge is distilled from the teacher to the student, the teacher model is actually compressed into the student model. Besides model compression, KD can also be utilized for targets besides model compression, by using different manners to define the students and teachers. In this chapter, we introduce how to leverage KD in model training to improve the robustness of computer vision models in Sect. 1, and to reduce the communication cost of updating neural network-based software in Sect. 2.

1 Robust Computer Vision with Self-Distillation

Dramatic achievements have been attained with the help of deep learning in various domains, including computer vision [1–4], natural language processing [5–7] and so on. However, image corruption, which can be widely observed in real-world application scenarios like rotation, blur, rain, and noise, leads to severe accuracy degradation due to the vulnerability of neural networks. A simple and effective method to improve model robustness is data augmentation [8, 9]. However, directly adding corrupted images into the training set always leads to an unacceptable accuracy drop on clean images [10]. Moreover, model robustness to different kinds of corruption always influences each other. For instance, Gaussian noise data augmentation leads to a robustness increment on noise corruption but reduces model robustness on the images with different contrast and saturation [11]. Most recently, one research trend is to improve model robustness without sacrificing accuracy on clean data [12, 13], but it's still challenging to develop a training approach that improves both accuracy and robustness simultaneously.

In this section, we introduce a novel neural network training framework named auxiliary training which consists of two types of training samples. One is the clean images from a dataset, and the other is the corrupted image,s which are generated

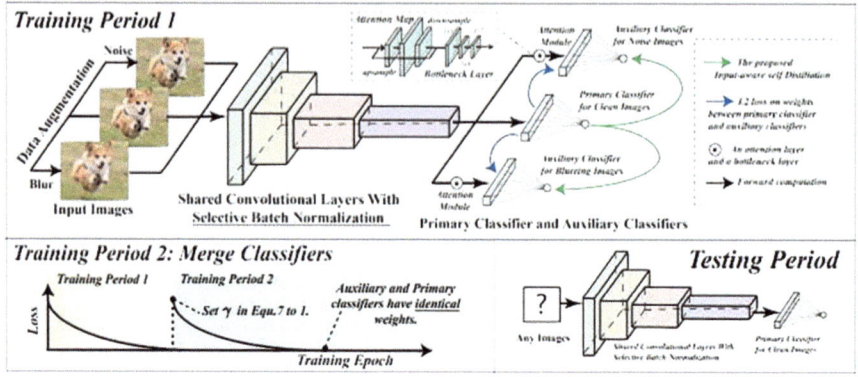

Fig. 1 Details of the proposed auxiliary training. (**a**) Training Period 1: (i) The images involved in the training include the clean images from datasets and corrupted (e.g. blur, noise) images generated from data augmentation. (ii) All of the images are fed into the same convolutional layers with the proposed selective batch normalization to obtain representative features. (iii) The features of the clean images are then fed into the primary classifiers, which are composed of one fully connected layer. The features of corrupted images are then fed into the auxiliary classifiers, which consist of an attention module and a fully connected layer. (**b**) Training Period 2: (iv) At the end of the training period, a L_2 loss is utilized to force weights of auxiliary classifiers to orientate the primary classifier until they have identical weights. (**c**) Testing Period: (v) In the testing period, all the input images are classified by the primary classifier, and the auxiliary classifiers can be dropped to avoid additional parameters

by adding corruptions to clean images. The corruptions in this section consist of noise, blur, and other kinds of image corruption. In our training framework, given a network, the feature extraction layer is kept, but auxiliary classifier,s which are copies of the final classifier layer (denoted as primary classifier) are introduced to facilitate the training of the primary classifier. In the first stage of training, both two kinds of images are fed into the same convolutional layers to obtain representative features but each individual classifier is only trained by samples from a certain kind of corruption. In the second stage, a L_2-norm loss is applied for penalizing the weights between the primary classifier and auxiliary classifiers such that they attain identical weights. As a result, the auxiliary classifiers can be dropped and only the primary classifier is kept. Therefore, the original network architecture does not change and extra computations and parameters are needless in the inference period. Figure 1 illustrates the flow of our approach.

Moreover, we propose input-aware self-distillation and selective batch normalization to facilitate model training. The input-aware self distillation regards the primary classifier as the teacher model and auxiliary classifiers as student models. It transfers the knowledge from clean images to corrupted images and enables the primary classifier to learn robust information from auxiliary classifiers. The selective batch normalization computes the mean and variance of clean images and corrupted images respectively and updates its parameters only by clean images, thus avoiding the negative influence of corrupted images.

Besides, the formulation of the proposed auxiliary training is motivated by the connections of perturbations between the input space and parameter space. Since the corrupted image can be seen as a small perturbation in the feature space, it is equivalent to a small perturbation of the parameters by using first-order approximation. Thus, it naturally leads to the soft constraints between the primary classifier and the auxiliary classifier which guarantee the mathematical rationale of our approach.

1.1 Training Auxiliary Classifiers with Self-Distillation

1.1.1 Formulation

Let $\mathcal{X}_C = \{(x_i, y_i)\}_{i=1}^m$ be a set of clean training samples, $\mathcal{T} = \{T_1, T_2, \ldots, T_t\}$ be a set of corruption operations and $\mathcal{X}_j = \{(x_i^j, y_i) x_i^j = T_j(x_i), (x_i, y_i) \in \mathcal{X}_c\}$ to be the corrupted training set by j-th corruption. Thus, the whole training set consists of

$$\mathcal{X} = \mathcal{X}_C \cup (\cup_{j=1}^t \mathcal{X}_j) = \cup_{j=0}^t \cup_{i=1}^m \{(x_i^j, y_i)\}, \tag{1}$$

where $x_i^j = T_j(x_i)$ and assume T_0 is the identity map. Let $f(x; \theta_f)$ be the feature extractor which can be a convolutional neural network and $g(x; \theta_g)$ be the classifier and the feature map associated with the j-th corruption be

$$\hat{x}^j = f(T_j(x), \theta_f), \quad \forall j = 0, 1, \ldots, t. \tag{2}$$

The traditional augmentation training method seeks the best parameters via the following minimization:

$$\min_{\theta_f, \theta_g} \frac{1}{t+1} \sum_{j=0}^t \left\{ \frac{1}{m} \sum_{i=1}^m \ell(g(\hat{x}_i^j(\theta_f); \theta_g), y_i) \right\}, \tag{3}$$

where $\ell(\cdot, \cdot)$ is the loss function, e.g. L2-norm, cross entropy and Kullback-Leibler (KL) divergence and where $\hat{x}_i^j(\theta_f) = f(T_j(x_i), \theta_f)$ denotes the feature map of i-th sample corrupted by j-th corruption. In (3), all the corruptions are treated equally which might not be consistent with the true distribution. Thus, assuming the probability of the j-th corruption is $\alpha_j = p(T_j)$ and introducing the auxiliary classifier $g(x; \theta_g^j)$ for each corruption, the minimization (3) can be formulated as

$$\min_{\theta_f, \{\theta_g^j\}_{j=0}^t} \sum_{j=0}^t \alpha_j \left\{ \frac{1}{m} \sum_{i=1}^m \ell(g(\hat{x}_i^j(\theta_f); \theta_g^j), y_i) \right\} \triangleq L_1, \tag{4}$$

s.t. $\theta_g^0 = \theta_g^1 = \cdots = \theta_g^t$.

Due to the existence of nonconvexity in (4), finding a stationary point of (4) with high accuracy and robustness is difficult. To facilitate the training for obtaining a desired classifier, we train the primary classifier with only clean samples and propose to introduce auxiliary classifiers so that each one is only trained by specific corruption samples. Finally, we merge the information from the auxiliary classifiers by the regularization. More concretely, assume $g(\cdot; \theta_g^0)$ is our desired primary classifier and the classifier $g(\cdot; \theta_g^j)$ is well trained for j-th corruption, then it implies

$$g(\hat{x}^0; \theta_g^0) = g(\hat{x}^j; \theta_g^j). \tag{5}$$

Let j-th corruption be parameterized by ξ, then in feature space, we have $\delta x^j = \hat{x}^j - \hat{x}^0$ in a neighborhood of $\hat{x}^0$. When the capacity of the feature extraction network is large enough such that it can learn certain invariant features for the corruptions, i.e. δx^j is small, the first order Taylor expansion implies that

$$g(\hat{x}^j; \theta_g^j) \approx g(\hat{x}^0; \theta_g^j) + \frac{\partial g}{\partial x} \delta x^j. \tag{6}$$

If there is a small perturbation $\delta \theta_g^j$ such that

$$\frac{\partial g}{\partial x} \delta x^j \approx \frac{\partial g}{\partial \theta} \delta \theta_g^j. \tag{7}$$

Together with (5)–(7), we arrive at a necessary condition for robust primary classifier $g(\cdot; \theta_f)$:

$$g(\hat{x}^j, \theta_g^0) \approx g(\hat{x}^j, \theta_g^0 + \delta \theta_g^j), \tag{8}$$

by the first-order approximation, i.e. our auxiliary classifiers are $\theta_g^j = \theta_g^0 + \delta \theta_g^j$ and the perturbation is implicitly given by the corruption for the input images. Therefore, the trajectory of the corruptions for clean samples corresponds to the trajectory of the robust classifier. Therefore, to achieve the robustness of the primary classifier, it could be better to choose it smoothly along the tangent direction of the trajectory of corruption. However, it is hard to analyze the tangent direction of the perturbations in feature space. Instead, we impose the smoothness of the primary classifier around θ_g^0, i.e.

$$\theta_g^0 \approx \theta_g^j, \quad g(\hat{x}^0, \theta_g^0) \approx g(\hat{x}^j, \theta_g^j). \tag{9}$$

This motivates us to relax the equality constraints by the penalty function Ω as:

$$\Omega(\theta_g^0, \theta_g^j) = \ell_{KL}(g(\hat{x}^0; \theta_g^0), g(\hat{x}^j; \theta_g^j)) + \gamma \theta_1 - \theta_2\_2^2. \tag{10}$$

Therefore, the total loss in our auxiliary training is:

$$\min_{\theta_f, \{\theta_g^j\}_{j=0}^t} L_1 + \lambda \sum_{j=1}^{t} \Omega(\theta_g^0, \theta_g^j). \qquad (11)$$

There are three hyperparameters α, λ, γ in (11), and all of them are fixed for all the experiments in this section.

1.1.2 Rationality of Auxiliary Training

Input-aware Self Distillation The knowledge distillation consisting of the teacher-student structure has proven to be a useful method for accuracy improvements. However, the performance depends on how "smart" the teacher is. In practice, it is difficult to find a universal "smart" teacher. In the proposed auxiliary training, the "decentralization" idea is applied to encourage knowledge communication among classifiers. More concretely, each classifier is only trained by the data with certain augmentation and the penalty term Ω defined in (10) imposes the knowledge transfer between the primary classifier and auxiliary classifiers under the simultaneous training strategy. In other words, each classifier can be seen as a domain expert and they learn from each other. Therefore, instead of the teacher-student structure, the auxiliary training approach is more likely to be a "student $\rightleftarrows$ student" framework which is more efficient for knowledge transfer.

Privileged Information The framework of learning using privileged information is first introduced in [14] and it is connected to the knowledge distillation in [15]. Let (x_i, x_i^*, y_i) be the i-th training sample where (x_i, y_i) be the feature-label pair and x_i^* is the additional information of x_i provided by the teacher network. In our proposed auxiliary learning framework, as both clear sample x_i^0 and corrupted samples x_i^j, $j = 1, 2, \ldots, t$ share the same label information, the privileged information can be $x_i^* = f(x_i^0; \theta_f)$ where f is a feature extractor. In the generalized distillation framework [15], the primary classifier is the teacher and the auxiliary classifiers are the students. Since a good feature extractor f can provide certain invariant properties for the corrupted images, it is reasonable that the auxiliary classifier is relatively easy to learn in feature space which leads to better generalization error [15]. From this perspective, it motivates that the proposed architecture contains a common feature extractor but different classifiers for corruption.

1.1.3 Techniques for Auxiliary Training

As shown in Fig. 1, two techniques are proposed to facilitate both the robustness and accuracy of neural networks, which are introduced as follows.

Auxiliary Classifiers Different from the primary classifier which is a single fully connected layer, the auxiliary classifiers in this section are constructed by three components: an attention module, a bottleneck layer, and a fully connected layer, according to the shallow classifiers in SCAN [16]. The attention modules consist of one convolutional layer and one deconvolutional layer, aiming at helping the auxiliary classifiers obtain the useful features [17, 18]. A bottleneck layer [19], which is composed of 1×1, 3×3, and 1×1 convolutional layers, is attached after the attention modules. Since all the auxiliary classifiers are only utilized in the training period, they don't bring additional storage and computation costs.

Selective Batch Normalization Batch normalization [20] is widely utilized in all kinds of convolutional neural networks to stabilize the training of models. However, recently, Galloway et al. found that batch normalization reduces model robustness to both adversarial attacks and corrupted images [21]. Zhou et al. show that models with batch normalization may not outperform models without batch normalization, especially when data augmentation is utilized in the training period. Their experiments demonstrate that batch normalization leads to a 2.9% accuracy drop on ResNet32 trained on CIFAR10 with data augmentation [10].

To alleviate the accuracy degradation from batch normalization on corrupted data, we propose selective batch normalization (SBN), aiming to eliminate the influence of corrupted data in batch normalization. The proposed SBN is based on the observation that the statistics parameters of batch normalization are vulnerable to the shift in input data, i.e., the corruption in input images. With the proposed SBN, the mean and variance of corruption data and clean data are computed respectively in both the training period and the inference period.

Let $\mathcal{X}^b$ be a training batch sampled from $\mathcal{X}$. The training batch is composed of clean samples $\mathcal{X}_C^b$ and corrupted samples $\mathcal{X}_j^b$, which can be formulated as $\mathcal{X}^b = \mathcal{X}_C^b \cup (\cup_{j=1}^t \mathcal{X}_j^b)$. In traditional batch normalization methods, the features of clean samples and corrupted samples are computed together, which can be formulated as

$$\tilde{x} = \gamma \cdot \frac{\tilde{x} - E[\mathcal{X}^b]}{\sqrt{Var[\mathcal{X}^b] + \varepsilon}} + \beta, x \in \mathcal{X}^b, \qquad (12)$$

where γ and β are two parameters for scaling and shifting trained by back propagation. ε is a number with a small value to avoid the zero-division error and $\tilde{x}$ denotes the features in the convolutional layers of a sample x. Compared with traditional batch normalization, the proposed SBN computes clean and corrupted samples respectively, which can be formulated as

$$\tilde{x} = \gamma \cdot \frac{\tilde{x} - E[\mathcal{X}_C^b]}{\sqrt{Var[\mathcal{X}_C^b] + \varepsilon}} + \beta, x \in \mathcal{X}_C^b, \quad \tilde{x} = \gamma \cdot \frac{\tilde{x} - E[\mathcal{X}_j^b]}{\sqrt{Var[\mathcal{X}_j^b] + \varepsilon}} + \beta, x \in \mathcal{X}_j^b \qquad (13)$$

During inference, $E[\cdot]$ and $Var[\cdot]$ are replaced by statistics mean μ and variance σ^2. In the training period of traditional batch normalization, μ and σ^2 are updated by both clean and corrupted samples in the batch, which can be formulated as

$$\mu \leftarrow \frac{1}{n}\sum_{i=1}^{n} x, \sigma^2 \leftarrow \frac{1}{n}\sum_{i=1}^{n}(x-\mu)^2, x \in \mathcal{X}^b, n = \mathcal{X}^b \tag{14}$$

In contrast, the proposed SBN updates μ and σ^2 by only the clean samples, which can be formulated as

$$\mu \leftarrow \frac{1}{n}\sum_{i=1}^{n} x, \sigma^2 \leftarrow \frac{1}{n}\sum_{i=1}^{n}(x-\mu)^2, x \in \mathcal{X}^b_C, n = \mathcal{X}^b_C \tag{15}$$

1.2 Evaluation and Discussion

1.2.1 Experiments Settings

Experiments of the proposed auxiliary training are conducted on four kinds of convolutional neural networks, including AlexNet [8], ResNet [19], Wide ResNet [28] and ResNeXt [29] and three kinds of datasets, including CIFAR10, CIFAR100 [30] and ImageNet [31]. Moreover, robustness benchmark datasets including CIFAR-C and ImageNet-C [32] datasets are utilized to evaluate model robustness in 19 kinds of common image corruption, containing all kinds of noise, blur, weather, and so on. The robustness of neural networks is measured by the relative value between the error rate of neural networks and AlexNet. It's named the corruption error (CE) [32], which is computed by the following formula

$$CE_{\text{Network}} = Error_{\text{Network}}/Error_{\text{AlexNet}} \tag{16}$$

where $Error$ denotes the error rates. A lower CE indicates that neural networks have better robustness to image corruptions.

1.2.2 Experimental Results

Improvements on Accuracy Tables 1 and 2 show the accuracy of neural networks by auxiliary training on CIFAR10 and CIFAR100, respectively. It can be observed that: (i) In CIFAR10, a 1.43% accuracy increment can be observed on the models trained with auxiliary training, ranging from 0.75% on ResNeXt50 as the minimum to 3.15% on AlexNet as the maximum. (ii) In CIFAR100, a 2.21% accuracy increment can be detected on the models with the proposed auxiliary training, ranging from 2.74% on ResNet50 as the maximum to 2.74% on Wide ResNet50 as

Table 1 Comparison of accuracy (%) between models trained by auxiliary training and standard training on CIFAR10

Model	Our approach	Baseline	Increment
AlexNet	91.43	88.28	+3.15
ResNet18	96.02	94.75	+1.27
ResNet50	96.31	95.22	+1.09
ResNet101	96.47	95.27	+1.20
WRN50	96.49	95.42	+1.07
ResNeXt50	96.34	95.59	+0.75

Table 2 Comparison of accuracy (%) between models trained by auxiliary training and standard training on CIFAR100

Model	Our approach	Baseline	Increment
AlexNet	70.09	68.44	+1.65
ResNet18	79.47	77.09	+2.38
ResNet50	80.16	77.42	+2.74
ResNet101	80.51	77.81	+2.70
WRN50	80.84	79.08	+1.76
ResNeXt50	81.51	79.49	+2.02

Table 3 Comparison between auxiliary training and standard training on on CIFAR10-C (lower CE is better)

Model	Ours	Base	Δ
AlexNet	69.98	100.00	+30.02
ResNet18	57.01	85.91	+28.90
ResNet50	58.15	84.26	+26.11
ResNet101	50.03	87.08	+37.05
WRN50	59.43	87.19	+27.76
ResNeXt50	52.96	84.50	+31.54

Table 4 Comparison between auxiliary training and standard training on on CIFAR100-C (lower CE is better)

Model	Ours	Base	Δ
AlexNet	80.03	100.00	+19.97
ResNet18	69.34	92.21	+22.87
ResNet50	69.13	92.28	+23.15
ResNet101	66.10	88.35	+22.25
WRN50	68.89	87.33	+18.44
ResNeXt50	69.13	92.29	+23.16

the minimum. (iii) Compared with the advanced models such as ResNeXt and Wide ResNet, more accuracy gain can be observed on the ResNet and AlexNet models.

Improvements on Robustness Tables 3 and 4 show the experiments results of six neural networks on CIFAR10-C and CIFAR100-C. It can be observed that (i) The proposed auxiliary training leads to consistent and significant robustness improvements. On average, there are 30.15% and 21.64% CE improvements on CIFAR10-C, and CIFAR100-C respectively. (ii) Although many kinds of corruption such as snow, fog, and JPEG compression are not involved in the training period, experiments show auxiliary training also improves model robustness in these corrupted images, indicating there is a good generalization ability of auxiliary training (Table 5).

Table 5 Top-1 and Top-5 accuracy on ImageNet (%)

Model	Top-1	Top-5
ResNet18		
Base	69.21	89.01
+Aux.	69.94	89.51
ResNet34		
Base	73.17	91.24
+Aux.	74.14	91.94

Comparison The comparison between the proposed auxiliary training and the other three robust training methods is shown in Table 6. It's observed that (i) Data augmentation can improve model robustness at the expense of model accuracy. (ii) Some robust training methods such as self-supervised training and Gaussian patch can improve model robustness with almost no drop in accuracy. (iii) In contrast, the proposed auxiliary training can improve both accuracy and robustness simultaneously and outperform the other three robust training methods by a large margin.

Experiments on ImageNet and ImageNet-C Experiments on ImageNet are conducted to show the effectiveness of auxiliary training on large-scale datasets. Tables 5 and 7 show the accuracy and robustness of four neural networks on ImageNet. On average, 0.85% top-1 and 0.60% top-5 accuracy increments on ImageNet and 7.61% CE (robustness) improvements on ImageNet-C can be observed.

Experiments on Adversarial Attack Although the proposed auxiliary training is designed for the robustness to natural corruption, experiments show that it also leads to accuracy gain on adversarial attacks. In this experiment, the primary classifier is trained on adversarial samples by PGD [22], and the auxiliary classifiers are still trained on images with natural corruptions. PGD attack, basic iterative attack [23], FGSM attack [24], momentum iterative attack [25], and the decoupled direction and norm attack [26] are utilized to evaluate the model accuracy and robustness to adversarial attack. As shown in Table 8: (i) Auxiliary training outperforms the state-of-the-art defense methods—adversarial training [27] by a large margin, on both clean data accuracy and adversarial samples accuracy. (ii) 1.86% clean data accuracy improvements can be observed in the proposed auxiliary training compared with the adversarial training. (iii) 3.17% accuracy improvements on 7 kinds of adversarial attack methods can be observed in auxiliary training. The consistent and significant improvements indicate that the proposed auxiliary training method can also be utilized in the defense against adversarial attacks.

Table 6 Comparison of training methods on CIFAR10 variants. CE refers to corruption error via Eq. (16) (lower is better). Best results in bold

Model	Baseline		Self-supervised		Gaussian patch		Data aug		Auxiliary	
	Accuracy	CE	Accuracy	CE	Accuracy	CE	Accuracy	CE	Accuracy	CE
ResNet18	94.75	85.91	95.23	63.09	95.13	63.17	93.53	60.03	**96.02**	**57.01**
Wide ResNet50	95.42	87.19	95.47	63.77	95.66	66.63	93.86	60.64	**96.49**	**55.41**
ResNeXt50	95.59	84.50	95.67	61.86	95.52	60.13	93.72	50.52	**96.34**	**49.37**

Numbers in bold indicate the highest results

Table 7 Comparison of robustness between models trained by auxiliary training and normal training on ImageNet-C. Model robustness is measured by corruption error (CE) in Eq. (16). **A lower CE is better**. "+Aux. Training" indicates training by auxiliary training

Model	Mean CE	Noise				Blur					Weather				Digital					
		Gauss.	Speckle	Shot	Impulse	Glass	Gauss.	Zoom	Motion	Defocus	Snow	Frost	Fog	Bright.	Satura.	Contra.	JPEG.	Elastic.	Spatter.	Pixelate.
ResNet18	84.11	87	85	89	91	90	85	88	87	84	84	85	79	72	70	81	91	91	80	79
+Aux. training	78.86	79	78	81	82	89	79	84	83	85	79	80	72	66	74	75	78	89	75	70
ResNet34	85.54	87	86	89	89	93	86	88	90	91	85	87	81	73	72	81	89	93	81	81
+Aux. training	75.58	78	76	80	81	85	77	82	79	77	75	76	70	64	62	73	77	84	71	66

Table 8 Comparison of adversarial training and the proposed auxiliary training with several adversarial attacks, ResNet18 on CIFAR10. The following adversarial attack methods are utilized for evaluation: PGD Attack [22], Basic Iterative Attack [23], Fast Gradient Sign Method [24], Momentum Iterative Attack [25], Decoupled Direction and Norm Attack [26]

Training method	Clean	PGD-L_2	PGD-L_∞	BIA-L_2	BIA-L_∞	FGSM	MIA-L_2	DDN-L_2
Normal training	94.75	23.37	4.88	24.62	6.49	18.34	24.62	1.42
Adversarial training [27]	83.90	45.54	43.52	79.94	44.88	51.99	74.04	24.36
Auxiliary training	85.76	49.35	46.45	82.56	47.07	54.38	76.97	26.53

2 Efficient Model Updating via KD

With the availability of large-scale datasets [31, 33, 34] and high-performance computing platforms, deep neural networks have achieved remarkable achievements in various visual tasks such as image classification [19, 29, 35, 36], and object detection [37–40]. Encouraged by their impressive performance, numerous software developers have effectively integrated neural networks into their software products and deployed them on edge devices such as mobile phones and tablet computers. Typically, the development roadmap for neural network-based software follows the paradigm illustrated in Fig. 2a. Initially, users install the software by downloading all the neural network parameters from a cloud platform. Subsequently, as the software interacts with its users, abundant new training data and requirements can be collected. Then, software developers can retrain the neural network with the collected data and update their software to enhance its performance. However, during the retraining phase, all the parameters of the neural network are typically changed compared to their values before updating. Consequently, users are forced to download all the parameters of the neural network again from the cloud platform, severely impairing their experience. While recent research has explored text prompts and adapter layers to fine-tune a large-scale pretrained model at a low training cost [41, 42], there has been no previous effort to reduce the download cost during model updates, which has a more direct impact on users with edge devices.

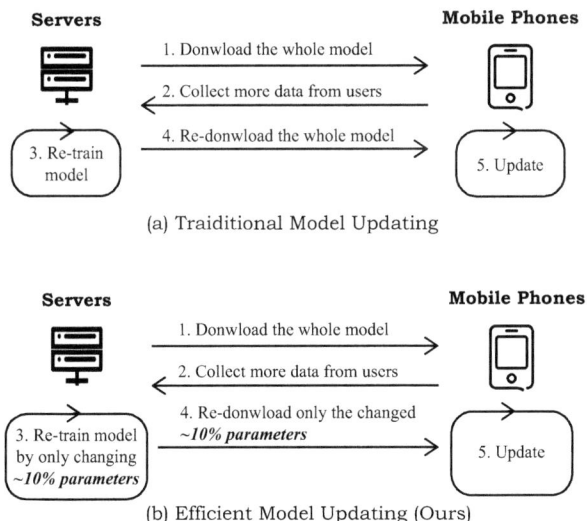

Fig. 2 Comparison between (**a**) the traditional model updating scheme and (**b**) the proposed efficient model updating. In efficient model updating, only around 10% parameters in the neural network are actually changed and thus users only need to download these changed parameters for updating

This section proposes the challenge of *efficient model updating* with the objective of reducing the download overhead of neural network-based software during updating. As depicted in Fig. 2b, during the retraining phase, efficient model updating introduces an additional constraint that limits the change of only a small subset (e.g. 10%) of the neural network parameters compared to the pre-updating model. Consequently, users only need to download a few parameters that have actually changed, instead of all the parameters in the neural network. In general, efficient model updating raises two questions: *how to find the optimal parameters that should be changed in the neural network*, and *how to achieve comparable accuracy with the fully-updated model* (i.e., the model with all parameters changed during updating).

To tackle this challenge, we propose a novel neural network training framework named Tiny Updater. Motivated by previous works in model compression, Tiny Updater is composed of the variants of two typical model compression techniques—neural network pruning and KD. Firstly, to determine which channels or layers in neural networks should be modified during updating, Tiny Updater applies the pruning technique. As shown in Fig. 3, it iteratively calculates the L_1-norm distance between the pre-updating model and the post-updating model parameters. The channels with smaller distances are considered unnecessary for updating and are pruned to their original values before updating. Conversely, the channels with larger distances are considered essential for updating, and thus they are actually changed. Secondly, during the retraining period, we propose to improve the performance of the partially-updated model by distilling the knowledge from a fully-updated teacher model. The partially-updated student model is trained to give predictions that are similar to those of the fully-updated teacher model by optimizing the KD loss. This ensures that the partially-updated model achieves comparable performance with the fully-updated model.

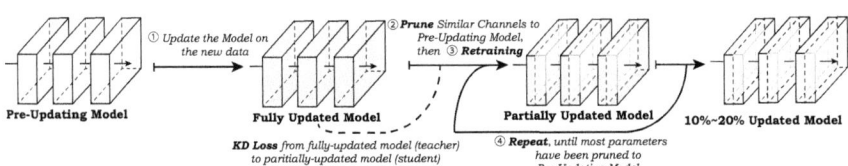

Fig. 3 The details of Tiny Updater. (1) Tiny Updater retrains the model with the new data collected from users (named as fully-updated models) by changing all the parameters. (2) Secondly, Tiny Updater finds the channels in the fully-updated models that have similar value to the pre-updating model and prunes these channels to their value before updating (the obtained models are named as partially-updated models). (3) Then, Tiny Updater retrains the unpruned weights. During retraining, the fully-updated model is utilized as the teacher model for the partially-updated model with KD (KD) loss to improve its performance. (4) Tiny Updater repeats step-2 and step-3 until most channels have been pruned to their value before pruning. (5) Finally, users only need to download very few parameters which are actually changed for updating

2.1 Reducing the Number of Updated Parameters

2.1.1 Efficient Model Updating

Given a training dataset $\mathcal{D} = \{(x_1, y_1), \ldots, (x_n, y_n)\}$, the software developers firstly train a deep neural network $\mathcal{F}$ with parameter Θ for their software. After deploying $\mathcal{F}$ on the edge devices, abundant new training samples $\{(x_{n+i}, y_{n+i})\}_{i=1}^{m}$ can be collected from users and the dataset can be extended as $\mathcal{D}^+ = \mathcal{D} \cup \{(x_{n+1}, y_{n+1}), \ldots, (x_{n+m}, y_{n+m})\}$. Then, software developers can retrain $\mathcal{F}$ on $\mathcal{D}^+$ to obtain better performance, whose parameters can be denoted as Φ. Usually, during this retraining step, all the values in θ can be totally different from that in Φ. Thus, the users have to download all the parameters of Φ to update the software, which harms the user experience and limits the frequent updating of neural network-driven software. In this paradigm, we name the model before updating as the pre-updating model, the model after updating as the post-updating model, the model with all the parameters updated as the fully updated model, and the model with partial parameters updated as the partially updated model. The target of efficient model updating is to obtain a partially updated model which has most of the parameters unchanged while achieving similar performance to the fully-updated model.

2.1.2 Tiny Updater

Fruitful previous works in model compression have successfully proven that even a very tiny neural network can have powerful representation ability, which motivates us to propose to learn the knowledge in the collected training data $\mathcal{D}^+$ with only a few parameters instead of all the parameters. The optimization objective of Tiny Updater can be formulated as

$$\arg\min_{\Phi} \frac{1}{n+m} \sum_{i=1}^{n+m} \mathcal{L}_{\text{task}}(x_i, y_i) \quad \text{subject to} \quad \frac{|\Theta - \Phi|_0}{\text{Card}(\Theta)} < \tau \quad (17)$$

where $\mathcal{L}_{\text{task}}$ indicates the original task-specific loss function, such as cross-entropy loss for image classification. $|\cdot|_0$ indicates the L_0-norm, which measures the number of non-zero elements in a tensor. Card($\cdot$) denotes the cardinality, which describes the number of parameters in a tensor. τ is a ratio threshold that determines how many parameters should be changed during updating. It is observed that when θ in Eq. (17) becomes zero, the optimization objective is similar to another deep learning technique—network pruning. Thus, we propose to solve this problem by introducing iterative pruning methods. Besides, KD is also introduced to improve the model performance with only a few parameters changed during updating with the teacher from a model with all the parameters changed. Please note that Tiny Updater is a framework that applies pruning and KD to tackle the challenge of efficient model updating and it does not propose any new pruning and KD method.

2.2 Evaluation and Discussion

2.2.1 Image Classification

The performance of Tiny Updater on CIFAR10&100 and four fine-grained image classification are shown in Figs. 5 and 4, respectively. It is observed that: (i) Tiny Updater achieves consistent effectiveness on all seven datasets. By changing around 20% parameters during updating, the neural networks trained with Tiny Updater achieve similar performance with fully-updated models on all these datasets. (ii) With the proposed Tiny Updater, when a large ratio of parameters is changed, it even leads to higher performance than the fully-updated model. For instance, on Oxford Flowers datasets in Fig. 4, the 84% updated model trained with Tiny Updater has 0.25% higher accuracy than the fully-updated model. We suggest this accuracy benefit is caused by the KD loss in Tiny Updater. As pointed out by previous research [43, 44], even if the student and the teacher have similar performance, KD can still lead to consistent accuracy benefits.

Ablation Study Tiny Updater is mainly composed of two modules—pruning and KD. Ablation studies on CIFAR10 and CIFAR100 are shown in Fig. 5. It is observed that: (i) Compared with Tiny Updater with random pruning, Tiny Updater with L_1-norm based pruning leads to consistently higher accuracy (around 6%) especially when only a low ratio (0 ~50%) of parameters are changed, indicating L_1-norm is an effective metric to find which channels are actually important for model updating. (ii) Significant accuracy boosts can be observed by applying KD during retraining. For instance, on CIFAR100, when around 10% and 20% of the parameters are changed, 1.79% and 1.15% accuracy boosts can be observed with KD, respectively.

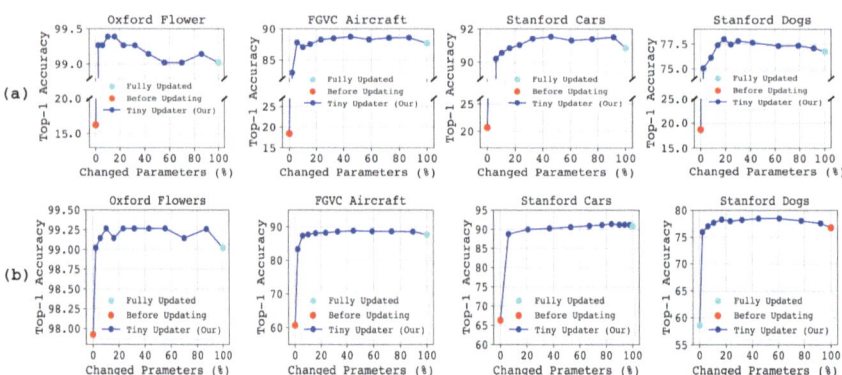

Fig. 4 Experiments on four fine-grained image classification datasets with ResNet50. The pre-updating and post-updating models are trained with 25 and 100% training data, respectively. In (**a**), the newly collected images come from all categories uniformly. In (**b**), the newly collected images come from only the categories that are not available before updating

2 Efficient Model Updating via KD

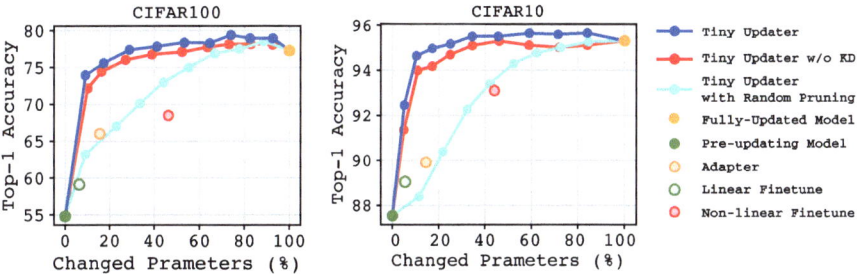

Fig. 5 Experiments on CIFAR with ResNet50. The pre-updating models and fully-updated models are trained with 25 and 100% training data, respectively. Tiny Updater with random pruning indicates pruning the randomly selected channels

These observations indicate that the pruning and KD in Tiny Updater have their individual effectiveness.

Categorical Incremental Updating Figure 4b shows the performance of Tiny Updater in the categorical incremental settings, where the pre-updating models are trained with 25% training data belonging to 25% categories. During the updating period, the model is further trained with data of all the categories. It is observed that Tiny Updater still achieves comparable performance by changing only ∼10% parameters, indicating that it generalizes well in different updating settings.

Comparison with Finetuning and Adapter Finetuning and adapter-based methods are two well-known efficient training methods and the parameters changed in these two methods are also much fewer than global finetuning. Figure 5 gives the comparison between Tiny Updater and these two methods on CIFAR10, CIFAR100 with ResNet18. It is observed that when the same number of parameters is changed, Tiny Updater outperforms these two methods by a clear margin, indicating that it is more effective than directly applying previous methods.

2.2.2 Video Recognition

Experiment Setting We evaluate Tiny Updater in video recognition datasets including UCF-101 [45] and Diving-48 [46] with video recognition models including SlowOnly [47] and Inception3D [48]. *UCF-101* is an action recognition dataset with 101 action classes over 13,000 video clips [45]. *Diving-48* is a fine-grained video dataset of competitive diving. It has around 18,000 video clips belonging to 48 dive sequences [48]. Both top-1 and top-5 accuracy are reported.

Experiment Result Figure 6 shows the performance of Tiny Updater on video recognition. It is observed that on both SlowOnly and Inception3D (I3D), UCF-101 and Diving-48, the model with only 20% parameters changed trained by Tiny Updater achieves comparable and even higher performance than the fully-updated

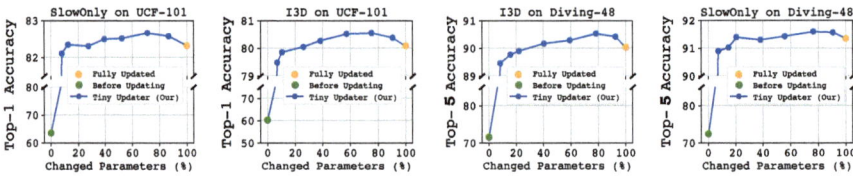

Fig. 6 Experimental results of video recognition on UCF-101 and Diving-48 with SlowOnly and Inception3D (I3D). The pre-updating models are trained with 25% training data

models. Moreover, the model with only 10% parameters changed during updating leads to only around 0.5% accuracy loss.

3 Brief Summary

In this chapter, we reveal that KD can be utilized as a more general training method for targets besides model compression. Although the original KD is only defined to transfer the knowledge between models in different parameter sizes, we show that KD can be widely utilized in a wide range of tasks, such as model robustness boosting and efficient software updating, where a stronger model can be built to guide the learning of a relatively weaker student. It may prompt more research on the training and optimization methods for modern intelligent models.

References

1. Huang, G., Liu, Z., Van Der Maaten, L., Weinberger, K.Q.: Densely connected convolutional networks. In: IEEE/CVF Conference on Computer Vision and Pattern Recognition (CVPR), pp. 4700–4708 (2017)
2. Liu, W., Anguelov, D., Erhan, D., Szegedy, C., Reed, S., Fu, C-Y., Berg, A.C.: Ssd: Single shot multibox detector. In: European Conference on Computer Vision (ECCV), pp. 21–37 (2016)
3. Ronneberger, O., Fischer, P., Brox, T.: U-net: Convolutional networks for biomedical image segmentation. In: International Conference on Medical Image Computing and Computer Assisted Intervention (MICCAI), pp. 234–241. Springer (2015)
4. Long, J., Shelhamer, E., Darrell, T.: Fully convolutional networks for semantic segmentation. In: IEEE/CVF Conference on Computer Vision and Pattern Recognition (CVPR), pp. 3431–3440 (2015)
5. Bahdanau, D., Cho, K., Bengio, Y.: Neural machine translation by jointly learning to align and translate. In: International Conference on Learning Representations (ICLR) (2015)
6. Vaswani, A., Shazeer, N., Parmar, N., Uszkoreit, J., Jones, L., Gomez, A.N., Kaiser, Ł., Polosukhin, I.: Attention is all you need. In: Advances in Neural Information Processing Systems (NeurIPS), pp. 5998–6008 (2017)
7. Devlin, J., Chang, M-W., Lee, K., Toutanova, K.: BERT: pre-training of deep bidirectional transformers for language understanding. In: Conference of the North American Chapter of the Association for Computational Linguistics: human Language Technologies (NAACL-HLT), pp. 4171–4186. Association for Computational Linguistics (2019)

8. Krizhevsky, A., Sutskever, I., Hinton, G.E.: Imagenet classification with deep convolutional neural networks. In: Advances in Neural Information Processing Systems (NeurIPS), pp. 1097–1105 (2012)
9. Simard, P.Y., Steinkraus, D., Platt, J.C., et al.: Best practices for convolutional neural networks applied to visual document analysis. In: ICDAR, p. 3 (2003)
10. Zhou, A., Ma, Y., Li, Y., Zhang, X., Luo, P.: Towards improving generalization of deep networks via consistent normalization. ArXiv. abs/1909.00182 (2019)
11. Yin, D., Lopes, R.G., Shlens, J., Cubuk, E.D., Gilmer, J.: A fourier perspective on model robustness in computer vision. ArXiv. abs/1906.08988 (2019)
12. Hendrycks, D., Mazeika, M., Kadavath, S., Song, D.X.: Using self-supervised learning can improve model robustness and uncertainty. ArXiv. abs/1906.12340 (2019)
13. Lopes, R.G., Yin, D., Poole, B., Gilmer, J., Cubuk, E.D.: Improving robustness without sacrificing accuracy with patch gaussian augmentation. ArXiv. abs/1906.02611 (2019)
14. Vapnik, V., Vashist, A.: A new learning paradigm: learning using privileged information. Neural Netw. **22**(5-6), 544–557 (2009)
15. Lopez-Paz, D., Bottou, L., Schölkopf, B., Vapnik, V.: Unifying distillation and privileged information. In: International Conference on Learning Representations (ICLR) (2016)
16. Zhang, L., Tan, Z., Song, J., Chen, J., Bao, C., Ma, K.: Scan: a scalable neural networks framework towards compact and efficient models. ArXiv. abs/1906.03951 (2019)
17. Wang, F., Jiang, M., Qian, C., Yang, S., Li, C., Zhang, H., Wang, X., Tang, X.: Residual attention network for image classification. In: IEEE/CVF Conference on Computer Vision and Pattern Recognition (CVPR), pp. 3156–3164 (2017)
18. Liu, S., Johns, E., Davison, A.J.: End-to-end multi-task learning with attention. ArXiv. abs/1803.10704 (2018)
19. He, K., Zhang, X., Ren, S., Sun, J.: Deep residual learning for image recognition. In: IEEE/CVF Conference on Computer Vision and Pattern Recognition (CVPR), pp. 770–778 (2016)
20. Ioffe, S., Szegedy, C.: Batch normalization: accelerating deep network training by reducing internal covariate shift. ArXiv. abs/1502.03167 (2015)
21. Galloway, A., Golubeva, A., Tanay, T., Moussa, M., Taylor, G.W.: Batch normalization is a cause of adversarial vulnerability. ArXiv. abs/1905.02161 (2019)
22. Madry, A., Makelov, A., Schmidt, L., Tsipras, D., Vladu, A.: Towards deep learning models resistant to adversarial attacks. ArXiv. abs/1706.06083 (2017)
23. Kurakin, A., Goodfellow, I., Bengio, S.: Adversarial machine learning at scale. arXiv preprint arXiv:1611.01236 (2016)
24. Goodfellow, I.J., Shlens, J., Szegedy, C.: Explaining and harnessing adversarial examples. arXiv preprint arXiv:1412.6572 (2014)
25. Dong, Y., Liao, F., Pang, T., Su, H., Zhu, J., Hu, X., Li, J.: Boosting adversarial attacks with momentum. In: IEEE/CVF Conference on Computer Vision and Pattern Recognition (CVPR), pp. 9185–9193 (2018)
26. Rony, J., Hafemann, L.G., Oliveira, L.S., Ayed, I.B., Sabourin, R., Granger, E.: Decoupling direction and norm for efficient gradient-based l2 adversarial attacks and defenses. In: IEEE/CVF Conference on Computer Vision and Pattern Recognition (CVPR), pp. 4322–4330 (2019)
27. Madry, A., Makelov, A., Schmidt, L., Tsipras, D., Vladu, A.: Towards deep learning models resistant to adversarial attacks. arXiv preprint arXiv:1706.06083 (2017)
28. Zagoruyko, S., Komodakis, N.: Wide residual networks. In: British Machine Vision Conference (BMVC) (2016)
29. Xie, S., Girshick, R., Dollár, P., Tu, Z., He, K.: Aggregated residual transformations for deep neural networks. In: IEEE/CVF Conference on Computer Vision and Pattern Recognition (CVPR), pp. 5987–5995 (2017)
30. Krizhevsky, A., Hinton, G.: Learning multiple layers of features from tiny images. Technical report, Citeseer (2009)

31. Deng, J., Dong, W., Socher, R., Li, L-J., Li, K., Fei-Fei, L.: Imagenet: a large-scale hierarchical image database. In: IEEE/CVF Conference on Computer Vision and Pattern Recognition (CVPR), pp. 248–255 (2009)
32. Hendrycks, D., Dietterich, T.G.: Benchmarking neural network robustness to common corruptions and perturbations. ArXiv. abs/1903.12261 (2019)
33. Lin, T-Y., Maire, M., Belongie, S., Hays, J., Perona, P., Ramanan, D., Dollár, P., Zitnick, C.L.: Microsoft coco: common objects in context. In: European Conference on Computer Vision (ECCV), pp. 740–755. Springer (2014)
34. Cordts, M., Omran, M., Ramos, S., Rehfeld, T., Enzweiler, M., Benenson, R., Franke, U., Roth, S., Schiele, B.: The cityscapes dataset for semantic urban scene understanding. In: IEEE/CVF Conference on Computer Vision and Pattern Recognition (CVPR) (2016)
35. Dosovitskiy, A., Beyer, L., Kolesnikov, A., Weissenborn, D., Zhai, X., Unterthiner, T., Dehghani, M., Minderer, M., Heigold, G., Gelly, S., et al.: An image is worth 16×16 words: transformers for image recognition at scale. In: International Conference on Learning Representations (ICLR) (2020)
36. Tan, M., Le, Q.V.: Efficientnet: Rethinking model scaling for convolutional neural networks. In: Proceedings of the International Conference on Machine Learning (ICML), vol. 97, pp. 6105–6114. PMLR (2019)
37. Ren, S., He, K., Girshick, R., Sun, J.: Faster r-cnn: Towards real-time object detection with region proposal networks. In: Advances in Neural Information Processing Systems (NIPS), pp. 91–99 (2015)
38. Lin, T-Y., Goyal, P., Girshick, R., He, K., Dollár, P.: Focal loss for dense object detection. IEEE Transactions on Pattern Analysis and Machine Intelligence (TPAMI) (2018)
39. Redmon, J., Divvala, S., Girshick, R., Farhadi, A.: You only look once: unified, real-time object detection. In: IEEE/CVF Conference on Computer Vision and Pattern Recognition (CVPR), pp. 779–788 (2016)
40. Tan, M., Pang, R., Le, Q.V.: Efficientdet: scalable and efficient object detection. In: IEEE/CVF Conference on Computer Vision and Pattern Recognition (CVPR), pp. 10778–10787. Computer Vision Foundation / IEEE (2020)
41. Liu, P., Yuan, W., Fu, J., Jiang, Z., Hayashi, H., Neubig, G.: Pre-train, prompt, and predict: A systematic survey of prompting methods in natural language processing. arXiv preprint arXiv:2107.13586 (2021)
42. Wang, R., Tang, D., Duan, N., Wei, Z., Huang, X., Cao, G., Jiang, D., Zhou, M., et al.: K-adapter: infusing knowledge into pre-trained models with adapters. arXiv preprint arXiv:2002.01808 (2020)
43. Mobahi, H., Farajtabar, M., Bartlett, P.L.: Self-distillation amplifies regularization in hilbert space. arXiv preprint arXiv:2002.05715 (2020)
44. Allen-Zhu, Z., Li, Y.: Towards understanding ensemble, knowledge distillation and self-distillation in deep learning. CoRR. abs/2012.09816 (2020)
45. Soomro, K., Zamir, A.R., Shah, M.: Ucf101: a dataset of 101 human actions classes from videos in the wild. arXiv preprint arXiv:1212.0402 (2012)
46. Li, Y., Li, Y., Vasconcelos, N.: Resound: towards action recognition without representation bias. In: Proceedings of the European Conference on Computer Vision (ECCV), pp. 513–528 (2018)
47. Feichtenhofer, C., Fan, H., Malik, J., He, K.: Slowfast networks for video recognition. In: Proceedings of the IEEE/CVF international conference on computer vision, pp. 6202–6211 (2019)
48. Carreira, J., Zisserman, A.: Quo vadis, action recognition? A new model and the kinetics dataset. In: Proceedings of the IEEE Conference on Computer Vision and Pattern Recognition, pp. 6299–6308 (2017)

Conclusion and Challenges

Abstract This book establishes KD as a cornerstone for efficient vision intelligence, highlighting both its fundamental problems and applications. Despite its current success, KD still suffers from reply on the experience of human experts and overlarge training overhead in large models, which provides challenges and opportunities for future research. By bridging performance and practicality, KD remains vital to advancing scalable, next-generation computer vision.

1 Conclusion

This book explores how to achieve efficient visual intelligence through KD. Starting with an overview of the research background and related work, we then present the contributions across three parts: the two fundamental problems in KD (chapters "Student and Teacher Models in KD" and "Distilled Knowledge in KD"), the application of KD (chapters "Application of KD in High-Level Vision Tasks" and "Application of KD in Low-Level Vision Tasks"), as well as the usage of KD beyond model compression (chapter "Application of KD Beyond Model Compression").

In chapters "Student and Teacher Models in KD" and "Distilled Knowledge in KD", we study the two fundamental problems in KD, including "how to build the student model and the teacher model", and "what kind of knowledge should be distilled". After carefully analyzing the previous literature, we have found that most KD methods can be summarized under these two fundamental problems. For the first fundamental problem, we introduce self-distillation as a new framework for building students and teachers, which first shows that the teacher model is not indispensable in KD. Self-distillation has been considered a pioneering work in teacher-free KD. For the second fundamental problem, we have proposed task-irrelevant KD, which demonstrates the influence of distilling different kinds of knowledge from teachers. These results successfully demonstrate the importance of selecting information for distillation in KD, providing researchers with a new perspective on understanding the process of KD. These two fundamental problems in this chapter form the basis for the subsequent chapter.

In chapters "Application of KD in High-Level Vision Tasks" and "Application of KD in Low-Level Vision Tasks", we have applied KD to a wide spectrum of visual tasks in real-world applications, including 2D object detection and point cloud-based 3D object detection for high-level vision, and GAN-based image-to-image translation, diffusion-based unconditional generation for the low-level vision. In these works, we consistently follow the same research philosophy: We first give an in-depth analysis of the crucial property of the given task and data, and then design specific KD tailored to the given tasks by thinking about the two fundamental problems introduced in chapters "Student and Teacher Models in KD" and "Distilled Knowledge in KD". This methodology enables the rapid application of KD to various tasks that truly serve real-world scenarios, thereby bridging the gap between AI research and application. Additionally, these works further support the findings in chapters "Student and Teacher Models in KD" and "Distilled Knowledge in KD" and validate the importance of the two fundamental problems in KD.

In chapter "Application of KD Beyond Model Compression", based on the first fundamental problem outlined in chapter "Student and Teacher Models in KD", we illustrate that KD can be utilized for targets beyond model compression. By employing various strategies to build student and teacher models and customizing distillation approaches to meet specific task requirements, we demonstrate the adaptability of KD to achieve broader goals such as model robustness boosting and efficient model updating, thereby expanding its application scope beyond traditional model compression. we hope that these insights will render KD a more versatile approach to neural network optimization.

2 Challenges

Despite the numerous advancements and significant breakthroughs in addressing both fundamental and applied problems through KD, there are still several unresolved challenges and opportunities for future research. In this subsection, we introduce two of them, including automatic design for KD and training-efficient KD.

2.1 Automatic Design for KD

In chapters "Application of KD in High-Level Vision Tasks" and "Application of KD in Low-Level Vision Tasks", we have explored the application of KD to various visual tasks. Generally speaking, we first analyze the key property of the given task and then propose the corresponding solutions tailored to it by addressing the two fundamental problems, including how to build students and teachers, and what kind of knowledge should be distilled. Although this approach has proven effective, it inherently demands expertise in both KD and the given task, which is a requirement not easily met in industrial applications. This gap has limited the broader adoption of KD. In previous works, fruitful automatic machine learning (AutoML) methods [1] have been introduced to automatically solve machine learning problems from the perspective of data [2] and neural network architectures [3]. AutoML has notably reduced the need for data science expertise, enabling software developers without a machine learning background to employ sophisticated models, particularly in deep learning. However, despite AutoML's successes, there's a noticeable absence of evidence supporting its applicability to the design of training methods such as KD.

Typically, automatic machine learning includes two steps, which are the construction of the search space and searching for the optimal solution in the search space. Fortunately, a similar methodology can also be applied to KD. Concretely, KD methods can be basically divided into two fundamental problems including how to build the students and teachers, and what kind of knowledge should be distilled. Besides, it also has some other sub-problems such as the design of loss functions. These orthogonal problems have formed the search space of KD. Besides, traditional search techniques such as evolutionary algorithms and meta-learning could be applied to find the most effective KD strategies within this searching space.

Automatic KD design also faces some unique challenges. For instance, the evaluation of the performance of KD methods is much more complex than the evaluation of neural network architectures. Additionally, leveraging past experimental outcomes to expedite the search process remains difficult, leading to more training costs in the search process. In summary, as a crucial requirement in industrial applications, automatic design for KD may be solved with the methodology in traditional AutoML methods, but it still has many challenging problems.

2.2 Training-Efficient KD

The emergence of large-scale models such as ChatGPT and Stable Diffusion [4] in 2022 represented a leap forward in generative capabilities across language and vision, approaching human-like performance. These models, including GPT-3 [5] with its 175 billion parameters and Google's Switch Transformer with 1.6 trillion parameters [6], underscore the trend towards increasingly large model architectures. Despite their enhanced learning capabilities, enabled by unsupervised training on extensive datasets, these models introduce significant requirements on their compression and acceleration with knowledge distillation.

In the compression for traditional models, the training cost is not a crucial problem. However, the tremendous size of large models renders the additional training costs of KD prohibitive. Addressing this challenge necessitates the development of training-efficient KD. Potential solutions include optimizing student initialization, combining KD with efficient model finetuning methods, and reducing the cost of teacher model inference during training. Such approaches aim to mitigate the resource demands of distilling knowledge into large-scale models, ensuring their practicality and accessibility. Nonetheless, striking a balance between reducing the training costs of KD and maintaining the accuracy of students is still challenging.

References

1. He, X., Zhao, K., Chu, X.: Automl: a survey of the state-of-the-art. Knowl.-Based Syst. **212**, 106622 (2021)
2. Cubuk, E.D., Zoph, B., Mané, D., Vasudevan, V., Le, Q.V.: Autoaugment: learning augmentation policies from data. ArXiv, abs/1805.09501 (2018)
3. He, Y., Lin, J., Liu, Z., Wang, H., Li, L.-J., Han, S.: Amc: automl for model compression and acceleration on mobile devices. In: The European Conference on Computer Vision (ECCV), pp. 784–800 (2018)
4. Rombach, R., Blattmann, A., Lorenz, D., Esser, P., Ommer, B.: High-resolution image synthesis with latent diffusion models. In: Proceedings of the IEEE/CVF Conference on Computer Vision and Pattern Recognition, pp. 10684–10695 (2022)
5. Brown, T., Mann, B., Ryder, N., Subbiah, M., Kaplan, J.D., Dhariwal, P., Neelakantan, A., Shyam, P., Sastry, G., Askell, A., et al.: Language models are few-shot learners. Adv. Neural Inf. Proces. Syst. **33**, 1877–1901 (2020)
6. Fedus, W., Zoph, B., Shazeer, N.: Switch transformers: Scaling to trillion parameter models with simple and efficient sparsity. J. Mach. Learn. Res. **23**(1), 5232–5270 (2022)

If you have any concerns about our products,
you can contact us on
ProductSafety@springernature.com

In case Publisher is established outside the EU,
the EU authorized representative is:
**Springer Nature Customer Service Center GmbH
Europaplatz 3, 69115 Heidelberg, Germany**

Printed by Libri Plureos GmbH
in Hamburg, Germany